Selling FOR DUMMIES®

2ND EDITION

by Tom Hopkins and Ben Kench

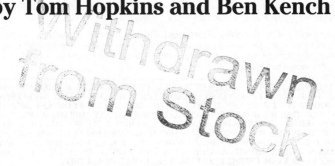

WILEY

Selling For Dummies®, 2nd Edition

Published by
John Wiley & Sons, Ltd
The Atrium
Southern Gate
Chichester
www.wiley.com

This edition first published 2013

Registered office

John Wiley & Sons Ltd, The Atrium, Southern Gate, Chichester, West Sussex, PO19 8SQ, United Kingdom

For details of our global editorial offices, for customer services and for information about how to apply for permission to reuse the copyright material in this book please see our website at www.wiley.com.

The right of the author to be identified as the author of this work has been asserted in accordance with the Copyright, Designs and Patents Act 1988.

For general information on our other products and services, please contact our Customer Care Department within the U.S. at 877-762-2974, outside the U.S. at (001) 317-572-3993, or fax 317-572-4002.

For technical support, please visit www.wiley.com/techsupport.

A catalogue record for this book is available from the British Library.

ISBN 978-1-118-48943-7 (pbk), ISBN 978-1-118-48944-4 (ebk), ISBN 978-1-118-48953-6 (ebk), ISBN 978-1-118-48954-3 (ebk)

Printed in Great Britain by TJ International Ltd, Padstow, Cornwall

10 9 8 7 6 5 4 3 2 1

WILEY

Contents at a Glance

Table of Contents

Chapter 15: Managing Your Time Efficiently 253

Introduction

●●●

*W*elcome to *Selling For Dummies*. Although this book
is about selling products and services to businesses
and consumers, it goes beyond that knowledge. This book is
really about people skills. After all, knowing how to get along
well with others is vital, especially if your career involves
persuading them toward ownership of your ideas, concepts,
products, or services. In this way, selling is a life skill that you
use in many situations, both at home and at work. Life is a
sales game and you fare better when more people see things
your way!

To be successful in sales, you must be able to co-operate,
have good listening skills and be willing to put others' needs
before your own. With the selling skills that we cover here in
your arsenal, you'll have more happiness and satisfaction in
all areas of your life, not just in your selling career (although
your selling will certainly benefit too).

About This Book

Selling For Dummies, can help you get more happiness and
contentment out of your life right now by helping you gain
more respect, more money, more recognition for the job
you do, more agreement from your friends and family, more
control in negotiations and, of course, more sales. Above all,
this book is a reference tool, so you don't have to read it from
beginning to end. Instead, you can turn to any part of the
book that gives you the information you need, when you need
it. And you can keep coming back to the book over and over
again throughout your selling career.

As the original dummies in sales, we're the perfect people to
write this book.

Ben started his career selling double-glazing. He remembers vividly his mother's reaction to his new job: 'Oh well, that'll do until you get a proper job.' But somehow, he never got the proper job. At the time, double-glazing sales, for many, epitomised the lower end of the selling spectrum – national television at the time spent most Sunday evenings exposing 'cowboy' selling tactics. However, the job served Ben well. He started in January with no money, no proper overcoat and a battered, barely legal Hillman Avenger car that had no heater. The experience was tough, but it served as excellent leverage. Ben wanted money, so he had to make the job work!

Ben listened and copied and learned and developed. He was constantly hungry for a new idea or pitch style, and when he added in his cheeky personality, he soon started winning – big. But he has never forgotten the lessons he learned at the start of his career. Today, Ben is recognised as the UK's number one sales and business growth specialist, and, within his successful business coaching and sales training entities, he still applies himself to constant learning. He's delighted to be able to share all the knowledge gained through his experience and hard work, so that you can enjoy, as he has, a life dedicated to sales . . . 'not a proper job'!

Tom started his selling career in property at the age of 19. Property may have been a great career choice, but at the time he owned neither a suit nor a car. All he had was a band uniform and a motorcycle. And selling properties on a motorcycle wasn't easy; rather than loading up the prospective buyers in his car, he had to tell them to follow him to the properties and hope they didn't get lost along the way. When they finally came to their senses and realised that this kid couldn't possibly be for real, they'd keep going straight when he'd make a turn. (To make things even worse, wearing a woollen band uniform in Southern California's summer heat didn't allow him to present the coolest image, either.)

But he stuck it out, because he knew there was big money to be made in the selling business – if he could just find out what the successful people were doing that he wasn't. He learned the hard way, through trial and error. Early in his career, a professional, experienced salesperson told Tom that he had to learn how to *close*, meaning 'to close the sale'. Tom responded, 'I don't have many clothes.' See why he only averaged $42 a month in his first six months of selling property?

Needless to say, Tom has come a long way since then, and it thrills him no end to give you the chance to benefit from the mistakes he made, as well as from the subsequent success he's had. Yes, he's had successes. He achieved his goal of becoming a millionaire by the age of 30, beating his own deadline by nearly three years! At age 27, he was one of the most successful estate agents in the United States – a guy who started without a decent suit or a vehicle with four wheels!

Just goes to show you that it doesn't matter how much of a dummy you are on this subject when you start. With this book by your side, serving as a reference for all the selling situations you encounter, you'll master the selling, persuasion and people skills you need to really shine.

Conventions Used in This Book

To help you navigate this book, we include the following conventions:

- ✔ **Boldface** highlights key words in bulleted lists and action steps that you should follow in a specific order.
- ✔ New terms and words we choose to emphasise are in *italics*.
- ✔ Web addresses appear in `monofont`.

When this book was printed, some of the web addresses we reference may have needed to break across two lines of text. If that happened, rest assured that we haven't put in any extra characters (such as hyphens) to indicate the break. So, when using one of these web addresses, just type in exactly what you see in this book, pretending the line break doesn't exist.

We also use some terms interchangeably in this book. For example, the people you look for to present your offering to may be called *prospects* in one area. In other areas, we refer to them as *potential clients*, which we believe creates a more positive, powerful mental image about who they are.

What You're Not to Read

If you're reading this book just to get a better understanding of the more serious bits of how to sell your product or service, skip past content preceded by the Anecdote icon. These are stories from our pasts or experiences of our students that demonstrate a point but may not be necessary to your understanding of the topic at hand. The same goes for sidebars, which are the grey-shaded boxes sprinkled throughout this book.

Foolish Assumptions

When writing this book, we assumed that its readers would either already be in sales careers or considering going into sales. It doesn't matter whether you're selling corporate jets or chocolates, the basic selling strategies apply simply because you're selling to *people.*

We also assumed that you like people in general and that you enjoy working with them: you're not a hermit or a recluse, you don't have an extreme case of anthropophobia (a fear of people) and you aren't painfully shy.

Another assumption is that you're interested in learning and willing to experiment and apply the strategies in this book. If you're not serious about at least trying something new to get different results from those you're getting now, you might as well give this book to someone else. This book contains answers, strategies and tactics for successfully selling products and services, but they won't work until you put them to work.

How This Book Is Organised

Selling For Dummies is organised into six parts, and the parts are divided into chapters. In the following sections, we give you a quick preview of what to expect from each part so you can turn to the part that interests you most.

Part 1: Laying a Solid Foundation for Selling

In this part, you find out a little about what selling is and what it isn't. We share ideas on what selling skills can do for you in all areas of your life, and give you a quick tour through the seven steps of the selling cycle. We also let you know how important your attitude is to the art of selling – encouraging you to have fun and get all the satisfaction and success out of selling that you get out of the things you do for fun.

Part II: Doing Your Homework before You Sell a Thing

Just as with virtually any pursuit in life, preparation is the key to success in the world of selling. In this part, we cover the steps to preparation – everything from knowing your clients to knowing your products – that will set you apart from average persuaders and help you hear more yeses in your life. We talk about the importance of understanding the cultural needs of your clients, and how to use this understanding to your advantage in the preparation stage of the game as well as in making your selling life more successful. We also cover many ways technology can make your life less complicated as you navigate the sometimes challenging course of business.

Part III: The Anatomy of a Sale

In this part, we give each of the seven steps of the selling cycle its very own chapter. We pack in lots of useful information – including some suggestions for wording and nonverbal communication tips – in each stage of the process. You'll discover how to find the people you can sell to, how to get an appointment with those people and make a good impression, how to build better relationships that increase the likelihood of sales, how to give fantastic presentations, how to address customer concerns, how to close the sale and how to get referrals . . . so you can start the process all over again.

Part IV: Growing Your Business

This part is where you begin to separate yourself from average salespeople to become one of the greats. Average salespeople make their presentations, win a few, lose a few and move on. But the great ones view every presentation as an opportunity to build a long-term business. So in this part, we give you tips for staying in touch with your clients, making more sales through the help of the Internet and managing your time wisely so that you always have time for your clients as your business grows.

Great salespeople build not only businesses but also relationships, because *relationships* take them further and bring them a lot more satisfaction in the long run. We also cover strategies and tactics for partnering with other non-competing business professionals to tap into their clientèle who just might have a need for your services as well.

Part V: You Can't Win 'Em All: Keeping the Faith in Sales

Rejection is a part of life. So you need to expect it, accept it and get over it. The fact that a prospect rejects your product or service doesn't mean that he's rejected you as a person. But when you're in the world of selling, where rejection is just part of the territory, your self-esteem can easily suffer. So in this part, we help you imitate a duck by letting things run off your back like water. We show you how to think like a pro – not an *average* salesperson – and how to work through challenging times without losing faith. We also help you understand how best to use your time and keep focused on the big-picture goals so the little negativities of life don't bring you down. *Remember:* With every no, you're that much closer to a yes.

Part VI: The Part of Tens

The short chapters in this part are packed with quick ideas about selling and persuading that you can read any time you have a few minutes. They're a great way to get yourself psyched for a presentation or for making calls. And they're good for pumping up your attitude and invigorating you for each day. *Remember:* No one will ever want what you have, if you're not excited about it.

Icons Used in This Book

Icons are those little pictures you see in the margins throughout this book, and they're meant to draw your attention to key points that are of help to you along the way. Here's a list of the icons we use and what they signify.

When you see this icon, you can bet that stories from our years of experience in selling and from our students' experiences are nearby. And, oh, what stories we have to share. . . .

This icon highlights advice to follow to go beyond the basics and become a true champion at selling. When you see this icon, you'll find examples of exchanges between you and your prospective client so you can see exactly how a conversation can develop if you know just what to say.

Instead of being the typical warning that red flags usually indicate, this icon highlights the crucial pieces of information and skills you need for selling anything. When you see this flag in the margin, take notice. Great selling tips are at hand.

Some things are so important that they bear a little extra attention. So this icon – like a string tied around your finger – is a friendly reminder of information you'll want to commit to memory and use over the long haul.

When you see this icon in the margin, the paragraph next to it contains valuable information on making the sales process easier or faster – anything from prospecting to closing and beyond.

This icon highlights things you want to avoid and common mistakes salespeople make. An important part of achieving success is simply eliminating the mistakes. And the information marked by this icon helps you do just that.

Where to Go from Here

Glance through the Table of Contents and find the part, chapter or section that flips your switch. That's the best place to begin.

To benefit the most from the material in this book, do a little self-analysis to see where you're the weakest. We know admitting your faults is tough, even to yourself. But reading the material that covers your weaker areas will bring you the greatest amount of success.

Studies have shown that most traditional salespeople are not highly skilled at relationship building. They visit a lot of people and try hard but just never quite get enough connection and interest to wrestle the sale from another competitor, or never quite make the sale happen for them when they'd like. If you're in traditional sales and you aren't sure whether relationship building is your weakness, Chapter 9 may be a great place to start.

The most successful people in life are those who continue to grow. The fact that you're reading these words now puts you into that realm – because it isn't how much you know that counts, but how much you can discover *after* you 'know it all'. Congratulations for believing in yourself, in your ability to change for the better, in your ability to improve your lifestyle *and* in your ability to improve the lives of the people you help with this book's many tips on the art of selling. We wish you greatness!

Part I
Laying a Solid Foundation for Selling

'We're looking for a salesperson who can get his foot in the door – Are you that person, Mr Snartley?'

In this part...

*H*ere you discover the components of the selling cycle and how you can use the process to generate greater success for yourself. We also look at the importance of attitude in your sales role. Whether you're a new starter or an old hand, this section offers excellent, simple suggestions and key reminders to keep you upbeat and focused for success.

Chapter 1

Selling Is All Around You

● ●

In This Chapter

▶ Defining selling

▶ Recognising some common methods salespeople use to get their messages across

▶ Improving your life by improving your selling

● ●

*S*elling is happening everywhere around you, and everybody does it almost every day, in one form or another. In fact, selling is a life skill that affects every waking moment of your day. So in this chapter, I let you know what exactly this thing called *selling* is, how it's done and how you can use selling skills to make your life and your career better.

Understanding What Selling Is

In the strictest sense of the word, *selling* is a process of communication in which the seller imparts a feeling to another person or group in order to win the buyer over to the seller's ideas, concepts, products or services. This feeling comes from the high level of emotion that you have for your idea, concept, product or service, and when you speak with other people about it you radiate your feeling! You glow! Indeed your enthusiasm for 'it' is contagious, and other people take it on board too! In its truest form, that is selling.

When you think about it, you can be sold a concept or an idea: a religion or political persuasion, a belief about an issue or a favouring of a person or thing. Selling is about getting someone to feel whatever it is you want them to feel, and you do this and see it being done every day. For example, you persuade your partner to go along with your choice of holiday or your choice of a night's entertainment, or you encourage your work colleagues to adopt a new process or a course of action. All these areas involve you selling: a process whereby you persuade and encourage other people to feel the same way as you do.

In the more traditional sense of the word though, people think of *selling* as a work skill that involves moving goods and services from the hands of those who produce them into the hands of those who'll benefit most from their use. Selling involves both educational and persuasive skills and a combination of methods, including personal approaches alongside print, audio, video and online messages – all selling either the particular item or the brand name as being something the customer would want to have.

Some people say that nothing ever happens unless someone sells something to someone else. Without selling, products that have been manufactured would sit in warehouses for an eternity, people working for those manufacturers would become unemployed, we wouldn't need transportation and freight services, and people would be living isolated lives, striving to eke out livings from whatever bits of land they owned. Or would people even own land if no one were there to sell it to them? Think about it.

Look around you right now. You can probably spot hundreds, if not thousands, of things that were sold to get where they are right now. Even if you're totally naked, sitting in the woods, you had to be involved in some sort of selling process to have this book with you. If you choose to ignore material possessions, take stock of yourself internally. What do you believe? Why do you believe what you do? Did someone – like your parents or your peers – sell you a set of values as you were growing up? Did your teachers persuade you to believe, through demonstration, that $2 + 2 = 4$? Or did you figure that one out on your own? Odds are that whether you're living in a material world or you've forsaken nearly all possessions, you've been involved in selling, one way or another.

The preceding paragraph should have persuaded you to look at selling a bit differently than you have in the past. We did this, though, without pushing facts and figures on you. Good selling isn't pushy; it's a process of helping people to think a bit differently than they have before by using a variety of techniques and tools.

The selling triangle

When Ben gives seminars about mastering the fundamentals of selling, he uses a triangle with equal sides, like the one here, to illustrate the three main elements of selling:

✔ On one side are product knowledge (see Chapter 5) and presentation skills (see Chapter 10).

✔ On the other side are relationships and people skills (see Chapter 9).

✔ And on the base of the triangle are attitude, enthusiasm and energy (see Chapter 17).

The three sides of the selling triangle are equally important. If product knowledge was all that mattered, then technical designers, manufacturers or assemblers of products would make the best salespeople. Of course, these folks often know the products quite literally from the inside out and can even be skilled in presenting them. But until they understand how much of a role attitude and energy play in sales, their sales approach is often 99 per cent description of product and 1 per cent relation of the product to the needs of the individual clients – and that rarely results in a sale.

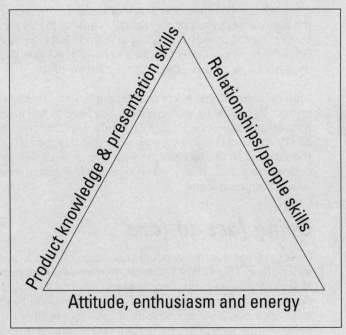

(continued)

(continued)

Great selling skills and enthusiasm alone won't get you far either. Even if you're comfortable talking with practically anyone, if you don't have a clear understanding of what your product, service or idea will do for your customers, they simply won't buy because they don't understand what it does for them.

And if you're excited about selling but you have little knowledge or experience about how important relationships are to selling, then your enthusiasm might open the door, but you'll get your fingers slammed in it when you start pushing products (because *pushing products* isn't how you sell anything).

Remember: A professional who hasn't developed any one side of the triangle is failing to reach his full potential and is letting down clients, who expect to work with a competent person. Do your best to develop all three areas of your selling life in order to reap the rewards.

Identifying Key Selling Methods

Although the definition of selling may be fairly straightforward, the approaches to selling are virtually endless. In this section, I cover the primary ways that people sell products and services (in order from most direct contact to least) and I give you some important tips for using them to the greatest effect.

Understanding at the onset that selling is about feelings is critical. For a sale to be successful, you need to feel an affinity with and have a belief in your product so that you can be effective in encouraging your potential buyer into feeling the same. With that in mind, as you look for various ways to achieve your goal, you're better equipped to decide which selling method is best.

Going face-to-face

On an average day, many people conclude sales in a face-to-face fashion. Diners buy breakfast, lunch and dinner in person at favourite restaurants. People physically register into hotels or check in at airport counters. Retail stores abound with sales opportunities, and millions of salespeople sit across desks, conference tables or kitchen tables turning prospects into clients. Person-to-person selling is the single largest type of selling that's conducted worldwide. Because of this, much of the content in the balance of this book is aimed at person-to-person selling.

The fun part about person-to-person selling is that you can watch prospects' body language and speak with yours. You can hand them information, have them handle your product or experience the service first-hand and involve all their senses: have them taste, touch, smell, hear and see just how cool your widget is. (We cover methods for doing this in Chapter 10.)

Ringing around with telemarketing

With a telephone, salespeople have the potential to reach nearly any other person on the planet. And what you say when your prospective client answers the phone, if he answers at all, is critical. In some industries, you try to sell the product on the first call, and in other industries you sell interest – enough interest that the person to whom you speak gets out of his home or office to come and see you, or lets you visit him in his home or place of business. Either way, you're selling what your business is all about, leaving the person on the other end with a very distinct impression of you and your company – good or bad.

Although telemarketing is a thriving method for reaching potential clients, many telemarketers are finding it more and more difficult to reach the target contact when making their calls. If you plan to use telephone sales, be prepared to deal with call-handling people who are specifically trained to be 'gatekeepers' and not let you through, or even just plain answering machines. Either way, you need to be ready to say enough to spark the interest of the target prospect so that they call you back.

If you hear a target prospect say 'Hello' on the other end of the line, you have cause for rejoicing – and you'll have to be prepared for that happening. Be clear about what you're selling, whether it's a product, a meeting or simply getting permission to send the person information.

Despite the difficulty telemarketers often have in getting through to people who are willing to listen to them, telemarketing is widely accepted and recognised as a true sales profession. It requires tact, training and the ability to articulate a compelling message in a very brief amount of time, as well as the skill of helping others recognise you as a warm, caring individual who has their needs at heart. Companies across many industries realise that gifted telemarketers can help bring a product or service to market in a much more efficient and cost-effective manner than face-to-face selling.

Sending email

Many companies are doing less telemarketing and direct-mail selling (I discuss direct mail later in this chapter) and are, instead, sending more email solicitations. In fact, an entire industry revolves around email marketing and the strategies required to get your messages through the many spam filters employed by individuals and companies alike.

Why has email become so popular? Primarily because it sprang into life as a free alternative to telemarketing and direct-mail, with the added bonus that the email used to go directly to the person to whom it was sent. These days, as with telephone calls and direct mail, many recipients find themselves inundated with email, and so some people delegate reading emails to a secretarial-type gatekeeper. Even though the days of free bulk email are gone, the cost of sending email messages is minimal compared to the cost of printing a mail piece and adding the postage to it.

Secretaries and receptionists may receive copies of emails, but they usually don't delete email messages from their bosses' computers. Home email, on the other hand, may not be thought of as quite so sacred. In fact, some couples share an email address. In that case, one party may see and delete your message when it was intended for the other, but it still has a good chance of being seen by the person you want to reach.

To make sure that your intended recipient receives the message you're sending, we suggest giving a lot of attention to the subject line. Amazingly, many people decide to auto-delete unless the five or six words in that subject line grab their attention. A useful technique is to put the recipient's name in the subject line (for example, 'Personal Message for John Doe').

The computer revolution – and your role in it

If you plan to have a future career in sales, you need to become computer-savvy. Let's face it, even if you're still selling something as simple as home-made birthday cakes, you need to track your client contacts in the most efficient manner possible to maximise your sales. You also need to have access to the phenomenal volume and quality of information available on the Internet and, perhaps more importantly, be able to access this phenomenal source of potential customers. Not being familiar with computers but thinking you can succeed in business and selling is like King Canute trying to hold back the tides . . . it just isn't going to happen!

Understanding the basics of today's technology is also crucial so that you can do business with clients who are in tune with it. Nothing ruins your credibility faster than saying that you don't have email or don't do computers when your prospect is using the latest notebook computer or web-enabled phone. You're especially well-advised to take advantage of contact management software (CRM), which allows you to maintain customer lists, prospect information, schedules, contact information and a variety of other sales-related tasks. Talk with others in your particular field to determine which software has the features you'll benefit from the most, or see whether your company has made arrangements to use a certain program in-house (see Chapter 6).

If you use email to connect with prospective clients, you can include your message in the body of the email itself, or type a few lines only but include a link to a web page with the information you want to deliver.

Email, when used properly, is an extraordinary vehicle for getting your message out. However, you need to be aware of the laws governing the use of email. Sending follow-up emails or proposals and presentation materials is fine, but if you're planning to use email as part of a larger sales campaign (similar to the way you would use direct mail), you must first get the permission of the recipient of the message, or what is commonly referred to as an *opt-in email list*. We discuss email lists in more depth in Chapter 8.

Selling online

Fundamentally, online sales and business transactions have made the biggest shake-up of the practice of sales and business since coins replaced barter. Simply put, people today live in a society where they believe time is short and they're used to an 'immediate' mindset. Internet selling gives people what they're looking for – speed.

Thus, imagine that you're a customer, and you really, really want a new widget in a razzle-dazzle raspberry colour. If you want to see it right away to be sure the colour matches or complements your other widgets, what's the best solution? You can place a call to a physical widget manufacturer and wait for a salesperson to contact you and then send you a brochure or catalogue. Or you can visit the manufacturer's website and, within a few minutes, see the actual widget in all its razzle-dazzleness and buy it now! As a busy customer, the choice is an obvious one.

Wouldn't your customers want to take advantage of the same opportunity? Yes, because if you don't offer your customers that opportunity, your competitors will. In today's environment, giving your customers the ability to buy online is essential. For this to happen, the Internet shopper needs to be aware that you're online, and you need to ensure that you're online presence is of a good quality and level of functionality. You need to look good online so as to be comparable with other online competitors.

Efficiency is the name of the game when it comes to technology. And you have to take advantage of every method possible to increase your efficiency while remaining easily accessible to your client base. The key is not to invest so much time in mastering the technology that you have no time remaining to do what you're paid for – to sell products and services.

The people you approach to do business will likely have a great deal of knowledge about your product or service, so you better know those products and services better than they do (see Chapter 5 for more on this important topic). Look at the same resource information that your customers see. In fact, add to your repertoire a question about where they did their research on your product. Find out where your customers are

going for information. If you have any impact on what's put
there, make sure it's positive.

Using direct mail

Every piece of mail you receive, whether it's a circular sales
letter, a coupon book or a catalogue, is devised for a single
purpose – to sell you something. Companies play the odds
that enough people will stop long enough to look at and order
their products before the direct mail hits the rubbish bin.

Believe it or not, today's response rate for direct mail is often
as low as 0.5 per cent for a *first* or *cold mailing*. (The reference
'cold' denotes a recipient that hasn't had contact with you
and is not already warmed to your offer. Subsequent mailings to known contacts are referred to as *warm*.) That means
only one out of two hundred catalogues may actually have an
order placed from it. One hundred and ninety-nine of those
catalogues are thrown away without ever generating a penny
for the company that sent them. Considering that those catalogues may cost several thousand pounds to produce and
distribute, especially if they contain a lot of full-colour photos,
that's a huge gamble. So why is direct mail still so prevalent?

The reason is simple: when you order from a company,
you'll probably order something else from that company in
the future. You've become a customer, and good companies
work very hard to keep you coming back for more. Warmed
contacts are a very good source of sales as they're already
familiar with the company making the offers. Thus, direct mail
as a selling strategy works when done properly – and the com-
pound effect is extremely effective if you can afford the entry-
level cost of building up a client base.

Appreciating What Selling Skills Can Do for You

Selling skills can do for you what a way with words did for
William Shakespeare. They can do for you what sex appeal did
for Marilyn Monroe. They can do for you what powerful communication skills did for Martin Luther King, Jr. Selling skills

can open doors and increase incomes and make you the most popular person in the company or town. They can mean the difference between getting the promotion or new job, landing the girl or guy of your dreams, or having to settle for less in life than you deserve. In short, improved selling skills can transform your life.

If you're good at selling, you probably earn a satisfactory income and have rewarding personal relationships. If you're not completely satisfied with your income level or with the quality of your personal relationships, make the development of selling and people skills a priority, and you'll reap the rewards.

Having a strong set of selling skills is like having a golden ticket for an easier life. All you have to do is invest a bit of your time and effort into understanding and applying this book's tried-and-true, proven-effective skills in your everyday life. Before you know it, they'll be such a natural part of you that no one, including yourself, will even recognise them as selling skills. People around you will just see you as a really nice, competent person and, believe us, you'll then be in the class of people who make the world go 'round.

Salespeople are everywhere – even where you least expect them

The person who isn't selling isn't living. Think about that: at some point nearly every day, you're involved in a selling situation of some sort. You may call it by a different name or not even recognise it as an act of selling, but all the same, selling it is. Here's just a short list of the people who sell things and whose 'products' you buy:

✔ **Actors and actresses:** If you've ever watched a TV show, film or play and been caught up in the story, you've been a part of a selling situation. The actress has given a believable performance – she's sold you on her portrayal of a character. Your getting involved was as a result of being sold.

✔ **Waiters and waitresses:** The wise waiter gives you choices of drinks, appetisers, meals and desserts. He doesn't just ask to take your order. Why? Because when he employs a bit of salesmanship, he's almost guaranteed to increase the order value and be recognised as more effective by his employer.

- **Lawyers:** Lawyers need selling skills in every aspect of their profession. Lawyers have to sell not only to get business but also to persuade judges and juries that their clients are in the right.

- **Politicians:** How does the public develop its expectations about political candidates? How do politicians get elected? They persuade the most people that, if they're elected, they can and will do the job the voters want done. Every time you've voted or thought of voting one way, you've been sold on the politician and his cause.

- **Parents:** Whether by words or example, parents constantly sell their children values and beliefs. They convince or persuade their kids on what to wear or eat, how to act, who to have as friends, how to be a friend and thousands of other things children need to learn to grow into happy, well-adjusted adults.

- **Children:** Children are the best! We've all seen it: a child asking for something, being told 'No' and then coming out with all the reasons they should have that sweet or toy. Notice what kids say and how they act when they try to persuade Mum or Dad to get what they want. It's selling at its best.

- **Spouses-to-be:** If you get married someday, you'll put forth one of the most important sales presentations of your life in persuading your significant other of the value of spending the rest of his or her life with you. And if you're already married, the trick is to keep persuading your significant other to stay with you.

- **Friends:** If your friends enjoy a film, they'll probably want to tell you about it – and sell you on going to see it yourself. Your friends may recommend a place to eat or persuade you to go to concerts or sporting events with them. All these are examples of selling, but they're also examples of ways your friends build relationships with you. The more memories you share, the closer you continue to be – and so it is with the art of selling.

You're not immune from selling situations in your daily life – even if you don't come into contact with professional salespeople – and you may not even be aware that selling has occurred.

Thus, you can see, selling is a life skill, and you benefit in all areas when you improve this skill.

Chapter 2

Working Through the Seven-Step Selling Cycle

*W*e like to think of selling as a cycle because, if it's done properly, the last step in the cycle leads you back to the first. Your new, happy client gives you the names of other people she feels would benefit from your product or service, and then you have your next lead or prospect to work with.

Selling breaks down neatly into seven steps that almost everyone can remember. But don't worry, you can always refer back to this chapter if you don't memorise them immediately.

The seven steps we cover in this chapter are an overview of what you'll find available in greater detail in Part III. Each step is equally valuable to you. Rarely can you skip a step and still make the sale. Each step plays a critical role and leads you to the next step in a natural, flowing manner.

The cycle sets out with finding *prospects* (people who you target at the outset of the selling cycle who haven't yet purchased from you, but who might do so) to turn into *customers* (people who spend money to buy goods or services) and *clients* (usually people who represent a professional organisation or business), with the ultimate aim of converting them to *advocates* (people who sing and dance about your product to others and hopefully bring in even more sales for you).

Step 1: Prospecting Effectively

Prospecting means finding the right potential buyer for what you're selling. When planning where's best to sell your product or service, ask yourself, 'Who would benefit most from this?' For example:

- ✔ If the end user is a larger corporation, you need to establish exactly who's involved in the buying process. Typically, you have a purchasing director and then a layer or two of managers involved. You need to make contact with all if you're to be successful.

- ✔ If your end user is a family with school-aged children, you need to go where families are for example, football clubs and school events such as summer fêtes or Christmas bazaars. Or you can simply connect through strategic alliance partnerships with others who serve a similar audience. (More on that in Chapter 16.)

To make an informed decision about which prospects to approach, you need to find out some information about the people or companies you've chosen as possibilities. Do some research about any prospective client company at the local library or online. This legwork is a sort of prequalification step in prospecting. You'll do even more qualification when you meet a prospective client – but why waste time on an appointment with a company or person who wouldn't have a need for your offering?

Pre-qualifying is your own personal market research. In fact, one of the best places to begin your research if you work for a larger company is your company's marketing department. The marketing department may well have done research during the product development stage to determine what people want in the product or service you sell. Study their results, and you'll get a handle on where to begin.

If your company engages in advertising to promote your products, you'll likely receive *leads* – names of people who called or otherwise contacted the company for more information about the product. Treat any client-generated contact like gold. What better person to contact than one who's called you for information first!

In truth, potential is all around you and you need to always have your radar on alert and your ears and eyes open.

A word of advice here that applies to all selling situations: never begin any selling cycle until you've taken a few moments to put yourself in the shoes of the other person. Take yourself out of the picture and look at the entire situation through the eyes of the buyer. Mentally put yourself in her shoes and think about what would motivate you to invest your valuable time in reading a letter about your product or taking a salesperson's call. If you can't come up with solid answers, you may not have enough information about your product to even be selling it in the first place. Or you may not know enough about your potential audience to sell to them. If that's the case, it's back to the books for you. Study more about both areas until you're comfortable with being in that person's shoes. In other words, don't start prospecting until you have something of value to share with your prospects – something you're confident is worth their while to investigate and, hopefully, purchase.

If you ever face challenges getting through to potential clients, you may want to take a slightly different approach to get their attention or bring about a positive response. Some ideas our students have used include:

- ✔ **Enclosing a professional photograph of you smiling:** If you're selling into the domestic home environment, then naturally people are more cautious. Being open and honest enough to publicise your photo carries a lot of weight and will definitely increase your success rate. Showing that you're a real person dramatically improves connection.

- ✔ **Enclosing a newspaper or media article about the situation your potential customers find themselves in without your product or service:** If you source an article about something going wrong that your product or service solves, potential customers notice and remember when you follow up with a telephone call.

✔ **Adding a clever quote or anecdote to the bottom of your covering letter:** You can find books that have quotes for nearly any occasion, or simply surf the Web and tap into an on-going supply. Indeed, you can even download an application on your smart phone that provides regularly updated, inspirational and humorous quotes, so you're never without something quirky to add to your approach letter.

✔ **Sending a lottery ticket with the mail piece:** Use a cheeky headline question like 'Is this the best plan for your brighter future?' or 'If this doesn't work, what's your plan B?' and stimulate the idea that maybe the customer could look at other ways to secure her future. Whatever happens, the customer will remember you as different and speak with you when you call.

✔ **Sending a small toy to the target prospect:** It's entirely possible that your prospect has a hobby or pastime in which she's heavily involved. Discovering this and then sending something that resonates with the pastime is a brilliant door opener. For example, Ben once discovered that a prospect in a major target company was keen on vintage cars and so he sent a toy car along with a note saying, 'Here's a new jaguar to add to your collection!' His prospect saw the funny side, and when Ben dropped in, he remembered him and welcomed him in for a chat.

These ideas might, at first glance, appear a bit gimmicky, and you must adapt to suit your own style, but always remember that being noticed is half the battle won. The idea is to open your creative mind to unusual ways of reaching people and capturing their attention.

Step 2: Qualifying Your Prospect and Making Appointments

If prospecting is where you identify those who might be qualified to purchase your offering, then the next stage is to qualify the prospect. Then you make an appointment with the prospect so that you can proceed with your selling mission.

You need to find out not just who the prospect is, but also what she does specifically, what she has in terms of existing provision for what you sell and what she needs in terms of ways to improve production or efficiency or cut costs and so on.

You don't have to take on every client who qualifies for your product or service. Every now and then you meet a potential client and you instinctively know from your first conversation that you won't get along. You sense that as a customer the person will just be too demanding or never satisfied. If this happens, try passing the prospect on to another colleague or, failing that, to a similar competitor. If a business relationship isn't right at the beginning, it isn't going to be right down the line, so walk away and avoid the disputes and stress this client could cause you.

If you've done your homework and looked up information about the prospect, you know what questions to ask. The more specific your questions, the more impressed your potential client will be with your expertise. Asking pertinent questions shows that you're interested in more than just a closed sale and that you're looking into the future as a valued business partner with your client.

Your prospects no doubt receive calls almost every day from someone trying to sell them something, and so they too are wary and are qualifying you. Be aware of their time constraints and how to the point you are. Making appointments requires not merely conversation, but enough dialogue to engage interest, as prospects don't know you and are put off by fake friendly chat.

The goal of your qualification discussion is to determine how well-suited your product or service is to the prospect's situation – whether she can afford it and who the real final decision-makers are. Ask questions to get the prospect talking about what she has now, how it's not fulfilling her current needs and how much of a budget she has for making an improvement. These questions are the same whether you're selling to a business or an individual consumer. (Flip to Chapter 9 for the full scoop on the qualification process.)

Your goal is to make agreeing to an appointment as easy as possible. We strongly recommend giving your prospect two options with regard to dates and times. Say something like, 'I have an appointment opening on Tuesday at 9:30 a.m., or would Wednesday at 3:00 p.m. be better for you?' This makes the prospect look at her calendar and consider the open blocks of time in her schedule. Whereas if you just say, 'When can we get together?' she's likely to look at how busy she is and hesitate to commit.

When you get a commitment, confirm all the details, such as where the meeting will take place – and get directions if you haven't been there before. Also, get a commitment as to who'll be present. If you sell products to consumers and you know you'll need to have the agreement of both spouses, for example, you need to confirm that they'll both be present. If you're talking with a young, single person, she may decide to have a parent or other adult present to help her make her decision.

Step 3: Building Relationships

You've found the right people to be your potential buyers, you've qualified them and made the appointment, and now you feel that it's right to proceed and focus on the task at hand – selling. You meet with the prospects in a physical sense, and your aim is to persuade them to buy from you.

Remember the old adage 'first impressions last'. How you look, walk, talk and act plays a part in the prospect's mind even before you start to discuss the offering that you represent.

When you visit with a potential client, be sure to appear at ease so that your prospect is comfortable with you, and pay attention to dress codes so that you're suitably attired for the environment. If you're meeting in a business office environment, then wear a business suit; whereas if you're meeting in an outdoor arena, such as farming, jeans and boots may be more acceptable.

In a prospective client's mind, any shabbiness in your appearance translates into shabbiness in work habits or a lesser-quality product or service.

Because this is a business situation, be prepared to shake hands, make eye contact and build rapport. Building rapport is the getting-to-know-you stage that comes with any new contact. You must immediately begin building trust. People buy from people they like and trust. They must feel your trustworthiness as early as possible in the contact you make.

Having overcome the very first hurdle and survived the initial few minutes, your task is to build a relationship that's conducive to a sales-winning connection. Remember that the person sitting just the other side of the desk is just another person – not an alien! That means that she has feelings and concerns as she thinks about you, her job and the product or service that you offer. Treating the prospect as being the same as you is your best strategy.

Building relationships means that you need to communicate on personal stuff as well as business detail. Yes, you close the sale because the customer needs what you offer, but whether the sale is made with you or another very similar competitor is down to the human and personal connection. It might have been true a few years ago that the focus of a sale was simply product variables, but those days are gone. Very little difference exists in the provision between major competitors, and so the buyer needs to feel that she can get along with and trust the person she's about to buy from.

More than ever before, the selling process is mainly about opening than about closing. This means that you have to 'open' the person to being a friend and, in many ways, a business partner. In selling, the best client is one with whom you have a win-win arrangement, a partnership, in effect. And you build partnerships on people. It's the people in a company who deliver the service to install or service the machine that keeps production going. It's the people who allow communication on cash flow when times are tougher. It's the people who pass referrals on or who come up with solutions to challenges. Selling is a *people* business and so your mission is to build a *personal* relationship. Here are some ideas to help:

> ✔ **Talk about you:** Sharing some truths about your life, family, hobbies and so on paints you as a real person, not merely a selfish salesperson who might be perceived as caring very little about anything except commissions. Bring in the you factor and relationships flow. Don't brag

or try to impress; simply be yourself. The customer will likely share some of the same aspirations or challenges, and then you form a connection.

✔ **Talk about the customer:** Discuss the person in front of you, not merely their business function. It might be important that she's a chief purchasing officer, but it might be more important that she's a parent and is having challenges with teenagers – an issue on which you share common ground. Everyone loves to talk about themselves. Get people talking about themselves and they open up, and then your relationship strengthens.

✔ **Talk about careers:** The customer has a whole history of ups and downs and trials and tribulations. Get her sharing the good times. Ask about how she got through the tough times, ask about where she aims to be when she retires and congratulate her upon her achievements so far. All this career talk builds powerful relationships.

✔ **Talk about leisure:** Everybody needs and loves holidays, even the hardest workaholic, and so share stories about holiday experiences and, hopefully, common destinations. The customer sees you're just the same as her, and that means she can trust you – a major factor in the sales process.

Your sales visit is your absolute optimum time to win the deal, and this is singularly the biggest influencer in the whole selling process. Your ability to create rapport with prospects directly reflects in your sales results.

You won't win by being the cheapest, because people still (rightly) believe that you get what you pay for. You won't win by being the most exclusive, because people often can't afford what they'd like and have to settle for the mid-market option in which several players are deliberately very similar. Thus your only real edge is *you*.

Spend a lot of time practising conversation and people-connection skills and your sales career will dramatically expand. You still won't win every sale, because circumstances are sometimes beyond your control, but you will win more than most and be recognised as a high performer. Better than that though, by being better at building relationships, not only do you make more sales but you make a whole heap of great friends and business connections that carry you through and make every day much more enjoyable. (For plenty more pointers on relationship building, read Chapter 9.)

Step 4: Delivering Your Sales Presentation

Your presentation of your product, service or idea requires the most preparation. In your preparation, make a list of the benefits that you think are your strongest persuaders in placing your product, and make a list of the most common objections or questions that prospects raise. Then create different ways to explain the benefits while answering the objections or questions. Think ahead and prepare, so that you effectively draw attention to the strengths of your product, service or idea and cover any predictable objections so that the prospect can't raise them as objections after your presentation.

For example, suppose you're selling a business-to-business graphic design service where you know that you can provide superb designs and help the prospect with her marketing and promotional success. Because your service is new, you don't have a track record of success to brag about. So here's where you may start:

> PROSPECT: Well, it sounds like a potentially good idea, but I'm not sure if you can really deliver what we're looking for.

> SALESPERSON: Okay, I understand what you're saying. I don't have a huge portfolio of work to bounce off, and so I suggest that I create a series of examples that I think might work for you, at no cost initially. And then, when you see something that you do like, well, at that point you'll be able to do business with confidence, won't you?

The real issue is not that the service is new but that the client doesn't feel confident that you'd deliver what she's looking for because you're unknown. By showing that you're supremely confident in your ability to deliver what the prospect is looking for, and by taking away her fear of loss, you gain the chance to win the account.

To demonstrate personal dependability and trustworthiness, tell the prospective client an anecdote from another client situation or even from an outside activity of yours. For example, tell the story of how you got started and won your first account purely on your innovative designs, producing unexpectedly good results for the business, and that you believe you could do the same for today's prospect. Find a way to bring up those kinds of stories and paint pictures of reliability and delivery performance.

Your clients buy more than your product – they buy you.

Amazing things can happen during the presentation stage of a meeting. One of Ben's colleagues was delivering a presentation after having built a good relationship, when the prospect simply stopped him and asked, 'Will it be you who's looking after me, or will I get passed around the houses?' Quite evidently, the prospect's fear was that, as with similar situations when she'd purchased in the past, after she purchased she was not going to see the salesperson again. Ben's colleague simply stated, 'I'll always be your first point of contact, and I personally account manage in a very hands-on way. Rest assured, when we go ahead it will be me you're dealing with.' The prospect wanted to close the deal right then, even though my colleague hadn't done more than one-third of his presentation. The sale was made on the relationship feel and the first main point or two of the presentation.

Check out Chapter 10 for additional pointers on making winning presentations.

Step 5: Handling Objections

No matter how good your relationship building and presentation are, sometimes prospects raise objections. It's important, therefore, to understand how to handle customers' negative comments or concerns.

Don't allow an objection to become an argument! Never attack if you feel an objection was an attack on you.

Calmly and without emotion, clarify the objection. Did the customer in fact mean what you interpreted as the meaning?

For example, the objection might be: 'That's no good for me; it just wouldn't work.' A bold, defensive statement, but rather than confront it with a direct 'What do you mean it just won't work! It does work for thousands of other customers,' say, 'That's a very interesting comment, Mrs Prospect. Can I just ask for clarification: which bit of it in particular do you feel wouldn't work for you?' The prospect will most likely then expand her statement and expose an area where you can easily adjust what you provide, and then you reach a happy outcome. The key point is that your response is to gently question for more information, rather than defend your standpoint.

If you sidestep obstacles during your presentation, there's a good chance they'll come back to haunt you if you do get the sale. Find a way to bring up and elaborate on any concerns about fulfilling the needs of the buyer as early in the presentation as is appropriate. Don't let unfulfilled expectations bring your potential for a long-term relationship with a potential client to a bitter end. Cover all her concerns and make sure that she understands how those concerns will be handled – and that she's comfortable with it.

The most common concern you encounter is the good old standby stall: 'I want to think about it.' When someone says she wants to think about it, she may simply not be interested and doesn't want to be rude to you, or she may be interested in owning your product but genuinely need to think about the purchase or discuss something with someone else before she can give you an answer.

Your best strategy is to ask a gentle question to clarify *exactly* what she wants to think over. With emphasis on the word exactly, your prospect usually gives you a key reason. Sometimes she needs a little more information or some clarification of the finer points of your presentation. But, in the majority of cases, you find that money has caused her to stall. Surprise, surprise! Everyone wants a bargain. Unless your product or service is severely underpriced, most of your potential clients want to bargain or hesitate to see whether you'll offer to include something else just to get her to buy. The 'objection' then actually leads into a discussion about finer monetary details and hence to a closing situation. We cover this and other aspects of addressing client concerns in more detail in Chapters 11 and 12.

Step 6: Winning the Business

If you've researched your prospect properly, given yourself enough valuable preparation time, built a good strong relationship connection and handled all the previous steps in a professional manner, you'll likely close the sale. Closing should follow naturally and smoothly after you address your prospect's concerns. But if your prospect doesn't automatically pick up a pen to approve your paperwork or write a cheque, don't panic . . . and don't turn into the stereotypical nightmare salesperson and apply pressure to get what you want.

If you haven't got enough of a warm connection to openly discuss the reasons your prospect isn't going ahead today, then you've missed something earlier on. The prospect interprets closing with smart questions as pressure, and you lose the ground you might have already gained. However, winning your prospect's business might be as simple as saying, 'If today isn't ideal for you, when would you prefer to proceed with this order?' At this point, if you're confident about being able to give her what she needs, you should begin taking verbal ownership of your future business relationship with assumptive statements and questions.

When it comes time to close, you've hopefully reduced any sales resistance the person had early on and increased her level of sales acceptance so that it's just a matter of agreeing on the details of start-up or delivery dates and/or financing arrangements. We cover many methods of getting that final agreement in Chapter 12.

Step 7: Getting Referrals

After you close the sale, take a moment to ask for referrals. This can be as simple as asking, 'Because you're so happy with this decision today, would you mind if I ask you for the names of other people you know who may also be interested in learning about this product?' If you're selling a service to the home owner and the client has mentioned other family members in the area, ask, 'Who in your family would also enjoy the benefits of our fine lawn service?' Or, 'Which of your neighbours takes the most pride in their garden?'

In a corporate situation, ask about other departments within the company that may need your same service. Then ask about other office locations that the same company has. Finally, ask about associates of the purchasing agent who may work at non-competing companies.

If for some reason you and the prospective client find that this isn't the best time to go forward with the sale, instead of just saying goodbye and walking out of the door, make the contact a part of your network of people who can help you find *more* people who may benefit from your product or service. For example, another department in your prospect's company may have people who could benefit from your product or service. Or the prospect may know of other companies needing your product. Never walk away from an opportunity to network.

Turn to Chapter 13 for additional information on getting referrals.

Chapter 3

Selling and Your Mindset for Success

* *

In This Chapter

▶ Analysing your satisfaction with what you do for a living

▶ Seeing how thinking affects performance

▶ Becoming a lifelong student

▶ Getting out of your comfort zone and facing new challenges

▶ Selling what people want to own

* *

*T*he main factor that separates the top 5 per cent of people in sales from those who struggle to accomplish their goals is very simple: highly successful salespeople actually *enjoy* what they do. To the top professionals, selling isn't merely a job, it's a passion. They love selling.

The more involved you get with selling, the more selling you observe going on around you in all areas of your life. When you truly *study* selling, you see that selling pervades every communication you have with others, and, on a purely business level, you notice and compare the selling efforts of others to your own. The fun part is that people never know what you're up to. You get to make all the mental notes you want, and they get to be your teachers. The best opportunity for discovery often (if not usually) occurs in an informal, non-selling atmosphere. In times and situations that you may not previously have seen as sales situations per se, a realisation will creep right up on you and whisper, 'Hey, there's selling going on here. You should be taking notes.'

In this chapter, we show you the way people usually approach something that they love doing, such as their hobbies, and help you find a way to approach selling in the same way. We demonstrate how you can challenge yourself throughout your lifetime to discover new things and explore new pathways, and we give you an idea of what to expect along the way. Remember always that attitude and passion are a huge part of success – in sales and in life – and in this chapter we cover both so you can put them to work for you.

Making Sure You Get Job Satisfaction

You've probably heard the advice to 'never mix business with pleasure'. That advice is well-meaning and, indeed, helps you remember not to destroy your circles of friends by trying to sell to all of them! However, the advice is maybe a little wide of the mark if you take it literally: you *must* derive pleasure from your business of selling or you'll never succeed. When you position the role of selling in the same mindset as your hobby, you blur the distinction between what you do to live and what you live to do. When you get the hang of making your work your hobby, you *always* mix business with pleasure – quite successfully.

When you don't enjoy what you do to earn money, your life becomes a draining trade-off – you swap long hours at work for very short holidays. Our question to you is this: as short as life is, are those 2 fun-filled weeks every summer worth the 50 weeks of drudgery you have to go through to earn them? We certainly hope they are. After all, you're on this earth for such a short time that you may as well do something you enjoy.

If you're in sales, you can find a multitude of ways to enjoy what you're already doing. If you discover and practise the communication skills that are a part of selling in your every-day encounters, your life is guaranteed to be more interesting. And anything that you're interested in has to include at least a little fun or it won't hold your interest, will it?

Do you ever have to drag yourself to work? Do you really dislike the 'back to work' thought when your holidays are ending? If you answer 'yes' to those questions, you need to take a long, hard look at what you do for a living and how much satisfaction it's bringing you. You may even want to seek professional career advice. We urge you, don't do a job just because it provides for you and your family when actually, every day, you feel less than happy about it.

Love the one you're with . . .

A merging of passion and profession has occurred in Ben's life with selling. For Ben, selling began as a career opportunity that would fulfil a need – the need to make money. And so, despite his mum saying 'It'll do until you get a proper job!', he entered into the world of commission-only double-glazing sales. He very quickly discovered the incredible high of winning a sale and, indeed, the need to improve so that he could maintain that high and win more often.

It was at that point that Ben chose to turn selling into his hobby. When he started to educate himself – by watching everyday people and looking for little nuances of selling that worked for them, and by reading up on the subject – he also started making a lot of money. He watched every person he met, he watched and listened to every phone call that was made, he mimicked the styles of the company's top performers and he discovered the massive joy of winning more and more in all areas of life.

Since then he's managed to transform his job-turned-hobby into something much more: it has become a way of life. Today, he lives and breathes selling. He's built his business in such a way that he enjoys what he does for a living. He doesn't 'work' any more, if *work* means doing some particular thing when you'd rather be doing something else. Selling now pervades every communication he has with others, and he thoroughly enjoys his life these days.

If you're in a job you don't like in order to earn a living, stop for a moment and analyse what's going on. Why don't you like what you're doing? Chances are pretty good that it's because you're not growing, achieving or having fun. If this description fits your life, you have two ways out: either you can change what you do to something that's more fun, or you can get better at what you already do in order to make it more fun. That's the great thing about living today: you have choices. No one is going to hold a gun to your head and tell you that you have to have this career and no other. If you aren't happy with what you've got, thousands of other choices are available to you. You have no excuse for staying in a job you don't thoroughly enjoy, but it's up to you to do something about it.

Wouldn't it be much more fun to take each day and enjoy it to its fullest, looking forward to getting up every morning, bright-eyed and bushy-tailed, vibrant with anticipation for what the day will bring? Wouldn't it be better to enjoy your workdays as much as you enjoy your free time? What would your life be like if you could enjoy your job as much as you enjoy your hobbies? What kind of life and home environment would you be providing for those around you, if the central element of your life was no longer drudgery, but rather the joy that comes from self-fulfilment?

Now, we're not saying that you won't still get tough days, but for the most part a life selling something that you really enjoy selling makes life so much more liveable. And if you're willing to spend a little time examining how to view your sales job as you do your hobby (with the help of the rest of this chapter), you can make this dream a reality.

Thinking of Your Job as a Hobby

Think for a moment about how you view your hobbies and how you view your job. If you're like most people, you gladly talk about your children's lives, your last ski trip, your favourite authors, your holiday plans and your leisure pursuits. You may talk about your cycling or your remote-controlled car or your latest dinner party recipe or barbeque success. Most people shine as they talk about their passions and pursuits, which they just love.

What makes people successful in their hobbies? Have you ever noticed the difference in expression and animation in people when they talk about their hobbies compared to when they talk about their jobs? If you haven't noticed this up to now, test this theory yourself. Ask a few people this question and pay attention to their answers: 'How do you like to spend your days?' Rarely will you hear about people's jobs. Instead, the conversation usually turns to how they spend their recreation time.

We believe that if more people looked at selling as they do their hobby – with energy, enthusiasm, excitement, fervour, anticipation, devotion and sheer fun – they would be leaders in all walks of their lives.

In the following sections, we take a closer look at the way people view their hobbies and let you know how you can harness those same traits and apply them to your selling – a path sure to bring you success.

Attitude makes a difference

Studies have proven that having a great attitude is one of the major traits that separates average salespeople from their highly successful colleagues. And we believe this is true in life in general, not just in sales. Think about the happiest, most successful people you know. How do you usually find them? Are they depressed, negative or even apathetic? We doubt it. They're probably upbeat, smiling and positive about life.

Success can fit many definitions – including yours

We always enjoy asking seminar audiences for definitions of the term *success*. We've probably asked well over 4,000 people to define *success* for us over the years. We haven't kept strict records on their answers, but we'd have to guess that we've rarely had repeat answers. That's because success is something like a fingerprint; it's individual. Of course, many of the answers we've received have reflected a desire for monetary riches, love and security, but few people have been able to come up with a definition of success that all who hear it understand and agree upon.

We've thought a lot about a definition of success and developed this one:

> **'Success is being consciously happy and able to spend your time doing what pleases you.'**

We like the phrase 'to spend your time doing what pleases you' because we believe that to be the raison d'être for everyone. Success is a journey, not a destination – it's about each day, not about one end point. If your focus is only on one end goal, then you set yourself up either for disappointment when you possibly don't attain it, or disappointment when you do and no longer have something to aim for! However, being happy each day and enjoying the now truly is a wonderful state to be in . . . that is being a success.

Consider using this definition for yourself, and lay a course for an exciting journey toward success!

Why not take the same positive, interested attitude you have towards your hobbies and transfer that attitude to your ability to sell yourself, your ideas and your products or services? Challenge yourself to read up on selling strategies. Of course, you're doing that with this book, but what will you do after that? While you're driving, will you listen to the radio, or will you inspire yourself to greater success by listening to selling-skills CDs or MP3s?

Give yourself permission to explore some creative ways of starting conversations with others who may have a need for your product or service. Observe how the next salesperson you encounter makes you feel. What did he say or do that brought about that feeling? Challenge yourself to pay attention, and you'll soon find yourself eagerly anticipating the next selling situation.

Passion supplies meaning

Another key trait that hobby enthusiasts have that many people don't have with their work is emotional involvement – in other words, passion. Consider this example: if your hobby is an outdoor sport, such as mountain biking, nothing is more exciting than cresting mountain peaks at sunrise or soaring downhill so fast that you have a permanent grin on your face. It's not just a physical experience either: it's charged with emotional involvement. When you schedule a biking event, it becomes a highlight that gives you a great feeling whenever you think about it. You plan every detail to make the outing the best one yet. You live and breathe for the next opportunity to get out there with your mountain-biking cohorts. When you think about your biking events, you feel an emotional jolt. When you get right down to it, avid mountain bikers have become sold on their pastime because they want to experience the emotional involvement. Thus, emotional involvement or passion for what you do is key.

Sadly, people often lack that passion with their jobs. They then become disillusioned, detached from their work environment and waste away their days just existing. By way of contrast, those who are emotionally involved with their work bring enthusiasm to their jobs and life itself, which is much more interesting and fun. Our suggestion is that you find a way to bring that emotional involvement into your sales role and your whole life as well.

Sales, as a career, is one of the very few and rare environments where you have the opportunity to like so many aspects of the work and still get paid for it! Here are just a few elements of the job that many salespeople love:

✔ Meeting new people – they're interested in how other people live their lives and they seek out new ideas and opinions on topics that they previously barely knew existed

✔ The buzz from achieving the sale, and, especially in the beginning, the knowledge that only they set the limit on how much income they earn

✔ For those sales positions that require travel, meeting other travellers, seeing new sites, visiting different climates and finding out about different cultures

✔ The flexibility that's often available in certain sales positions, which allows them to schedule valuable family time or to participate in hobbies or sporting events that occur when the rest of the world works

✔ Entertaining clients, which can involve attending sporting events that some salespeople wouldn't otherwise have opportunities to attend

If you're having trouble finding even one little thing to like about your job, we suggest that you seriously consider making a change: either change yourself, or change your job. You don't have to suffer through a job you dislike. The world is a whirl of opportunity. But beware the temptation to always blame exterior causes when you can resolve the dissatisfaction with some honest internal dialogue and a fresh look at your attitude, energy and input.

Becoming a Lifelong Student of Selling

Starting the hobby of selling is pretty simple. You don't need any special tools or equipment. No large financial investment is required. And you don't have to travel far to participate.

So what do you need to do to start making selling your favourite pastime? Watch and learn! Pay attention to the way your children or parents communicate with you about family matters. Watch how sales assistants treat you, and notice how you feel about the shop in response. Get into the habit of really *reading* billboards and newspaper ads. Which ones are talking directly to you and why? Listen carefully to radio spots; those that hold your attention the longest deserve some analysis. In general, become an avid student of the selling that is presented to you daily by everyone from sales and marketing experts to your friends and family.

In the following sections, we explain the importance of setting aside time to learn about selling and we provide tips for working your way through the learning process.

Making time to learn about selling

Although people allow their children the privilege of ample time to learn, they often don't allow themselves as adults the same privilege. The large majority of people discontinue their conscious learning experiences in life when they complete their formal education. Hundreds of thousands of mature adults haven't learned in the past 20 years half as much as they learned in their years at secondary school.

Adults make excuses for themselves, saying that they don't have the time to take educational courses. Or they think that they can learn faster on their own. Or, dangerously, they assume that they don't really need to know much more than they already know . . . until they tune in to a quiz show on TV or take part in a pub quiz and find out exactly how much they don't know!

Most adults fail to continue the learning process not because of a lack of desire, but because of a perceived lack of time. They expect youngsters to spend most of their time on education, with a strong dose of fun thrown in for good measure. But somewhere along the way, as people grow into adults, that focus shifts to the responsibilities they have for financial and family matters. Their desire for achievement overwhelms them and taking time out for education just doesn't happen.

The good news is this: studies have shown that developing the habit of listening to educational programmes in your car during commuting time can provide you with just as much information as studying for a Master's degree. How hard can it be to carry some CDs or an MP3 player around with you all the time? You probably already do it with music. But when was the last time your favourite music group taught you anything that made you more successful in life?

Today, almost anything you want to learn about is available 24/7 via the Internet. You can watch videos on YouTube, download a thousand e-courses and free e-books from another thousand websites, all within ten minutes of surfing, and you can devour them on the move or in any environment with today's mobile world of smartphones and tablet computers.

 So, in eliminating convenience, what's left is time. Do you recall the old story about the two men cutting wood? One worked hard and steady all day. The other worked hard too, but every now and then would stop. At the end of the day the second man had cut more wood, much to the surprise of the first. When asked how he did it, he said, 'Every time I took a break, I sharpened my saw.' We challenge you to set aside a specific amount of time every week – or at the very least, every month – to sharpen your saw. Register for a seminar that's coming to your area. Invest a couple hours a week in a bookshop or library to find out about the latest books that have been published on the field of selling or on your industry in particular. Put your hands on one and read! After taking in that new information, you won't be the same person you were before. You'll see the world just a little bit differently, and your hobby of selling will progress even further.

From now on, challenge yourself to think of training seminars and educational events as professional necessities. Take these learning tools out of the realm of things to do 'when you have the time' and put them into the category of things that you *must* do to reach the levels of success you set for yourself. Shift your perspective only that much, and you'll *make* the time to continue your education – you'll become a lifelong learner.

Working in bite-sized chunks

When you begin to learn anything, you can absorb only so much before you experience what we call a *brain cramp*. This happens when you reach a point of information overload. You've taken in the information, but haven't yet processed how to make it work in your life. The perceived pressure to learn means you try to force all the info in at once, but that's not going to work.

The best approach to learning something new is to learn, digest and then relearn and practise the skill. Do your learning, and application of what you've learned, in bite-sized chunks. You can internalise only so much information at once, so break the learning down into smaller steps. Get a good understanding of one step before taking on the next.

If you're new to sales, you want to concentrate on prospecting and appointment-making strategies (which we cover in Chapters 7 and 8, respectively) and, in particular, you need to work on your relationship-building conversation skills (as we cover in detail in Chapter 9).

If you're a bit shy or uncomfortable with first-meeting greetings, work on just that step of selling for a while (see Chapter 8 for guidance). Write yourself a script and stick to it. Then change one word or phrase and continue to use it – refining it as you go until you find the one that breaks the ice faster with more new people.

True selling is the art of communication. This includes asking good questions and really listening to the answers. If this is your area of weakness, see Chapter 9.

Many novices who choose to consciously develop sales skills want instant success. We think it has something to do with the 'instant' mentality triggered by emails and SMS messaging. Also, when you see experienced professionals can make a skill look easy, you assume you can therefore easily master the skill. Not so! Don't look at others who are more successful than you are and try to duplicate their sales techniques overnight. They're successful because they've practised, drilled and rehearsed their material over a period of time. They've already experimented with the nuances of body language, voice intonation and inflection that you're just introducing yourself to. Keep in mind that old saying, 'Don't assume anything about another person until you've walked in his shoes.'

Knowing that it's okay to get it wrong sometimes

Giving yourself permission to be a lifelong student can change your life dramatically. But students don't always do things right the first time around. So when you give yourself permission to be a student, you also give yourself the right to make mistakes. Don't beat yourself up when you don't immediately get it as right as you'd like. Remember that there is no wrong, just a not-quite-right way – the mentality of Thomas Edison who, after recording 1,000 so-called failed attempts to create a light bulb, stated, 'I didn't fail. I simply found a way not to do it.' Having found one way not to do it, you're one step nearer to finding the right way!

If you have the attitude and mindset of a student, you don't beat yourself up over your failures and mistakes. Instead, you look at your mistakes as learning experiences. As a student, you must admit that you're fallible. Until you make that admission, you won't move far off the mark you're currently standing on.

After you do admit that you can make mistakes, though, seek out others who can teach you, people who can help you grow into the person you want to become. When you open yourself up to the possibility that you don't know everything and don't have all the answers, you start a quest to discover what you don't know – and that's an important step in the learning process.

One of our favourite reminders about learning is this: you can recognise true professionals by how much they learn *after* they 'know it all'. If you ever assume you know all there is to know about something, or even if you accept that you know enough, you've just doomed yourself to mediocrity.

Moving out of your comfort zone

To get to the level of comfort and success you want in your selling career, you need to step outside your comfort zone. Your *comfort zone* is where you are today, and unless you change who and what you are today, you'll never change what you're getting out of life.

Along with 'When you're green you grow, when you're ripe you rot', Ben's motto is 'comfort kills'. When you become comfortable, the push to go forward usually stops pushing. You start to say, 'Why push? I like where I am!' But you need to keep the forward momentum so that you're never satisfied with what you know and how good you are. If you accept that you want to be the best, then you always accept that you've more to learn, and so you can never be comfortable with your own level of growth. With that realisation, you make yourself *uncomfortable* with the extent of your own ignorance.

This striving for knowledge can become wonderfully habit-forming. It's such a kick to learn and benefit from new concepts and ideas that the highest achievers in life have become addicted to it. They wouldn't think of facing a single day without the anticipation of learning something new.

Rome Wasn't Built in a Day: Understanding Your Development Process

Learning anything takes time and practice. This is what people refer to as a *learning curve* – the time it naturally takes for someone to progress from a complete beginner to an expert. In any learning curve, you go through four major phases or levels of competency. We cover each of them in the following sections.

Unconscious incompetence

The first level of competency is known as *unconscious incompetence*. In this most elementary phase, you find people who don't even know that they don't know what they're doing. These people are the hardest ones to help because they haven't yet recognised that they need help, or won't admit it. In daily life, these are the people who stay in the same job year after year even though they constantly moan about it. They live in a set routine and even eat similar meals on similar days because they like their habits. They tend to live rather mediocre lives because either they haven't realised there's more to be learned – more to be aware of – or they've simply resigned themselves to be whatever they are at the present moment.

In business, this may include someone who has been in sales for a little while, has had just enough 'success' to have not lost his job and sees himself as having done it all. He knows the product and how to fill out the paperwork, and thinks that's all there is to the story. He thinks that the best performing salesperson achieves his results because of his relationship with the management and his getting all the best leads or territories. He doesn't even know there are things such as strategies, proper methods of asking questions and all the other good stuff that we explain in this book.

Conscious incompetence

The second level is *conscious incompetence*. People abandon unconscious incompetence when they suddenly realise that they don't know what they're doing. In the wonderful world of sales, you're very likely at the conscious incompetence level right now simply because you're reading this book. You've admitted that you don't have all the answers and that you want to find out more. You know that you still have something to learn and have taken steps to address the situation.

But here's the caveat – being aware of a need is only good when you take the action to address the need. Take action right away! Too many potentially great careers have been stalled at this level because people don't know where to turn for help or won't expend the effort to find the right kind of help. Your lack of competency can be overwhelming if you don't take charge. Don't be like the deer you see in your headlights at night, frozen to a spot on the road. You must *move* in order to rise to the third level of competency.

Begin by reading this book, of course. Then move on to *Sales Closing For Dummies* and *Sales Prospecting For Dummies*, both written by Tom. (The folks at Wiley are trying to be as helpful as possible in providing resources for you.)

If you're a person who learns better by connecting with a 'live' person, possibly in a seminar environment, then connect with Ben at www.benkench.com or search online for www.grow mysmallbusinessnow.com, where Ben coaches sales and business improvement techniques in live events every month. Listen to any recording or audio download a minimum of six times to achieve maximum retention of the material.

Once upon a time, a future sales success and professional speaker was totally lost for words

For an example of acutely conscious incompetence in action, think about the first time you had to give a presentation in front of a group. It probably wasn't much fun, was it? If it was anything like Ben's first time, you came off the stage vowing to never allow that to happen again. Ben explains:

'In my early days as a salesperson, I was deputised to take the sales meeting. Now to be fair I'd been with this sales team for a matter of just nine months. Nonetheless, I was a pretty confident young chap who'd proven over the last few months that my initial weeks of success weren't a fluke and that I could handle selling up against the old timers, despite all of the to-be-expected knock-backs and lousy appointments. The sales manager was called to another arrangement at the last minute and he asked me to chair the meeting. Well, I was ambitious and keen, so I ignored any doubts and agreed to the opportunity without thinking about preparation . . . until he left the showroom and it was all down to me!

'To say I didn't quite do as well as I might have is an understatement. I faced the team and immediately saw a look of indignation on many senior faces. They were wondering why this new kid was taking the meeting. I felt their resentment and the attitude that nothing I had to say was of any relevance.

'In the face of such hostility, I froze. I mumbled my way through an introduction and explanation as to where the manager was, and then rushed through my thoughts on last week's sales league tables and this week's performances – all the while conscious of my reddening face. I skipped the bit I'd watched my manager do each week about advising the team on how to handle a challenging sales situation and closed the meeting, promptly rushing to get a cup of tea in the sanctuary of the kitchen. A hideous experience!

'When my manager returned, I emptied my anger and frustration upon him. When I'd calmed down, he explained that had he given me more notice, I would probably have found an excuse not to do it and avoided the challenge. He went on to explain that I was ambitious and capable and that he believed I would make a great sales leader one day, but that I would have to master the art of holding an audience and that experience couldn't come too soon. A baptism of fire, yes, but for a genuine reason – and one I thanked him for later in my career.

'Although it was true that I didn't do too well, I faced the challenge. The audience might have been less than pleased but I had proven that this was a hurdle I could jump. Indeed, I discovered that speaking publicly is really no different from selling. So I learned to approach public speaking with the same confidence and energy as an everyday sales call. I focused on one person at a time in the audience and 'sold'. Doing so isn't that difficult, and now when I speak to audiences, the bigger, the better!'

Conscious competence

When you reach the third level, *conscious competence*, you find new challenges and new victories. By this point, your desire to improve has become strong enough to overcome the discomfort of learning something new. You're testing the waters now. You know how to do the thing you're learning, but you have to think about it, be conscious of it, in order to succeed.

You're practising the new material you've learned. You're rehearsing in your bedroom or car before an appointment, rather than on qualified clients and potentially losing them due to awkwardness with the material. You're trying new things and making adjustments – and that's good.

Be careful! Don't place too high a level of expectation on yourself, and then you'll do better, faster. Tensing up when you try new things takes your enjoyment from the experience. Relax a little and don't fear failure. Remember, you never fail as long as you keep trying.

Unconscious competence

At the fourth and final level of competence, *unconscious competence*, you apply all your previous knowledge without making a conscious effort to do so.

You're making headway and things are generally pretty good. Indeed, you're smack in the middle of an example of unconscious competence right now – you're reading this book. You probably aren't reading it as would someone who's just learning to read. Instead of uttering each syllable individually as you point and sound it out, hoping for eventual comprehension, you're able to cruise along and seek the content you're looking for, not even thinking about what you're doing.

As an unconscious competent salesperson, the strategies are now a natural part of your presentation. In fact, if you were to record your presentation, you'd recognise each nuance and recall when and why you added it – because it sounded good at the time. You've kept it because it works!

A tremendous advantage of being a lifelong student is that you no longer allow yourself the luxury of seeing yourself as a victim of circumstance. You take responsibility for your successes *and* your failures, and you're more likely to be honest with yourself when it comes to evaluating those successes and failures.

Knowing How to Sell What Your Customers Want to Own

As in any area of life, in the world of selling, if you have the wrong attitude, you can end up being your own worst enemy. Many people in selling situations have a challenge with their own likes and dislikes – they tend to sell only what they like and mostly to the people they like. You do need to like and believe in what you're selling. But if you're in a career sales position, you probably have to sell other items in the product line that may not be your favourites.

You must always keep what's right for the customer in the forefront of your mind. If you sell only what you like, you also severely limit your income and risk losing clients to a competing supplier who sells what you don't like to sell.

Your job is to enthusiastically sell whatever benefits your customers, whoever they may be. During your selling career, you have to work with some people whom you don't particularly like. (We discuss how to deal with several personality types in Chapter 7.) If you refuse to work with some people, both you and the customers lose. You lose opportunities to make sales, and the customers lose opportunities to have their needs satisfied. The people you turn down will just get their needs filled by someone else. The moral of the story: keep your mind and your opportunities open.

Be sure not to prejudge people when you're selling to them. Whether you realise it or not, you make some sort of judgement about people the moment you lay your eyes on them. You judge them based on their physical condition, their clothing, their hairstyle, their posture. In selling situations, though, acting on preconceptions is a dangerous habit that you need to control. If you're committed to becoming a professional, force yourself to look at every customer with clear vision. We could share with you hundreds of painful examples where a salesperson squandered an opportunity simply by erroneously pre-judging the prospect and the situation. Eliminate those preconceived notions before they start costing you money!

Always assume that the prospect is a buyer. Treat your prospects with the respect you would expect to receive were you in their shoes and extend to them the courtesy and hospitality that you would to a friend and you'll probably then make a friend in the process. This may sound suspiciously similar to the Golden Rule – 'Do unto others as you would have them do unto you' – as well it should, as it is timeless wisdom. Keep in mind the following tips about the kind of attitude you need to have in the world of selling, and your self-control will pay off in the long run:

- ✔ If you want others to agree with you, first be agreeable.

- ✔ Don't let people's outward appearances affect the way you react to them.

- ✔ Always act as though each person you contact is the most important person in your life.

With the right attitude, your selling career can take you as far as you want and introduce you to anybody or anything that you desire. The product or service that you offer can be a significant link for you to billions of other people who need what you have to offer.

Someone else's selling nightmare can be your dream come true

Ben vividly remembers a situation many years ago in which he had the opportunity to learn at first-hand a critical lesson about prejudging clients.

He was selling property to holidaying couples possibly looking for a holiday home or investment property. He was new to the company and waiting his turn to see a prospect.

A gentleman came into the reception of the company and explained that he'd like to have a look around. Well, frankly he looked decidedly scruffy! His clothing was old and dirty and his general appearance was dishevelled – hardly what Ben expected if the man had the wherewithal to afford a property worth £200,000 plus.

The reception staff and the more experienced salesperson whose turn it was to see the next client were unwilling to even entertain him, and consequently the man was passed over to a less experienced salesperson (Ben) so that he wouldn't waste anybody more valuable's time. To cut a long story short, the gentleman was indeed a serious customer, who purchased a property at full price and paid the £10,000 deposit from his carrier bag full of cash. Ben received a healthy commission; not so his more experienced colleague who had judged the man based on appearances.

That moment has stayed with Ben ever since and flashes through his mind whenever he finds himself tempted to judge a potential client in a selling situation.

Part II
Doing Your Homework before You Sell a Thing

'This is a more upmarket product for the brighter child – It contains punctuation.'

In this part...

In this part you find out about prospecting and client gathering. We share ideas to help you in your research so that your product knowledge and market knowledge are always valuable assets in your client interaction. We look at the involvement of technology in your selling role; particularly at how this can have a profound impact on your effectiveness and on time management challenges.

Chapter 4

Understanding Your Potential Clients

Sometimes the hardest thing in starting something new is breaking through old teachings or beliefs that you've always held as being the way to do something and adopting a new approach. We're sure you remember the old adages 'Ignorance is bliss' and 'What you don't know can't hurt you'. However, in today's world of selling, the fact is that what you don't know can hurt you massively! Times have changed, people and their expectations have changed and you need to change or adapt if you're to survive.

When you're simply an observer, you can believe that something that appears smooth and effortless is, in fact, easy to do. The real champions, however, master their craft, and what you don't seeing on the surface is all the practice and dedication that happens behind the scenes and over the years of effort to improve. When selling looks natural, you know that hours and hours of planning and preparation have gone before.

One of the reasons people don't succeed as perhaps they might is the 'I know' attitude. Being resistant to learning and defensively proud is the mark of an average performer. Winners recognise that constant improvement and active learning are keys to greater and greater success. Beware falling into the 'I know' trap!

In the world of selling, preparation is key, and this chapter is a great introduction to issues you may not have considered before. We cover some specific ways that you can prepare, so that you can serve your clients better – everything from researching your prospective customers before you even set up an appointment to knowing how to listen to them when you finally do meet.

Understanding Why Research Is Important

Why do you need to research your prospective clients and their businesses? So that, at the moment of truth, when you're giving a presentation or getting ready to close the sale, your lack of knowledge won't trip you up.

Your knowledge about a prospective client's situation – or lack of it – goes a long way on the making-an-impression scale. We've sat on the other side of the desk and we know how exciting it is to be present when someone who's really made the effort to research sits in front of you. And we've experienced the opposite situation, when the person is obviously ignorant and kills any chance of success as soon as that becomes evident.

Your time invested prior to attempting to present or approach a company can make all the difference between success and failure. So always research. In doing so you show that you care about your prospect and you're demonstrating professionalism, which the prospect is eager to experience.

For example, say you sell air-filtration systems to businesses, and you find out that a particular business must maintain a degree of air purity in their production environment. That's critical information that impacts the sale required. Not knowing this info would clearly demonstrate a lack of preparation and care, and most likely scare off the potential buyer who would fear production disaster if you got it wrong after the sale.

Adapting your message to what your clients tell you about themselves and their needs

If you doubt the validity of the premise that knowledge is power, take a look at how much information websites gather about the people who visit them. For example, Tesco no longer just sells groceries. It offers you an opportunity to purchase a comprehensive range of ancillary products and services with your groceries. It gives you special coupons for similar products to entice you back into its stores. The key is intelligence.

Tesco developed the Clubcard system, and it monitors everything you spend. By matching and comparing your data to other shoppers' data, Tesco builds up a buyer profile that allows it to consistently offer things

that suit the buyer. Tesco is brilliant in its execution of this strategy.

You can apply the same idea. Intelligence gathering on a wide range of subjects allows you to build similar profiles, and then you aim your marketing and sales messages directly at the prospect. When you approach prospects with an on-target message, your chances of a listening ear rise dramatically – and your sales success rises dramatically too.

Intelligence is the key to success, so always gather and store as much information as possible – it will come in handy one day and you'll be glad that you did. For tips on storing information, head over to Chapter 6 on technology.

Researching a company using any and all avenues, especially its website, gives you many important clues as to how best to deal with the prospect. For example, you may find information on awards and standards to meet, plus examples of the client base, illustrating the size and type of customer the business sells to. You may also find pricing information – if the company pitches its price structures as 'discount' or 'special offer', it's clearly very price sensitive and you'd do well to adjust how you position and price accordingly.

The same principle that you use when you sell to business applies when you sell to the consumer or in the domestic environment. The more you know about people's background, the better. You warm people up faster when you talk about their hobbies, jobs and kids than you do if you know nothing other than their address and phone number. For example, if you're selling air-filtration systems, and you know that one of the prospect's children has allergies or asthma, your demonstration of this knowledge and your presentation from a slightly different angle scores you valuable brownie points.

You may be wondering how you'd find out about a prospect's child's asthma or allergies. You can do that in one of several ways, including a brief survey-type phone call asking if anyone in the home has or has ever had allergies or other illnesses that are affected by the quality of the air in the home.

In addition, list brokers often have enough information about a potential client that you can find out what types of pets they have, cleaning products they purchase and whether they make a lot of long-distance phone calls. How do they get this information? Think about it. Have you ever filled out a survey about the products you use in order to receive free grocery coupons? Do you send in for rebates on products? If you do any of this sort of thing, those companies don't just send your coupons or rebates and toss your reply card. They store that valuable purchasing information about you in their databases for future reference.

Getting to Know Your Clients Inside and Out

To be successful at selling, you must be constantly looking out for and storing information. What type of information? Everything and anything about your product, your company, your competition and (most importantly) your prospect. And with the Internet just a mouse-click away, you really have no excuse for not being well informed. An abundance of information is available, quite literally, at your fingertips.

You've heard the phrase 'Knowledge is power' – but simply knowing it isn't enough. *Applied* knowledge – taking what you've learned and actively using it to demonstrate its benefit to clients – is where your power lies.

The most important thing to remember when you're selling is the benefit of being able to walk in someone else's shoes. Being able to see the situation from another person's perspective is a wonderful skill that, when demonstrated, will win you a lot of sales.

So where do you begin in your quest to walk in your prospects' shoes? Not at the shoe shop! Instead, you need to do some basic research into your prospective clients, their businesses and their goals. Start by following these tips:

✔ **Gather as much literature and other information as possible on a company before approaching it with your offering.** You want to be as prepared as possible before you make that first approach – that way, you're starting off on the right foot from the very beginning.

✔ **Visit the business's website.** Pay particular attention to the business's online product catalogue (if there is one), and look for press releases posted on the site so you're up to date on the most recent news related to the business. Plus, always look for an 'About Us' link on the website. The information you'll find there often gives you valuable insight into the management team and their backgrounds. And who knows? You may find out that you know someone who works there or you know someone who knows someone there.

✔ **Get copies of the company's product brochures and/or catalogues.** Talk with one of its customer service representatives about what the company offers. If you're familiar with the products that your prospective client sells, you're better able to sell her *your* product.

✔ **Visit your local library or surf the Internet and look up past news articles on the business.** If you're familiar with what's been happening in the industry in the past few months, you can work that information into your conversations with the people who work in the industry. The prospect gets the sense that you've done your homework about her – so you've probably done your homework about your own products too. And that's exactly the impression you want to make.

✔ **Check out the business's accounts, if they're available.** If what you sell requires a considerable financial investment, you don't want to find that you've done all the hard work and then the client can't finance the deal. Many companies these days have limited or no credit options and you don't want to be simply creating a debt situation for your company.

By law in the UK, all limited companies have to return a filing of their accounts to Companies House, and you can access this type of credit information prior to approaching any targeted prospects. Go to www. companieshouse.gov.uk for any company-related finance information, along with www.creditsafeuk. com. You can also use an organisation such as Experian (www.experian.co.uk) if your prospecting is within the domestic consumer market. All of these fine sites enable a company to search the creditworthiness of potential customers and to make informed choices, rather than risking accruing debts.

Be thorough and check all paperwork and links on a prospect when you do your research. Obviously, the larger the sale price, the more relevant the information gathering is. But the habit of due diligence is a great one in any case.

Experience will tell you how much you need to prepare, but you're better off erring on the side of preparing too much than not preparing enough. As you develop your career your confidence in your ability to judge how much background info you need will grow.

Working with Different Types of Buyer

When you work in the business-to-business arena, a key concern is who the true decision-maker really is. (The same goes for a domestic sale too, but identifying the decision-maker in a business can be more difficult.) The decision-maker may be the office manager, a purchasing agent or a department head, usually depending on the size of investment required: the greater the cost, the higher up the management ladder the person who makes the decision.

You can usually identify the decision-maker simply by asking the receptionist who is responsible for the area of business to which your products or services apply. After she tells you, ask a confirming question, such as, 'So, just to clarify, am I right in understanding that Ms Carter has the final responsibility of authorising purchase orders, is that right?' If Ms Carter does handle the area, but she has to get approval on purchase orders from someone like the comptroller, you need to know that going in (and your question will verify that for you).

When you have the name and position of the person responsible for purchasing in your area, you need to know a little about that person's style. Not everyone operates the same way. People have many different attitudes towards spending money and if you're to succeed then you need to identify the styles and adjust your approach accordingly. Your job is to become familiar enough with the types to quickly determine how to work with each.

Your range of delivery styles and your skill at presenting must be flexible enough to relate to all the different personality types. Never settle for having one presentation style. Having only one style severely limits the number of people you can serve. We're not advising you to develop multiple personalities. Just remember that if you don't like the personality of the decision-maker, you can still like the opportunity she's offering you to do business with her and go forwards on that basis.

Note: We've exaggerated the following personality types for the purpose of example, and they're not limited to the genders we've identified them with. They demonstrate characteristics of buyers, but the people you encounter in the real world won't fit into boxes quite as neatly as these examples do.

A buyer's attitude isn't personal. They believe they're operating with the company's best interests at heart.

Buyer 1: The Halfway-there-already Buyer

The Halfway-there-already Buyer is already sold on your company or brand. He knows just what to expect from your products and he likes their reliability and your reputation. He's easy to work with and, after you convince him of your personal competence, he'll remain loyal to you and your product. If this buyer isn't convinced that you're competent, he won't hesitate to call your company and request another representative.

How do you appeal to this personality type? Don't assume that the sale is already made and shorten the presentation or reduce your efforts to demonstrate the product or service just because he's already sold on its quality. You need to exhibit great product knowledge to personally win over his trust and belief in your ability to meet his needs. Providing dependable service and follow-up will help you close the sale and gain repeat business (and referrals from him).

Buyer 2: The Deal-maker

The Deal-maker is easy to identify because almost straight away she usually says something like, 'I hope you're going to give me a special price!' This buyer loves getting a deal.

You can sell to this buyer easily if you play along with the special deal and show that you like her as an individual. Then you play her and she talks herself into your proposed sale. (We say *play* because selling is a game, a series of counter offers, but one where both parties enjoy the banter and then agree on a mutually acceptable price or deal.)

Let the buyer know that she's important and special – that she drives a hard bargain and that you admire her business savvy. If you think that the business is worth giving something extra, give it, but possibly make the extra conditional on something in the future, or agree a lower price but counter with a shorter payment term, for example. That way the Deal-maker feels she's made a deal that's meaningful and hence is satisfied that she's done her job. You both walk away feeling good.

Buyer 3: The Cool, Clinical Cat

The Cool, Clinical Cat is a distant, matter-of-fact type who carries a high level of responsibility. (You often find her in business-to-business sales situations.) She remains cool and measured, and tries hard to stop emotions clouding her judgement. Often dominant and apparently selfish, this type of buyer has a defence mechanism that she uses to protect her company and herself from making mistakes. Her experience has taught her that when she gets warm and friendly, she's talked into a less favourable deal.

When you're dealing with this type of buyer, you need to throw her off guard. Where she's cool, be warm. Where she's short and to the point, demonstrate a totally relaxed air and be willing to give more than you need in information terms. Friendliness wins over her cool, business-like stance.

Talk deliberately about the feeling of security with ownership. Talk about the glow that she might bask in when her correct decision proves to be so further down the line.

You might have to persist for a little longer than just a few minutes! She's strong and won't want to give in too quickly. But she'll come over to you if your friendliness and warmth keep flowing her way.

Buyer 4: The Scarlet Pimpernel

The Scarlet Pimpernel is your most challenging buyer; after all, how can you sell to someone you can never get hold of? This buyer avoids your phone calls, he postpones appointments or reschedules at the last minute, he likes to shop around and keep you waiting in the meantime and he tests your patience at every turn.

If you've found yourself up against this type of buyer, enlist the aid of his secretary or support staff. (In a consumer sales situation, enlist the aid of his spouse or another family member who knows him well.) Ultimately, as with the cool and clinical type, this buyer sincerely believes that being evasive is serving his company's best interests.

Your task is to demonstrate that every moment the buyer resists buying costs him more than investing would. Then you help him be true to his perceived mission of not spending. You need him to see that by delaying, he's in fact exposing his company to risk. Clearly pointing this out in both written communication and via the ally that you enlist will see him quickly respond and invite you in.

Buyer 5: The Moaner

The Moaner always has something to complain about or something negative to say. He wouldn't be your first choice for a companion if you ever got stranded on a deserted island.

If you're dealing with this type of buyer, you have to decide whether the income his business generates for you is actually worth all the energy he'll steal from you. If his business is not one of your bread-and-butter accounts, you may want to consider finding other clients who don't take so much out of you. *Remember:* No client is worth risking your mental and physical health for.

The most important thing you can do for The Moaner is listen and be empathetic while also remaining professional. So don't engage in any negative dialogue about another person or supplier, and don't supporting negative requests. Often, your strength and example can turn a Moaner around and win you a wonderfully loyal account.

When you first get on the line, you may want to say something like this:

> I'm pleased that you called. However, I'm just heading out for an appointment, so how can I help you very quickly?

Stay pleasant and helpful; after all, that's why The Moaner gave you the business. If the moaning gets to be too much to handle, the easiest and least costly thing to do may be to refer him to someone else in your organisation or simply push towards email or written communication.

Buyer 6: The Bully

For The Bully, it's her way or the highway. Often a self-proclaimed expert, even though her expertise may be limited to her own company, this buyer is actually poor at delegating authority and quite insecure. The Bully's exterior is a mask, and when you understand this, dealing with her is easier. She doesn't want to fight; she just doesn't want to feel that she was steam-rollered into a deal. She isn't really hard or big headed; she just doesn't want to look ignorant and therefore weak. She may sometimes be rude and interrupt your presentation by taking calls or giving directions to subordinates.

When dealing with The Bully, be extremely polite, prepared and concise. Show clearly that you recognise her experience and valuable knowledge, and that her decision-making process has great merit. Demonstrate that you're willing to be submissive and allow her control. Give her a warm smile and deflect her attention into a satisfactory outcome, and then allow her to bask in that glory. She relaxes because she feels you're no threat.

You may encounter The Bully in a consumer setting as well. She's the lady who asks you a question and then takes a call on her mobile phone before you can engage her in conversation. It's important that you are agreeable with her and say things like 'This will only take a minute' or 'Let me take you directly to that product'. This strategy lets her know that you recognise how valuable her time is, and that you're thinking about her and not you, so as to serve her properly. You relax her but keep control of the sale.

Buyer 7: The Drifter

The Drifter is a common type. He has a lot on his mind and the purchase you're discussing is just one of many duties or tasks that he needs to handle. Your presentation must be designed to keep the buyer both mentally and physically involved or you lose him. It will take you longer to close the sale and complete the agreement.

This buyer is afraid of making a mistake, and so he pretends not to concentrate with an aim of getting you to *gear down,* or stop trying to sell to him at this time. He is actively trying to encourage you to switch off slightly as he wants to have time away from you to consider the purchase.

Often this type of buyer can be very attentive when he feels that you're accepting that he cannot be sold to in that visit, so a good strategy is to appease his wish by saying something like:

> I know how busy you are and I fully appreciate that you have many other important considerations on your mind. However, if you'd help me with information that I need in order to correctly design a solution for your company, I'll go away and do just that, and leave you free to concentrate on other important matters.

 If you notice that the buyer's attention has drifted, simply pause in your presentation as if you have lost your train of thought, or pause and ask a direct question such as, 'How do you feel it would work best?' If the buyer was genuinely drifting, then this questioning style helps them to re-tune without causing embarrassment. So, without addressing the drifting directly, you address the mindset and win.

Being Aware of Unique Cultural Needs

If you're planning to do business with people from cultures and backgrounds different from your own, you need to invest as much time into understanding their culture as you do into understanding their needs in terms of your products and services. The UK has rich and diverse communities, and many different expectations and preferred styles, so you need to know all about cultural needs to achieve success across all arenas.

Here are a few general pointers to help you in your sales career:

- Be patient when building trust and establishing relationships. People from all walks of life need time to build trust when dealing with someone different from their usual contacts. Slow down and observe formalities.

- Avoid slang, buzzwords, idioms, jargon and lingo. Anyone outside your world can easily misunderstand what you're saying.

- Pay attention to nonverbal interaction cues. For example, the word *yes* or an affirmative nod often means 'Yes, I hear you' in Asian cultures, not 'Yes, I agree'.

Culture has as much influence on people as their personal experiences, so knowing about your clients' customs and traditions only makes sense. That way, neither you nor your client feels uncomfortable. Knowledge is power!

Arranging meetings

As a general rule, try allowing the prospect to select the location for the meeting. That way, the prospect sees that you're considerate and care about their needs – a good start! When you have an appointment, confirm all the details by simply asking, for the sake of clarity, if you've recorded the meetings details correctly, and then do your homework on what to wear, what to bring with you and how to give your presentation. Always be punctual, but don't expect the other person to be. In many cultures, relationships are much more important than clocks. Value the time your client gives you, but don't count the minutes.

Dressing appropriately

Because your appearance is the first cue others get about how you feel about yourself and your business, take extra care in dressing for business meetings and events. As a simple rule, we might suggest you wear what you usually wear when selling in your normal day-to-day environment. That way you give off a genuine and authentic energy that the prospect senses and acknowledges – and that goes a long way towards overcoming any possible cross-cultural apprehension that might be present.

Meeting and greeting new people

When doing business in the UK, people usually shake hands. We recommend offering a handshake even when selling to other cultures in the UK. If, however, you travel to do business overseas, check the local custom for the place you're visiting.

Taking time to read up on the small details of how people meet and greet one another in the country you'll be visiting can make a huge difference to how the balance of your contact time goes with each potential client.

Presenting your business card

Business cards come in many shapes, sizes and styles. Your employer usually gives you your cards and encourages you to hand them out freely because they're inexpensive to produce.

When you give and receive a card, you gain a valuable connection if you pause and slow down for a moment to allow for the absorption of the information on the card. You show respect for the card that you receive and allow time for the other person to look at your card.

If you're travelling to win overseas business then be sure to find out what rules apply in the culture or country you'll be visiting. In any culture, taking the time to read the card of each person who gives you one before accepting another card is wise. Don't set the cards aside quickly – that's like dismissing the person to move on to someone else.

Respecting personal space

All people, regardless of their cultural background, have a need for *personal space* (the distance between you and another person when you're talking to one another). Personal space is just that – personal. But in each culture, the amount of personal space people need is different from what you may be used to.

If you want to be sure that people feel comfortable around you (a necessity in the world of selling), don't invade another person's space. If ever you're uncertain as to where to stand or sit then apply the golden rule and just ask politely what the other person prefers. That way you demonstrate openness and respect.

Making presentations

All cultures vary, and so do all people. Some like sales to be straight to the point; others prefer a slower, more considered style.

In some cultures, the negotiation is the best part of the game. Negotiation may include gesticulations and animation or simply silence. In other cultures, you present, and they either accept or decline and then move on with little or no chance for you to reiterate important points or give a benefit summary. So, your first shot needs to be your best shot.

Do your research and preparation, and then have an honest and open approach. You simply can't prepare too much for a presentation to someone from a culture other than your own. Expect to be asked for any and every little detail about your company, product, service and location, as well as about yourself. That way, no matter what comes up, you're ready.

Giving gifts

Be aware of the fine line between giving gifts and bribing someone. The further up the price scale, the less likely it is that you can give gifts. Your company probably has a policy both for receiving and donating gifts, so check with your HR department. When travelling and doing business with other cultures, apply the locally acceptable rules.

Personal gifts such as simple thankyou meals, a book by a noted favourite author and notes of thanks are always welcome and they don't need to be of great value to have great meaning. In all cultures, gifts show appreciation and gratitude.

Dining out with ease

In all spheres of business the idea of breaking bread with a potential supplier or client is a good one. Make dining out a regular part of your prospecting and relationship building, and always share the costs so that you're not buying favours.

Whenever you dine with a prospect or client, remember the saying: 'When in Rome, do as the Romans do.' And when you're entertaining clients from a different culture, do everything you can to make them feel at home.

Responding to Your Clients' Fears

In all its forms, fear is the greatest enemy you'll ever encounter in persuading your clients. The toughest part of your job is helping other people overcome their fears so you can earn the opportunity to do business with them. Fear is what builds those walls of resistance that salespeople so often run into. You need to know how to climb over or break through those walls if you're going to succeed in your selling career.

In the following sections, we identify eight common fears that you need to help your prospects overcome. When you recognise these fears as barriers to your ability to serve your prospects with excellent service, you're ready to discover how to dismantle those walls, one brick at a time, and gain your prospect's confidence and trust.

Your goal is to get your prospects to like you, trust you and want to listen to you. They do that when you serve them with warmth and empathy.

Fear of being sold to

At first, every prospect is afraid of you. Why? You're a sales-person, and you want something from them – a commitment, their time or their money. Plus, what you want usually involves some kind of a change on the prospect's part, and most people are afraid of change, at least to some degree. Even if you're sell-ing to someone you already know – a friend, an acquaintance or even a relative – when you meet that person in the role of a sales professional, certain fears inevitably arise.

As a salesperson, when you meet with someone who, like most people, tries very hard to hang on to his hard-earned cash (or at least not part with it too easily), you can safely assume a certain amount of fear is involved. Most people separate themselves from their money only for products and services they believe they need. Your job is to help them rec-ognise the need, and build the value of your product's ability to serve that need to a point where their fear now becomes a fear of what happens if they *don't* allow you to help them.

Most people, when you first encounter them, show their fear in their body language. They may cross their arms or lean back away from you. In retail settings, they may actually take a small step backward when you approach them on the sales floor. A wise tactic to help overcome this is to warmly invite them to stand or sit beside you while you show them all the good stuff your product does or has. This way, you're looking at it together. You encourage them to put their hands on the product, push buttons, turn dials and make things light up, heat up or move. When they get involved with the product, their fear of you lessens. After all, you're the one who intro-duced the prospects to the product, and look what great fun they're having now!

Fear of making the wrong choice

The fear of making the wrong choice is one you're likely to encounter in your clients, because virtually everyone has this fear to some degree. Why? Because everyone has made mistakes, and everyone has regrets. Whether your failure was in choosing the wrong hair colour or purchasing a vehicle that wasn't right for you, you know the frustration of making a mistake. Somewhere in your psyche, you have a fear, not necessarily because of your bad decision, but because you remember that mistake as being associated with a salesperson (the hairdresser who told you that you'd look great with green hair or the car salesman who convinced you that your five kids didn't have to ride with you all the time when he sold you a two-seater convertible).

No one wants to handle a transaction in which the customer may be dissatisfied with the result. The grief you get from a dissatisfied customer isn't worth the commission you'll earn on the sale. Although dissatisfied customers aren't (and shouldn't be) the norm, you must go into every presentation with a sharp interest in the who, what, when, where and why of your client's needs. When you've satisfied yourself that owning your product or service is in your client's best interest, then it's your obligation as the expert to convince her that this decision is truly good for her. Take the time to talk your prospect through every aspect of her decision very carefully, giving her the time she needs to make a choice she'll be comfortable with.

Fear of being in debt

Prospects are tremendously afraid of owing too much. The fear of debt stems largely from a scarcity mentality – people are raised to believe that there isn't enough to go around and therefore you always have to be careful and usually say no. Repaying debt isn't easy, so this is a very real fear for many people.

Most people won't attempt to negotiate with a company about its fees, but as a salesperson your clients don't see you as an institution. You're not cold, forbidding concrete walls and walkways. Instead, you're a warm, flesh-and-blood fellow human – and because of this, your clients will often try to negotiate with you. Depending on your clients' negotiation skills, they may do any or all of the following:

✔ Put off making a decision, forcing you to draw them out. We cover what to do in this situation in Chapter 11.

✔ Tell you point-blank that they're concerned about the cost. In this situation, you need to sell them on the value of the product or service you provide.

✔ Voice their concerns in a roundabout way. For example, a client may say something like, 'Another company I talked with will charge a lot less.'

If your client has reservations about the cost of your product or service, we recommend saying something like this:

> You know, I've learned something over the years. People look for three things when they spend money. They look for the finest quality, the best service and, of course, the lowest investment. I've also found that no company can offer all three. They can't offer the finest quality and the best service for the lowest investment. So, for your long-term happiness, which of the three would you be most willing to give up? Fine quality? Excellent service? Or the lowest fee?

Most people say that quality and service are of the utmost concern, which overcomes their concern about the fee. Your next move is to reiterate everything you'll do for them. Again, sell the value of the product that you and your company provide.

If you run into a client who's truly concerned only with getting the lowest investment and you can't provide it, you may have to bow out of the picture. Do it gracefully and stay in touch. Chances are good that she'll get what she pays for and she'll eventually see the wisdom in investing more for the quality product or service that you can provide.

Fear of being lied to

A common fear in buyers. As a general rule, clients who are afraid of being lied to doubt everything you're saying about how much they'll benefit from your product, service or idea.

When you face a client with this fear, a strong track record comes into play. Having a long list of happy clients should help you calm this fear, because the prospect will believe others who are like her and have no reason to lie. If you're new and you don't yet have an established track record, tell your prospect you made a point of choosing your company because it has a great track record. If you're doing something entirely new with a new company, new product or service, or new concept, you have to build on the personal integrity and credentials of those involved in the project. For some products, you have a salesperson (you), a technical adviser who reviews technical details of either the manufacture or installation of a product, the actual installer and the after-market customer service folks. Believing that *everyone* is a liar is hard, and so at some point the prospect has to admit to a truth, and you build on this.

You never have a reason to lie to a customer. If you're honest with your customers and always share the truth with them, even if it's bad news, they respect you and give you the benefit of the doubt. Honesty and integrity in every selling situation makes you a winner each and every time.

Fear of embarrassment

Many people fear being embarrassed with anyone who can possibly know about the decision if it's a bad one. Have you ever made a poor decision that was big enough that most of your friends and family members knew about it (and then kept reminding you about it)? They may have only been teasing you. However, you may have felt demeaned and embarrassed. Bad decisions make you feel like a child again – insecure and powerless. Because many potential clients have this fear of being embarrassed by a bad decision, they put off making any decision at all.

If you're selling to more than one decision-maker (such as a married couple or business partners), odds are that neither person wants to risk being embarrassed in front of the other. Chances are they've disagreed about something in the past and they don't want to have that uncomfortable situation arise again.

Knowing that this fear can block your sale, your primary goal when working with clients who are afraid of being embarrassed is to help them feel secure with you. Let them know that they're not relinquishing total power to you – you're merely acting on their behalf, providing a product or service for which they have expressed a need. Openness and techniques such as telling a story about when you made a mistake help here.

Fear of the unknown

Fear of the unknown is common in buyers. A lack of understanding of your product or service, or of its value to the prospect's company, is a reasonable cause for delaying any transaction.

Name recognition helps here, but if you work for a smaller or local company, getting past this fear can be hard. You can overcome it, though, by taking your time to learn a little about the prospect. Ask questions and listen for clues, and then simply ask for a chance to prove your point in a very open and gentle way. The prospect can overcome her fear when she trusts you.

Always spend a little extra time on what your product actually does and the benefits it brings, when you're working with a customer who's unaware of your offering – and afraid of the unknown.

Fear of repeating past mistakes

Having a bad past experience generates fear in the hearts of some potential customers. If they've used a product or service like yours before, find out what kind of experience it was for them. If they hesitate to tell you, you may assume that their past experience was bad and that you have to overcome a lot more fear than if they've never used a product or service like yours before.

Try offering the product or service on a sample or trial basis. Give the prospect the names of your satisfied customers who'll give unbiased testimony as to the value of your offering. (Check with those customers first to make sure they don't mind if you have prospects contact them.)

Fear generated by others

A prospect's fear may also come from third-party information. Someone she admires or respects may have told her something negative about your company, about your type of product or even about another representative of your company. In any instance, that third party stands between you and your prospect like a brick wall until you convince or persuade her that you can help her more than that third party can, because *you* are the expert on your product or service. You have to work hard to earn the prospect's trust. Enlist the aid of some of your past happy clients as references, if necessary.

Choosing Your Words Wisely

When you're getting to know your clients, you need to think about the effective power of language. Every word you utter creates a picture in the mind's eye of the listener. Do you use that power to your greatest advantage?

Every word has a meaning attached to it. In your mind, when you hear a word, you draw from your memory bank and 'see' an image of what that word represents. Each symbol often has emotions attached to it as well. Words – such as *spring, summer, autumn* and *winter* – can generate positive or negative emotions in you. If you love gardening, the warm spring air brings to mind beautiful blossoms, the opportunity to get your fingers in the dirt and prepare your soil for a summer crop. If you're a hay fever sufferer, the picture painted by the word *spring* is totally different.

The same rule applies to the words you use in your contacts with customers. You don't know in advance which words about you, your product and your company will generate positive feelings in your clients. So you need to become extra sensitive to the way you use words if you want to have a successful sales career.

In the following sections, we share the best selling-related words and phrases to use, we explain the importance of using the jargon your prospects use and we provide tips on fine-tuning your vocabulary to create positive mental pictures.

Knowing which words and phrases work best

Many words common to sales and selling situations can generate fearful or negative images in your clients' minds. The experience of hundreds of thousands of salespeople confirms that replacing such words with more positive, pacifying words and phrases (like the ones in Table 4-1) is crucial. We discuss these words and phrases in more detail in the following sections.

Table 4-1	Words and Phrases to Eliminate from Your Sales Vocabulary
Instead of . . .	*Use . . .*
Sell	Get them involved or help them use
Contract	Paperwork, agreement or form
Cost or price	Investment or amount
Down payment	Initial investment or initial amount
Monthly payment	Monthly investment or monthly amount
Buy	Own
Deal	Opportunity or transaction
Objection	Area of concern
Problem	Challenge
Pitch	Present or demonstrate
Commission	Fee for service
Appointment	Visit, as in 'pop by and visit'
Sign	Approve, authorise, endorse or okay

Concentrating on what appears to be such minor details may seem like overkill, but some of those details pack a hefty punch. You may consider the following words minor and feel that all our fussing over them is misplaced. But if you really think about it, language is a salesperson's only tool. The salesperson who uses language well, for the genuine benefit of other people, is a salesperson who sells and sells and sells. The words you use aren't minor details at all. They're at the very centre of your profession. So when you write down and practise your own product presentation, go through it and make sure your words stress comfort, convenience and ownership from your prospects' perspectives. After all, satisfying your prospects' needs is what the business of selling is all about – and the words you speak to prospects are the only way that you, and not your competition, can earn the opportunity to satisfy those needs.

Replacing 'sell' and 'sold'

The first terms we recommend that you remove from your vocabulary are *sell* and *sold*. Many salespeople tell prospects how many units of their product they've *sold*. Or they brag about having *sold* the same product to another customer. What are the mental images these words create? No one likes the idea of being *sold* anything. The word reminds people of high-pressure sales tactics and usually turns them off. It makes the transaction sound one-sided, as if the customer really had little say in the matter.

So what can you use in place of these common words? Replace *sell* or *sold* with *helped them acquire* or *got them involved* – phrases that create softer images of a helpful salesperson and a receptive customer becoming involved together in the same process.

Replacing 'contract'

A commonly used word in sales is *contract*. What images does that term bring to mind, especially when you picture yourself as a consumer? For most people, *contract* evokes negative images – something Mum and Dad have warned you about all your life. Contracts bring with them fine print, legalities and being locked into something. Where do you go to get out of a contract? To court – not a pleasant image for most people. So we recommend that you stop using the word *contract*, unless your particular line of business requires it. Instead, use *paperwork*, *agreement* or *form*. Do those words bring to mind threatening images? Maybe, but they're a lot less threatening than the images the word *contract* evokes. And that's exactly what you're going for.

Replacing 'cost' and 'price'

What about *cost* and *price*? When we hear those words, we see our hard-earned cash leaving our pockets. That's why we train people to substitute the words *investment* or *amount* for *cost* or *price*. When most people hear the word *investment*, they envision the positive image of getting a return on their money. For products for which the word *investment* just doesn't fit, use the word *amount* – it's been proven to be less threatening to most consumers than *cost* or *price*.

Replacing 'down payment' and 'monthly payment'

Most people envision *down payments* as large deposits that lock them into many smaller *monthly payments* for, if not an eternity, at least a few years. They see themselves receiving bills and writing cheques every month – not a pleasant image for most people. So replace those phrases with these: *initial investment* and *initial amount* or *monthly investment* and *monthly amount*. In the selling business, we call these terms *money terms*, and anyone who wants to persuade someone to part with money needs to use these terms well.

Replacing 'buy'

What about the word *buy*? When people hear the word *buy*, they see money leaving their pockets again. Use the term *own* instead. *Own* conjures images of what they'll get for their money, where they'll put the product in their home, showing it with pride to friends or relatives and many other positive thoughts.

Replacing 'deal'

One term overused by salespeople is *deal*. This word brings to mind something people have always wanted but never found. Images of used-car salesmen are only too closely associated with the word *deal*. Top salespeople never give their clients *deals*. They offer *opportunities* or get them involved in a *transaction*.

Replacing 'objection,' 'problem,' and 'pitch'

Customers don't raise *objections* about your products or services. Instead, they express *areas of concern*. We never have *problems* with our sales. Every now and then we may, however, face some *challenges* with our transactions. We never *pitch* our products or services to our customer. Instead, we *present* or *demonstrate* our products or services – the way any self-respecting professional would.

Replacing 'commission'

As an authority or expert on your product or service, you don't earn *commissions*, either. You do, however, receive *fees for service*. If a client ever asks you about your *commission* on a sale, elevate your conversation to a more appropriate level with language such as this:

> Mrs Johnson, I'm fortunate that my company has included a fee for service in every transaction. In that way, the fee compensates me for the high level of service I give to each and every client, and that's what you really want, isn't it?

Replacing 'appointment'

One word that can potentially raise concerns in the mind of a consumer is *appointment*. Now, in the business-to-business world, concerns may not be as strong. However, consumers view the appointment as interfering with their regular schedule, even if the schedule shows that time as free time. Rather than equate meeting with you to an appointment with a doctor or dentist, use the softer term *visit*:

> I'd love to have the opportunity to visit you. Would Wednesday evening or Thursday afternoon be better?

Better yet, offer to 'pop by and visit'. What mental image does that create? That you're going to pop in and pop out. That you'll only be there a short time. In the business world, a 'pop by' can conjure the image of a brief handshake and exchange of information in the lobby with no sit-down, conference-room involvement at all.

A gentle word of caution here – don't make the visit sound too casual or you might run into difficulties. The prospect may not see your visit as a sales call, and then either the decision maker isn't present or, when you turn on the selling process, the prospect is offended. Especially in a business-to-business environment, clarify the purpose of the visit:

> When I pop round we can freely discuss the offer in question to ensure that it's what you're looking for.

Replacing 'sign'

The last but definitely not the least important term we recommend that you replace is *sign*. If you replace nothing else in your selling vocabulary after reading this book, never again ask a customer to *sign* an agreement, form or paperwork. What happens emotionally when you ask people to *sign* something? In most cases, a warning goes off in their heads. They become hesitant and cautious. They want to review whatever it is they're signing, scanning the page for the infamous fine print. Any time now, they may even head for the door. It's been drilled into almost everyone from early childhood never to *sign* anything without careful consideration. And why would you want to create that emotion in anyone you were trying to *get happily involved* with your product or service?

Instead of asking your clients to *sign*, ask them to *approve*, *authorise*, *endorse* or *okay* your *paperwork*, *agreement* or *form*. Any of those word pictures carries the positive associations that you want to inspire in your clients.

A fun twist on getting the signature on the agreement that you need is to ask for a buyer's autograph. The buyer feels important, and you can add a quirky, 'If you're ever famous then at least I can have this in my scrap book' type comment to break the tension.

Using only the language your clients understand

Today more than ever, your selling vocabulary matters because of the phenomenon of *trade talk*, or jargon. *Jargon* is defined as words and phrases particular to a given field of work. If you sell medical supplies to doctors, you need to know the jargon medical professionals use and use it yourself, liberally. But if you sell medical supplies to the general public, limit your use of technical terms to the bare minimum until you can determine your client's level of knowledge about the product. You don't want to alienate or confound your customers by using acronyms or words they're not familiar with. **Remember:** Your goal is to make your customers feel important – and it's tough to feel important when you don't feel very clever.

The human mind can assimilate information rapidly only when it comprehends what someone is saying. If you're talking to an average consumer about bits and bytes and she doesn't understand those terms, her mind stops at those terms and tries in vain to find an image that fits them. Many people won't stop to ask you for explanations because they're afraid of showing their lack of knowledge and being embarrassed in the process. Others may get the gist of what you're talking about but struggle to keep up. While they're trying to keep up, they miss the next few valuable points you relay to them. In other words, you've lost them. If your subject sounds more complicated than your customer can comprehend, you risk squelching her desire to ever own or use your product or service *and* you risk losing the sale. More often than not, you lose such customers to a salesperson who uses lay terms and simple definitions.

Good things come to salespeople who take the time to find out how to speak their clients' language.

Developing your picture-painting vocabulary

Words are readily available to anyone who wants to use them. The dictionary didn't reserve certain words and their meanings for the rich. Everyone has access to the same dictionary, and everyone has the same opportunity to choose the words that make their speech outstanding and memorable. Every time you need to convey a concept to someone, you have a choice of any one of thousands of words to establish your meaning. You have no excuse *not* to choose your words carefully. Because you know that your words reflect the person you are, investigate the word choices you make and the reasons you make them.

Developing your selling vocabulary isn't about mastering the words you were tested on in school. It's about taking the time to make a list of powerful but easy-to-understand words and phrases that are specific to your product or service. The first time you use the terms with new or prospective clients, be prepared to give them the definition in lay terms if it's something vital to the transaction or if the term will recur frequently in your discussion with these customers.

You need to strike a balance between speaking the language of your clients and educating them about the terms they'll need to know if they're going to use your product or service. The key is to not make any assumptions about the terminology your clients are familiar with – and to be ready to explain any terms they don't know.

Anyone who wants to persuade others (and if you're in the selling business, that's you) should recognise and choose appropriate language. Take a look at the two following examples. Be aware of the differences in language between the two situations. Even though you can't *see* these two salespeople, pay attention to the mental picture you get of each of them and their selling styles.

Here's the situation: the manager of Continual Hair Care (CHC) has been courting an account with a major chain of salons (owned by someone named Mr Dunn) for two months. Mr Dunn's salons now carry the products of one of CHC's competitors, but Mr Dunn has agreed to hear a presentation by a CHC representative. The CHC manager needs to choose the salesperson who can consummate all the manager's hard work – making a sale and landing the account. The manager calls a meeting with each salesperson she's considering: Dawn and Sue. The one who succeeds in representing the company can receive a sizable increase in earnings. Which one would you choose?

Dawn goes first:

> MANAGER: Now that you understand what will be expected of you, how would you give this presentation?
>
> DAWN: I would just love the chance to tell Mr Dunn how much better our products are than what he's using. I would go to Mr Dunn's salon tomorrow morning. I know I can convince him to dump what he uses now and replace his stock with ours.
>
> MANAGER: What's your next step?

DAWN: Well, after I got all the information, I would tell Mr Dunn what we can do for him and I would try to get him on my side before the presentation to his staff so he can help me sell his stylists on the products.

MANAGER: I'm interested to hear how you would do this, Dawn.

DAWN: Well, I guess I'd tell him how much money he would save and how much more he'll make by selling our products.

Now, here's the same situation – a hopeful salesperson talking to CHC's manager – except now the salesperson is Sue:

MANAGER: Now that you understand what will be expected of you, how will you handle this presentation?

SUE: I believe the first step would be to contact Mr Dunn and request a meeting at his convenience. Then, with your approval, I would examine your files on the salon, so I'm prepared for the presentation.

MANAGER: What's your next step?

SUE: I will ask Mr Dunn to show me his salons. I will familiarise myself with Mr Dunn's needs, his stylists' needs and those of the salons' clientele. Then I will offer Mr Dunn the opportunity to use Continual Hair Care products and ask his permission to present the products to his stylists.

MANAGER: I'm interested to hear how you would do this, Sue.

SUE: Although considering his financial benefits is important, I will encourage Mr Dunn to examine the improved condition of hair that has been treated with Continual Hair Care products. Making hair more beautiful will give Mr Dunn happier customers as well as increased profits. Would it be possible to take a few company models with me on the presentation?

These two conversations have created two pictures in the mind of the manager. Who will represent her company with the most success? The answer is Sue. Why? Because Sue radiated calm enthusiasm and a thoughtful manner. But the turning point in Sue's interview is her choice of the phrase *I will* instead of the indefinite terms like *I guess* or even *I would* that Dawn uses. Sue speaks as if she's already been chosen, whereas Dawn uses iffier, less-confident language. This difference is subtle but very effective. And it isn't long before the manager agrees to send models out with Sue for her presentation.

Sue is an *above average* salesperson with a powerful command of language. She creates positive word pictures with every word she utters. Here are some words you may hear an *average* salesperson deliver. Think about the pictures they create in your mind.

> SALESPERSON: All the kids in your neighbourhood will love playing in your new swimming pool.
>
> PROSPECT: I'm probably going to have trouble getting my kids out of it.
>
> SALESPERSON: When should we start digging? Would this Saturday or next Monday be better?

What's wrong with this dialogue between the salesperson and the prospect? What image comes to your mind from the salesperson's statement that 'all the kids in your neighbourhood will love playing in your new pool'? Loads of kids jumping, splashing, running and yelling at the tops of their lungs comes to mind. It's not too peaceful a scene.

Think about the word pictures you paint. Just a few careless words can destroy hours of hard work. In this case, the salesperson would do better to say, 'Most of our customers tell us they enjoy spending quality time with their families in their new pools.' This image is much more pleasant – and it leaves the picture more open to interpretation. So if the client would *enjoy* a bunch of kids playing in the pool, that's what she can see, but if she would prefer a more laid-back atmosphere, she can see that as well.

The salesperson's next words – 'When should we start digging? Would this Saturday or next Monday be better?' – carry their own negative images. With the word *digging*, the prospect may envision a huge tractor roaring through her garden, digging up plants and mound after mound of dirt, making a general mess of the prospect's home – and on a weekend to boot.

The salesperson would do better to say this:

> Some people prefer to be present when we begin the first phase of their new swimming pool. Others prefer to just tell us when and then have us tell them when the pool is ready to swim in. We can begin Phase 1 on Saturday or next Monday. Which would you prefer?

We can't emphasise enough how important your choice of words is in your selling career. Your words can make or break the sale without you even knowing it. In many cases, if you ask a customer why she *didn't* buy from you, she may not be able to put her finger on any one deciding moment. She 'just didn't feel right' about going ahead.

Words create images, which in turn evoke emotions, so start paying careful attention not only to your prospects, but also to the effects your words have on them.

Becoming a Better Listener

The human body has two ears and one mouth. To be good at persuading or selling, you must find out how to use those natural devices in proportion: listen twice as much as you talk, and you'll succeed in persuading others nearly every time. When you do most of the talking:

- ✔ You aren't finding out about either your customer or your customer's needs.
- ✔ You aren't hearing buying clues or concerns.
- ✔ You may be raising concerns that the prospect did not have in the first place.
- ✔ You're shifting your prospect's attention from your offering.
- ✔ You're giving your prospect more opportunity to disagree with you, to distrust one of your statements, or both.
- ✔ You're taking centre stage away from the customer.

✓ You aren't able to think ahead.

✓ You aren't able to guide the conversation.

✓ You aren't able to convince the other person of the best decision for her.

Most people don't think they talk too much, but if you had listened to as many sales presentations as we have during more than 30 years of teaching, selling and sales management, you'd have developed a keen ear for how much talking sales-people do compared to how much they need to do – and the answer, all too often, is too much.

To develop your ear, try these two simple exercises:

✓ **Listen to a salesperson selling to others or trying to sell to you.** Pay attention to what her words are doing. While you're listening, ask yourself these questions:

- Do her words paint positive or negative mental pictures?

- Do her words say anything that may raise a new objection to her product or service?

- Are all her words necessary?

- Does she ask questions and then carefully listen to the prospect's answers?

- Does she move forward with questions, or does she get off course by talking about features and benefits the customer hasn't expressed a need for?

✓ **Record yourself when you're talking with a customer.** You may be shocked at how much chatter you can cut out. To detect what you need to cut, ask yourself these questions:

- What is the quality of the questions I ask?

- Am I asking information-gathering questions to help myself move forward with my sale, or am I just asking questions to fill a sound void? (Questions don't mean much unless the answers are helping you get the information you need to help you serve your customer better and keep the sale moving forward.)

Watch and listen to others and to yourself more carefully than you're used to when you're listening in everyday conversation. Acquaint yourself with what good listening really 'sounds' like. It should sound like the voice of others, not your own voice. As you discover more and more about selling well, the phrase 'putting your foot in your mouth' gains new meaning for you. After all, you can't put your foot in your mouth if it's closed. So close it, and listen more.

Chapter 5

Knowing Your Product

● ●

In This Chapter

▶ Noting the product details that your clients need you to know

▶ Getting the vital statistics on your product with a variety of techniques

● ●

*O*ne of the best advantages of a career in selling is that good selling skills are portable. By that I mean that after you master basic selling skills, you have the education you need to sell any product that interests you when you master your product knowledge. Product knowledge is one whole side of the selling triangle that we discuss in Chapter 1, which tells you that it's one-third of what you need to know to be successful.

In this chapter, we cover some specific suggestions for ways you can develop your product knowledge and be prepared for nearly any question that comes your way when you're with potential clients. Investing time in product research up front pays off when you're ready to put your selling strategies to work.

Knowing What You Need to Know about Your Product

To sell any product or service offering you need to know about what you're selling. Why? To excite and ignite interest, and so that you can answer any questions that are critical to the sales-ordering process.

What must you absolutely, positively, truly *know* about your product in order to sell it? Always begin with the obvious:

- ✔ **What the product is called and how it's perceived:** Know the specific product name and model, as well as the product/part number, so if your customers refer to it by a number, you know exactly what they're talking about. You also need to have a clear understanding of how your product is perceived in the marketplace. That includes knowing what the product does, because you're bound to run into potential clients who refer to it as 'that machine that prints as well as copying and does photos and everything'.

- ✔ **Whether the product is the latest model or release:** Many of the potential clients you'll encounter want the latest version of your product. Others hope to find a discount on a discontinued model. Either way, you need to be prepared.

- ✔ **How the product improves on a previous model or version:** Be able to list the new features or options and what they can do for your customers, or how they make your offer different from any competitor's.

- ✔ **How fast, powerful or accurate the product is:** Be able to offer up a comparison of your product to its competition so you can tell your customers how your product stacks up.

- ✔ **How to operate the product during demonstrations:** Be able to operate the product as well as you operate the car you drive every day – by reflex.

- ✔ **What colours the product comes in:** Being able to tell your customers right away whether you have a specific colour available will come in handy when they want to know whether it meets their needs.

- ✔ **What your current inventory is for setting delivery dates:** Your client may have seen a review of your product in a magazine, even though it's not due out for two more months. You'll need to know what he's talking about, be prepared to inform him of delivery delays or future release dates and see if he needs the benefits of the product sooner. If the product is currently in production, but on back-order, brag about its popularity and know the projected delivery dates. This is where you want to focus on the new model being worth the wait.

✔ **How much of an investment the product would be:** Be sure to phrase the price of the product in terms of an *investment* as opposed to a *cost* (as I note in Chapter 4). Also be prepared to reduce that amount to a monthly amount if your product is something that requires financing. Many purchasing agents will consider how much something will add to monthly overheads and how soon they can recover their investment. Other clients will want to know how quickly they will receive a return on their investment (ROI). Be prepared to do some maths with them as well. It can be as simple as calculating the cost of your product and dividing it by the annual, monthly, or weekly savings you project after your product is doing its job. The answer you get tells the client when you project he'll have earned his money back on the initial investment.

✔ **What terms and financing are available:** If your company offers financing, consider it another product and know how it works as well as you know the product itself.

✔ **If you work for a manufacturer, know whether there are distributors who may offer the product for less:** If there are, know who these distributors are and what price they're selling the product for. Don't be caught short-sighted by a client who is willing to do more research than you are.

Even companies with the most basic product training should cover these topics with new salespeople before sending them out to talk with customers. Unfortunately, however, some companies provide only the bare minimum of information, and you have to develop the rest on your own. Indeed, you can't find out all the information you may require in any training course when you start a sales role. Thus your learning is on-the-job and on-going. Provided that you recognise this and don't stop actively learning after your initial induction training is over, you'll do well.

However, from time to time you meet a client or prospect who has a question you can't answer. Don't panic, and certainly don't make up an answer! Instead, tell the person that you'd be happy to find out the answer to that question for him and then do it – quickly – before he considers the competition's product over yours. This 'need to know' answer seeking is excellent experience, and when you view it as such you welcome the awkwardness and know that it serves as a great stepping-stone to mastering your role.

How can you be sure you're armed with the product knowledge you need before you head out to make a sale? Take advantage of as many different resources as you can. If your company offers training sessions on the product, attend. If the company hands out brochures and pamphlets, know what's in them and be able to refer to them when required. But especially talk with your existing customers about the products they're using and what they think of those products. It's also worth knowing a little about your competition's product so you can tell your customers how your product measures up.

Product information doesn't just come from the technical booklet that comes with the product. It's everywhere the product has been. In seeking out as much information as possible, you earn and keep your expert status, and more people want to take your advice.

Attending training sessions and reading product literature

Your company or the manufacturer of the products you represent may hold regularly scheduled training sessions about the product. If they do then by all means go to these training sessions. They're your best opportunity for getting the scoop on your product from reliable sources. And *always* attend these sessions with a list of questions and a notepad for writing down the answers. If the speaker doesn't answer your questions during the presentation, find a way to ask your questions before this knowledgeable person gets away.

Average salespeople resist training after their initial orientation period with a new product. That's why they remain average. Keeping your eyes and ears open to new and better information or ways of selling your product is critical to achieving success in your selling career.

In between training sessions, watch for email or web updates of product information from the company as well. Visit your own company's website and regularly visit the websites of the product manufacturers you represent to keep up to date with specification or marketing changes. You should be able to show that your information is current.

If training sessions and product literature aren't available to you, and what you sell is a tangible product, get your hands on a product sample right away. Be like a kid with a new toy: play with it, experiment, read through suggested demonstrations and try it out as if *you're* the customer. Make notes on things you find hard to understand. Chances are good that at least one of your prospects will have the same questions or concerns that you come up with. Resolve those concerns now, and you'll be well prepared for your demonstrations.

Make sure that responding to customer support questions and concerns doesn't take up so much of your time that it interferes with your selling time. After all, you're paid primarily to find and serve new customers for your business, in addition to keeping those you've already gained.

Talking with current clients

This is the key arena for broadening your knowledge. No amount of 'official' information will be as useful to you in your sales career as the information from the ground-floor users. They tell you in different, sometimes colourful, language – but their language and feedback resonates with other clients and prospects, and it's here that you need to pay the greatest attention.

Get as much feedback as you can from the people who already use and benefit from what you sell. Ask what their experiences have been with your product. Do it in person as much as possible. The advantage of talking to people personally is that you can get the client talking and, hopefully, discover something new that will help you serve all your clients better.

You might find that your company has already carried out a client survey and this contains lots of useful info. But why not do one for yourself too, canvassing opinions from the users in your sales territory? A survey of a few simple questions can be hugely valuable. Try online survey provider Survey Monkey (www.surveymonkey.com) if you need to survey larger numbers. If you're looking for feedback from fewer people then a series of telephone calls over a few days does the job.

Your current customers are an extremely valuable resource – *if* you keep in contact with them. We cover several strategies for keeping in touch in Chapter 14.

Picking your colleagues' brains

Second only to the existing users' knowledge is that of your colleagues. Without a doubt, if you're aiming to be a top professional in the world of selling, then you need to be a hungry learner and an avid listener of those in your company who've been around for a while. Veteran and top salespeople have all kinds of information about products that they may never document. Talk with them as much as you can in order to put their knowledge to work for you.

Ask your sales manager for permission to do a ride-along with the top salesperson in your territory. You'll almost always get a thumbs-up because the request shows your manager that you're sincere in wanting to become the best salesperson you can be. Watch how the salesperson handles everything: himself, the client, brochures, proposals, visual aids and the product itself. Listen to the word pictures he uses in describing it. Notice the mood he sets. *Remember:* The *how* of handling products and information is as important as the *what* and *why*.

Ask long-standing professionals questions about how they learned and what they do when in certain situations. Their ideas have got them to the top, so by adopting them, you'll soon be up there with them.

Going directly to the source

Whatever type of product you sell, try to create an opportunity to tour the facility where your product is designed and built. Better yet, try to visit the originator of the idea. Find out what he was thinking when it all came together.

Being a student of selling

When you're in learning mode, you need to set the stage for learning. That may mean gathering pen and paper, brochures and a demo piece of equipment and locking yourself in the company conference room to study. It may mean setting appointments and interviewing with a training director, company owner or top salesperson. It may involve watching hours of product training videos or attending classes on the products. It may involve interviewing current customers.

It doesn't matter what the type of education is, you must begin every session with a clear respect for what's to come. Treat the sessions like gold. Show up on time, if not early. Have plenty of paper for note taking. Bring a couple of pens in different colours to highlight the most important information. And be courteous to those who are sharing their knowledge with you. What they're imparting will make you money. Treat them and their messages with the utmost respect. The better you treat the people who are helping you, the more they'll relax. You'll be making them like you and trust you, which will lead them to offer you even more valuable information. Hmm, sounds a lot like selling, doesn't it?

This might include attending a company meeting where the founder is present. If there's an opportunity for a question-and-answer period, be prepared to ask questions and take great notes. If the idea for your product came from someone else on the company team, seek him out. At the very least, make a connection with someone in the headquarters of the company who can provide you with background information.

With most products, the original idea came from a need that wasn't being met. Some were stumbled upon while seeking the answer for a completely different need. Knowing your product's 'story' comes in handy when selling to clients. If it's a particularly interesting story (and not too long), consider weaving it into your presentations.

Keeping an eye on the competition

You need to know at least a little about your competition. Competitive advantage is smaller now than ever before and shorter lived, because technologies mean other players catch up quickly. However, it's still valuable to at least know what others offer and how you stand when compared – because buyers will compare.

If your company has a person whose job it is to carry out competitor analysis, that's great – absorb the information. If not, then spend some time maybe once a month reviewing competitors' websites and keeping abreast of any changes or product updates.

Don't rely on just one source for information. If you're in business on your own and do not have the benefit of other departments or colleagues feeding information to you, you need to keep your eyes and ears open for any information available, and deliberately asking questions when talking with prospects is the best way to do this.

If you call on customers who've had past experiences with your competitors, ask them whether they'd mind sharing their thoughts on the product and service with you. Ask what they liked about the product – particular features and benefits. How was the competitor's customer service? What would the customer like to see improved upon? Asking in a sincere, caring manner sends the message that you want to do better, be better and help the customer have a better experience than ever before.

When customers tell their tales, take good notes and keep them handy for future reference. If a new customer has just switched from the competition to your product, find out exactly what the deciding factor was and work it into any presentations you make in the future, where circumstances are similar. Also, be certain that product feature has been kept, if the customer is thinking about making an upgrade.

Chapter 6

Making Technology Your Friend

In This Chapter

▶ Overcoming techno-phobias

▶ Making your selling career easier with gadgets, software and more

*N*ot so long ago, a professional salesperson might have organised themselves by using a card file and a filing cabinet and, maybe, a large wallplanner. Organised professionals used many useful physical aids. Not so these days. Professionals the world over are realising the massive benefits of technology.

For many, though, sales has always been about the 'on the go' mentality, and they have resisted getting technology because they view learning time as missing out on sales time, instead of leverage for future time-saving. The whole idea of using technology is that doing so saves you time and frees you up to do more selling . . . you just need to get to grips with the technology first!

In this chapter, we start by lessening some of your fears and motivating you to get up to speed. Then we share some great resources that can help you sell better.

'As the mind thinketh, it shall appear' – and so when you're frustrated by all the paperwork or reports or feedback that you're having to create and wish there was an easier way, well, there probably is! What we cover in this chapter is just the tip of the iceberg in terms of what current and developing technology can do for you in your sales career. Allow yourself at least 30 minutes a week to investigate up-and-coming technology, and make sure you always push for more efficiency of process so that you have more time for actual selling.

Readjusting Your Perceptions about Technology

Advertising has changed in recent times. Every ad includes a web address and many include text links. That's because marketing research has shown that people have become more techno-savvy. People are more mobile than ever before; to do business with you, companies need to be accessible on your terms. Your thinking has changed and your expectation as a consumer is very different. Thus you need to embrace those changes and apply the ideas to your sales process.

Setting aside your fears

If you've been in the sales profession for decades, the Internet revolution may have left you reeling. Many seasoned sales professionals have either expressed fear that technology will take over their jobs, or they've felt that, because selling is a people-to-people skill, there'll never be a real need for technology because it can't replace a person.

Technology can replace a salesperson in some fields – especially simpler products (such as books, groceries and wines, for example) – and yet in many areas the more we advance, the more we rely upon a person to tell us what the technological advancements really mean, in plain English!

Technology won't bring about the demise of the sales profession any more than automation eliminated the need for living, breathing people in the industrialised world. Sales aren't made to machines; sales are made to people. And even though more information is accessible than ever before, technology hasn't yet mastered people skills – and as a salesperson, you still have the upper hand if you develop those skills to better serve your customers.

The truth is that it is your *attitude* towards technology that has the greatest impact on your sales career. If you're a newbie in the field of sales, then you have a huge advantage over longer-standing professionals in that you've probably grown up in a world where technology is the norm. Indeed, these days, smartphones and laptop computers are commonplace, and people embrace technology because they appreciate how it enables dialogue or speeds tasks.

Selling will always be about being able to persuade potential clients to like you, trust you and want to listen to you when making buying decisions. Real people with real challenges will always want to talk with other real people – and that's where the fun is. Technology can't empathise with clients. It can't understand their needs and calm their fears the way a sales professional can. It can't build a caring, mutually respectful, long-term relationship either. But technology can speed up much of the admin and the sales process, expand your reach and increase your potential.

When it comes to using any of today's technology solutions, having some fear at first is completely natural. However, when you develop a positive attitude and focus on the benefits of using technology, your career in sales grows accordingly, no matter how long you've been in the game.

Understanding the benefits of technology

Many people hesitate to discover something new, even if they're assured it will make their jobs easier or make them more effective – or extend their lives (like exercise) or help them earn more money (like sales training). Fear of failure is at play: an inner voice warns of getting it wrong and looking stupid, and so people choose to stay in their comfort zone instead of pushing out. Another excuse is a simple 'I don't have time'. But deep down, you know you're busy, but equally you can make time if you're really determined to.

So, you need to find sufficient motivation to take away the fear and to encourage discovery. Technology and its advances are here to stay and so your career in sales, going forward, is likely to depend more and more upon them. Now more than ever is the time to look at how some of the benefits can truly add value to your life, and to see technology as your friend.

Flexibility and adaptability are the keys to success in today's ever-changing business world. Computer literacy is no longer just a business skill, it's a life skill – just like adding, subtracting or knowing how to drive a car. Using the Internet, wireless phones, handheld planning devices and certain common computer software programs all fall under this umbrella as well. The more you know and the more you're constantly willing to develop your skills, the more indispensable you are to your company – or the more valuable you appear to a new company, if you decide to change jobs.

When you understand this and embrace technology, you can reap a number of rewards:

✓ You can complete tasks more quickly, freeing up more leisure time for yourself.

✓ You can achieve a greater degree of accuracy and make fewer mistakes, so you become more efficient.

✓ You can communicate and connect with more people, so you're able to capitalise on opportunities that you mightn't have otherwise discovered.

✓ You can broaden your skill set, making yourself more valuable to your employer.

Using Technology to Make Your Life Less Complicated (Not More)

If you're new to some of the technological tools that are available for you to use in your selling career, you may think of all those gadgets as time-consuming things you have to spend hours figuring out. And to some degree, you're right. Any time you use a new product or program, you have to spend a little time up front learning how to use it – but if it's the right tool for the job you have in mind, then your time is well spent.

In this section, we highlight some key tools that you can use in your selling career to make your life simpler. If you do your homework and get up to speed on these tools, you can put them to use – and be more profitable in the process. How can these tools make you more profitable? Because, when used properly, they can free you up to focus on your clients' needs more completely (instead of worrying about some of the other details). And that's always a win-win situation.

The techno-salesperson you talk with about any new tool should do a good job of understanding your specific needs before recommending any device. If she doesn't invest that time, she may not have your best interests at heart.

Embracing mobile technology

Technology exists to handle most tasks. The trick to not owning so much technology that you can't carry it all around with you is to concentrate on your own priorities. Which tasks take so much of your time that it would be worth having them mechanised or, at the very least, simplified? Not only can today's gadgets organise and simplify your business and personal life, but they can also help you communicate. Many enable you to check in with your office via phone and also check your email.

In this section, we review some of the more common tools sales professionals use to get organised, plan their time and communicate – or at the very least, get from Point A to Point B with clients, both physically and verbally.

Smartphones

Pretty much everyone has a mobile phone these days. They're totally a part of modern life, and people expect you to have one. Therefore, being in any form of sales role where you can't be in touch via a telephone would be extremely unwise. With the advancements in technology and the many additions to simple telephones, *smartphones* – gadgets that combine little computers and phones – are a must.

With the newer smartphones, you can

- Keep all your contact records to hand
- Note ideas or points, either typing them in or recording them on the voice recorder
- Organise your diary

✔ Receive email and connect to the Internet

✔ Use satellite navigation programs, so that finding the route to the next sales visit is easy

Simply put, a smartphone is a must for a forward-thinking sales professional such as yourself. Invest in one and then play around with it, and soon you'll be singing its praises every chance you get!

If you're in doubt about what you need, talk to someone else within your company, or possibly to another friend in a similar job role, and find out what she uses on a regular basis. Seeking advice gives you an excellent guide when choosing the right smart phone for your requirements.

Tablet computers, netbooks and laptops

Tablet computers – the iPad and its competitors – have made a huge splash in the world of technology. These lightweight and highly portable tablet computers are ideal tools in the modern sales arena because their screens are much larger than that of a smartphone. They're sleek and fun to use and impressive when presenting. They fall right in between the technologies of laptop computers and smartphones.

Many people are also downsizing from the standard laptop computers to using *netbooks*: small, lightweight and inexpensive computers. They provide people with the opportunity to access and use web-based applications.

With a netbook, as with iPads and tablet devices, you have limited data storage on the machine. They're designed for cloud computing, and they encourage you to store your files elsewhere – for a small fee. An important benefit of this is that you're safeguarded from loss of files and expensive maintenance and backup challenges. Increasingly, each year, manufacturers and developers are taking technology into a world where your data files, pictures, videos and other files are stored in a remote server that you access using a local web connection.

Laptops have been around since 1975. They were designed specifically to allow people to take their desktops with them.

Ever since then it seems manufacturers' goals have been to increase their power while decreasing their size and weight. Laptops were a staple of salespeople for many years, and still are for some industries. One of their advantages over tablets and netbooks is that you can store your whole world on the laptop and take it with you. You can function as long as your battery lasts. You're not tied to working only where you can get Internet access.

When it comes to technology, the phrase 'horses for courses' applies, and your style of working might lean towards one device or another. Whichever tool you use, when used properly, enables you to serve the needs of your clients more effectively, communicate with your company efficiently and make more sales.

Being available, always

You probably have a lot of information on your business card – your company name, your company address, your direct phone number (or, at the very least, your extension number), your fax number, your mobile phone number, your company's website address and your business email address. So what's the best way for a client to reach you when she has a challenge or an enquiry? Well, most people dial a mobile number first, and failing that, an office number where they can leave a message. Of course, emails go directly to the handset along with SMS text messaging.

In short, you're always available. We recommend that you

✔ Have an answering machine service on all your numbers, so that callers can leave a message

✔ Respond to all messages in the form that they were sent (so if you receive an email, send one back) within two or three hours

That way you never spoil budding relationships over potential sales by irritating a client who can't contact you.

Making travel plans

A live person at a travel agency can be a great help when you're planning a business trip in advance, but if you discover that you have a more pressing engagement, then you need the immediacy of the Internet.

Modern technological devices allow you to be your own travel agent. No matter the time of day, you can connect to the World Wide Web and make the necessary arrangements. Whether you travel longer distances using airlines or shorter distances by car, your technology friend helps you find the best routes and cheapest options – and all at the click of a button, perhaps while enjoying a coffee in a local Wi-Fi café.

If you're more likely to be travelling by car, you can use Google Maps. You find this tool on all smartphones and tablet computers, or you can simply connect to the Internet, bring up `maps.google.com` in the web browser and plan any route to anywhere for free in minutes.

Using slides in your presentations

Giving presentations is a key element in selling, and Microsoft PowerPoint or Apple Keynote makes it easy for you to tell your prospective clients about yourself, your product or your service. Both are software programs that allow you to create simple or intricate slide-show presentations. When you're ready to give a presentation, you can use the slides you've created in a number of different ways:

- ✔ Print the slides and give them as hand-outs to your potential clients
- ✔ Display the slides on a wall or screen with a projector
- ✔ Show them on your laptop, tablet, netbook or smartphone

You can also customise the slide presentation for each prospect – and in much less time than it would take you if you were doing it all by hand, the old-fashioned way. Plus, you can include audio files in your presentation, time music to go along with the messages and add photos and diagrams to better make your points.

Some of our students take photos with their digital cameras and add them to their presentations. This is ideal in industries such as real estate or property maintenance, or indeed any arena where seeing a product or service in action adds weight, but where physically being present is not possible.

Using CRM software

If your business is a simple one and requires only name, address and telephone contact information on each client, you can get by with nearly any simple address book, such as the one found in Microsoft Outlook. But if you need to track each contact with your clients and have those contacts co-ordinate with your daily, weekly or monthly calendar, using something called *contact management software* (CMS) or *customer relationship management* (CRM) software makes more sense. CMS and CRM allow you to create databases of information – as much information as you'd like to include – about your future clients and long-term clients. You type in things such as:

- ✔ Client names (make sure you get the spelling correct)
- ✔ Company names
- ✔ Addresses
- ✔ Various phone numbers
- ✔ Email addresses
- ✔ Assistants' or secretaries' names
- ✔ Best times of day to reach the clients
- ✔ Dates, locations and times of appointments
- ✔ Notes on each conversation with the client
- ✔ Descriptions of correspondence sent
- ✔ Products or services ordered
- ✔ Delivery dates
- ✔ Challenges that arise and how you overcome them

✔ Future growth plans for the company or division

✔ Birth dates

✔ How long clients have been with their companies

✔ Hobbies (to establish common ground)

✔ Where clients went on their last holidays

✔ Just about anything you can possibly learn about the people you sell to

The best thing about CMS and CRM is that the information is quickly and easily accessible and alterable as your relationship with each client evolves. Some contact management programs also allow you to link to, say, Microsoft Word and generate a letter or process orders for a client. The program automatically places the name and address information in the letter so you don't have to worry about misspelling anything after you enter it correctly into the database.

Many of these programs even prevent you from scheduling a meeting that conflicts with another event you have already booked. That feature alone can help you save face with clients instead of having to call them to reschedule. Some CMS is even available online, so you don't have to be concerned about your laptop crashing and losing all your valuable information. Others are customised to the specific needs of salespeople – with forms for travel itineraries, charting of activity and productivity, meeting notes, expense reports and so on. Take some time to find one you think you'll be comfortable using.

Your company may want you to use a certain software program that the whole sales team uses. Many of these programs provide reporting information or sales analysis information for management so they can see how efficient their staff are being and where clients may be dropping off. So, your decision may be made for you by someone higher up. If that's the case, you simply need to take advantage of whatever training is available – even if that's just a training manual to read through – to gain the most benefit from it.

If your company doesn't offer or suggest a software program, or you're a small business owner and wish to enhance your sales and business effectiveness, you need to spend some time researching your options and choose the one that's right

for you. Although we don't recommend one program over another (because what works best for you is your call), we can share some basic information about some of the more useable programs:

- ✔ **ACT! by Sage** is an economical investment. It retails for about £90 per licence. If you buy from an online store, you can also download it directly onto your computer, instead of having to wait for the CD to be shipped to you. You can also purchase licences for five or more users so that you and four of your associates can use the same program at a discounted rate. ACT! is a starter level program, and as such it's slightly limited in its functionality and customisation ability. However, it's great for sales-people who work out of an office as opposed to actually going off-site to visit with clients. As with all brands of CRM, ACT! allows you to import contact information from Outlook, or almost any other format you may already have been using. You store the software on a computer as opposed to accessing it online. For more information on how to use ACT!, you can check out *ACT! For Dummies*, published by Wiley; different books are available, depending on the version of ACT! you have. To read about the many features of this software, visit www.act.com.

- ✔ **Salesforce.com online CRM service** allows you to keep your database online rather than on your own computer. That way, you're not bogging your system down with a huge amount of data, and the information is available to you online from any computer. No more lugging your laptop home every night. The investment varies depending on the number of people in a company or group who subscribe to the service. Visit www.salesforce.com for more information; you can also pick up *Salesforce.com For Dummies* by Tom Wong and Liz Kao (Wiley).

- ✔ **FuseMetrix by WebOffice Systems** is a superb solution. It's cloud-based, giving the user total access freedom. Wherever you are in the world, as long as you have Internet access, you can be 'at work'. This system is also massively expandable. It will grow and accommodate your growing business demands without any limit or need to upgrade, even in an out-of-the-box state. It's scalable – from one to a thousand users – and is available with no upfront fee to make it suit your business, from only £25 per user. It encompasses more than any other standard CRM:

- An email marketing program
- An accounting function similar to Sage
- Document storage for the whole company, not just the client in question
- Modules for manufacturing, delivery, project planning and e-commerce

To find out more about Fusemetrix, visit www.fuse metrix.com.

Part III
The Anatomy of a Sale

'What sort of sales training did you go through before you joined us, Thomas?'

In this part...

The chapters in this section cover the selling cycle in depth and include insights and stories to really improve your performance and up your enjoyment levels. We detail everything from appointment making and relationship building to handling objections and winning business that develops into long-standing relationships, giving referrals and repeat business. This section as a whole stands as a powerful resource.

Chapter 7

Finding the People Who Want What You Sell

● ●

In This Chapter

▶ Starting the search for qualified, potential leads for business

▶ Approaching prospects using methods that have been proven to work

● ●

*T*he first step in the selling cycle is what salespeople call *prospecting*. Prospecting is, essentially, searching for people to whom to sell your products or services. It's a lot like treasure hunting, except that instead of a metal detector and a spade you use telephones, email and word of mouth.

If you already know the people you'll be selling to, you probably don't need this chapter right now (although the tips and suggestions you'll find here may help you find even *more* qualified prospects, which is always a good thing). On the other hand, if you have a great opportunity, service, product or idea, but you don't know where to find other people who would be interested in getting involved, this chapter is exactly the place to start.

If you don't know whom to contact to help you get from Point A to Point B, you doom your product, service or idea right from the start. You soon lose your enthusiasm or invest too much of your own time and money with little or no payoff at all. You run out of steam before you even get on that road to success. That's why this chapter is vital. You can master everything else in this book, but if you never get the opportunity to get in front of the right people, all the selling techniques you've refined ultimately produce nothing for you.

Knowing Where to Start Looking for Prospects

When you're finally prepared enough with knowledge about your product, service or concept (see Chapter 5), and when you feel comfortable with your selling skills, you need to begin finding the people to sell to. In the early stages of your new career, you need to focus much of your time on lining up prospects. In fact, in the beginning, your daily plan should be to invest about 75 per cent of your time prospecting. The other 25 per cent of your time should go toward developing your product knowledge and presentation skills.

The key to success in a people-oriented business like selling is initially purely numbers. Selling is a numbers game. You must connect with as many targeted prospects as possible in the time you have.

The simplest place to start prospecting is with the people who've already become known to your company in some way, maybe from a past marketing campaign or an exhibition or previous enquiry.

Many successful sales professionals will tell you how important prospecting is, even after you build a large customer base. Successful sales professionals – those with a strong desire not only to reach the top but to stay there – make prospecting a part of their everyday selling strategy. They understand that achieving success doesn't mean they can stop looking for new business opportunities.

Starting with a few prospecting basics

The best place to start prospecting is with people who've already expressed an interest directly with your company in the past, or who've already paid money and are using products and services similar to yours. If you're selling exercise equipment, begin with people who jog, belong to health clubs or join local recreational sports teams. Why? Because you *know* they're already health conscious. The convenience of being able to exercise at home may be just what they're look-ing for. If you're selling graphic design, start with the people responsible for handling advertising for local companies. If you've already worked for people in a certain type of business, such as gift shops, you may want to concentrate on other gift shops in the area. The items in your portfolio will then be very appropriate outlets for your work.

To some degree, where you'll find your prospects depends on what you represent. If you sell products or services for a company, you probably discovered the likeliest places to find your products or services in use during your product-knowledge training (if you didn't, ask now). Those places are, obviously, the best places to begin prospecting. After you have some sales, you'll have time to get more creative with staking out other claims.

If you're on your own (as opposed to representing a com-pany), start with your local business networks such as the Federation of Small Businesses (FSB; www.fsb.org.uk) and your local Chamber of Commerce. (These chambers have regional web addresses dependent on where they're located. Find your nearest simply by typing 'Chamber of Commerce' and the name of your town into a major Internet search engine.) Both have membership bases that are considerable. If you conduct business in your local community, become a member of both and attend their events. Most are hosted specifically for members to get to know one another and they can be an excellent source of leads for your business.

Indeed, extending that process into other specifically designed business networking groups is the simplest and fastest way to grow into a community, if your employer doesn't already have a huge list of needy prospects. Among the better and more established national organisations are Business Network International (BNI; www.bni.eu), 4Networking (www.4networking.biz) and Business-Scene (www.business-scene.com). Use an Internet search engine to hunt down other local business networks.

You can also purchase marketing lists and even purchase a 'done-for-you' email marketing programme, although doing so can lead to high costs for poor returns, unless you really know your stuff. We advise you, instead, to do some legwork in the early stages and then, when you start to flow, your world of contacts will expand naturally.

In the case of needing consumer contact information versus business contacts, simple local marketing is a preferred strategy. Again, you can purchase lists – just ensure that they're reputable and verified distribution lists first.

A lot of companies are out there with lists that haven't been updated or may not have been collected in the most appropriate manner. If you plan to reach out to your clients via email, you want a list with a double opt-in process and names that have either been verified or added within the last six months.

Taking your search online

Unless you represent a product or service with a very small and particular demographic, the opportunities you have for making contact with prospective clients are practically unlimited. You simply need to test a variety of methods to narrow down those that bring you the best people.

If what you sell is good for businesses, you might want to begin with Yell.com (`www.yell.com`), which lists lots of businesses, and then of course sift through the myriad of other local directory listings that you find by the dozen when you search the Web. The popularity of the search engine has driven almost every company you might want to seek out to create a web presence, and the Internet is where 85 per cent of people who might be shopping for something start their search. This figure is only going to increase, so it makes sense that your prospecting starts there too. Spend hours in the early stages with Google or similar and save your searches into a separate folder on your computer and you'll never run short of cold prospects to approach.

In addition, you can post bulletins on Internet message boards related to your product or service. Provide valuable information in addition to selling your product or service. Seeking out a reputable forum or message board is not unlike finding a reputable list company. Begin by asking your fellow sales associates which ones they find most helpful. LinkedIn (`www.linkedin.com`) is a superb connection forum for business professionals. Every networking organisation has a members forum facility and each industry has an industry leaders forum. Also search through your industry news publications. Some of those sources may have forums for users of your type of product.

When you find a message board or forum that suits your product offering, follow simple etiquette rules for engaging others:

- ✔ Introduce yourself to the others who use the forum.

- ✔ Don't go straight into a sales presentation. Rather, ask questions of the other members about their uses of your product or how they feel about it.

- ✔ After you begin to see what needs are being expressed, offer advice in the form of solutions.

Using this type of strategy requires a soft-sell approach but can get you great exposure to a large database of people who are already interested in your type of product.

Because no Big Brother-like editor exists on the Internet, not everything you see there is 100 per cent accurate.

Employing someone else to prospect for you

If the idea of laboriously searching through data or treading the boards of local business meetings fills you with dread, then you can employ someone else to search out the interested prospects. However, this is *not* an ideal place to start.

Simply put, the experience gained from 'doing the hard bit' sets you up for much greater success . . . and conversely, the abdication of the task to another party straight away sets you up to be exploited and fleeced of your money! You're too raw in the beginning to know what a good deal is. So the hard work is the best option.

However, using a bona fide telemarketing company to telephone prospects and set up sales visits *is* an effective way, if you're sure of your closing ratios and your sales values. But, at several hundred pounds a day for their services, you have to be extremely confident of your results, before you blow a whole ton of money! Much the same applies with direct mail houses, where you can spend a fortune on mailing and production costs with little or no return.

Even if you do decide to risk your cash using a marketing support set-up, never stop prospecting for yourself. Always keep some self-generated enquiries coming in. That way, you ensure your survival if the other party lets you down.

Taking advantage of lists generated by your company

When you work for someone else's company, the company usually handles the details of advertising and marketing to generate leads for you and the other salespeople. You have a flow of enquiries from both existing companies and Internet shoppers and these are strong, 'hot' leads. But the leads are often in demand too, and you probably won't get fat living off your share!

You might be pro-active in helping your employer provide you with names of previously contacted companies, or you might ask for the opportunity to create your very own referral programme using the company's existing clients. But to become a great salesperson, you should always be prospecting on your own too. In sales there are always quieter times and busier times, and your habit of consistently prospecting for yourself, regardless of company-supplied leads, is your safety net.

Finding the Right People: Proven Prospecting Strategies

In this section, we cover the most effective methods we've used to find people who are the best candidates for what you have to offer. When you apply yourself to finding these people, and if you continue to do so on a regular basis, you'll be off and running on a successful selling career.

Going to the people you already know

No matter who you are or what you do, everyday life demands interaction with others. That means that you already know a considerable number of people who may be potential prospects for your product, service or idea.

Think beyond your closest circle of friends and relatives, and add to that list people in your local area or gym club or parenting group, and the number of contacts is pretty large. Then consider for a moment all the people your contacts know.

When you add two or four names per contact, your field of contact becomes exciting. In prospecting with the people you come into contact with on a daily basis, your job is simply to communicate. Letting others know what you're selling and some of the benefits of what it can do opens many doors of opportunity for you. All you need to do is start a conversation.

Make a list of all the people you know, and start there. Here's a list to get you started:

- ✔ Your parents
- ✔ Your grandparents
- ✔ Your siblings
- ✔ Your aunts, uncles and cousins
- ✔ Your colleagues at previous employers
- ✔ Members of your sports team
- ✔ Parents of your children's friends
- ✔ Your neighbours
- ✔ Your hairdresser
- ✔ Your friends
- ✔ Members of business or community groups you belong to
- ✔ Your mechanic
- ✔ Customer service 'friendly faces' at your local supermarket
- ✔ Your dry-cleaning shop
- ✔ Your pet's veterinarian
- ✔ Your doctor
- ✔ Your dentist
- ✔ Your lawyer
- ✔ Your accountant
- ✔ Your financial adviser
- ✔ The teachers at your children's school
- ✔ Those who might coach your children in various activities
- ✔ Customer service representatives at your bank

Prospecting . . . an imaginative way

One student of Tom's always wore his company logo on a lapel pin – upside down. He made a specific point of putting it on upside down when he left the house. Hardly a day went by that some well-meaning do-gooder didn't tell him it was upside down, thus opening the door to a pleasant conversation about his business. As soon as he left that person's presence, he would turn the pin upside down again and move on to the next do-gooder.

Tapping your business contacts

Whether or not you're new to selling, you've probably been involved in some sort of business or at least have some loose connections in the community where you live and with the shops and businesses with which you've interacted.

Business contacts can sometimes be easier to talk with than some social contacts, because business contacts prospect all the time too. But be aware that they're also on the receiving end of many prospecting approaches and can sometimes be overloaded. So if a business contact is curt with a reply, don't be put off.

Visit the websites of the companies where your business contacts work and learn a little about the industry sector, the size of the company and its client base. You get a fairly accurate indication as to the likelihood of prospecting in their direction being fruitful.

When you're prospecting, think not only of the people you know in your business life, but also get involved in clubs or organisations for business professionals and prospect there.

Pay attention to emails you get from your business associates. You may have received an email as part of a group of recipients – and one of those people may be a prospective client for you. Getting a new lead may be as simple as having the person who sent you the message give you those other people's contact information so you can reach out to them. Or see whether you can get permission to contact each person who received the email along with you.

When you receive a group email from a business contact, you may be able to see the email addresses of all the recipients. If you want to try prospecting with them, contact the person who sent the email and see whether the people you want to contact would mind if you contacted them (as opposed to just sending emails without checking first). That way, you can contact the person and say, 'John Smith asked me to contact you,' which is much more professional and courteous to all parties involved.

When you're sending emails to more than one person, put your recipients' email addresses in the *blind carbon copy* (BCC) field instead of the *To* or *CC* field. That way, you're not sharing your personal or business lists with others.

Remember that prospecting is all about numbers, and leveraging your contact base or sphere of influence through organised networking is the fastest route to larger numbers. In addition, at most networking meetings you have opportunity to stand and introduce yourself for a minute or maybe more, and this is excellent practice for your effectiveness as a speaker and a wonderful opportunity for prospective clients to get to know you. Indeed, many industries also have their own associations where you can network and establish a contact group, and some of these will become extremely valuable as your career progresses.

Ask your company to purchase a Dunn & Bradstreet (www. dnb.co.uk) data file, or a similar file from Creditsafe (www. creditsafeuk.com). This file contains financial information that can tell you straight away whether your prospect is a good bet financially, which can save a lot of wasted time or pain later!

Talking to salespeople you currently buy from

Talking to salespeople you buy from is one of the most overlooked strategies of prospecting. Other companies send you highly knowledgeable, professional salespeople who already know loads of other people. They wouldn't be coming to you if you were in a similar business, right? So, because you're in a non-competing business, why not talk with them about any leads they may have? Or at the very least, ask them to keep you in mind the next time they call on their customers.

A sort of 'brothers in arms' camaraderie exists among those in the selling profession, and sharing ideas and banter with a colleague can open the door to powerful relationships and enquiry-swap arrangements. Never miss this opportunity to extend your connection and prospecting power!

Staying alert as a consumer

Imagine that you're at a restaurant and your server does an especially excellent job. If you're looking for someone to join with you in business (such as network marketing), not work *for* you, and if this person already has great people skills and is competent at performing his duties, he may be a good candidate for being in business for himself. You probably run into these kinds of people every day, everywhere you go – so take advantage of the situation and talk with them about the opportunities (or products or services) you have to offer.

Be careful how you approach people while they're working. Professional etiquette dictates that you don't interfere with other professionals while they're conducting business.

So what do you say to such people when you have the opportunity to talk? Here are some words that are proven to work in this particular situation:

> I can't help but notice that you have a nice way with people. I'm genuinely impressed. And because of that I'd like very much to chat with you – possibly on another occasion – about an opportunity in my business that I'm confident you would totally enjoy and be very successful at.

If the person asks, 'What's this about?' say

> Ethically, because you're working now, it isn't the right time. However, if you'd like to jot down a number and time I can reach you when you're not working, we can chat and see whether it's a win-win possibility.

You can then either arrange a time to call or, at the very least, leave him with your card and a time to contact you. It's a harmless strategy, but it gets the person's attention.

Another way to prospect through other businesses is to send the business a letter or thankyou note for providing you with excellent service. Many businesspeople publish or display these letters in their places of business or on their marketing literature. If they have your permission to use your name in promoting their business, they're also pretty likely to list your profession or business name. When other people read your words, they'll see how professional you are and, hopefully, remember your name when they need services such as the ones you offer.

If you market a consumer item, chat with people you meet when doing your own shopping to see whether they're good potential candidates for your product or service as well. Always remember that any and all consumers are just like you and have needs, wants and desires for all sorts of things! Keep your ears open, always be friendly and conversational, and within a short time you'll see enquiries everywhere you go.

The key to successful prospecting is to acquire the mindset that *every* person you meet is either a potential client or knows someone else who's qualified.

Remembering that nothing is permanent

Face it: nearly every tangible product brought to market has a limited lifespan. At one end of the spectrum, you have computer software and hardware, which can have a lifespan as short as six months. At the other end of the spectrum, you have things like refrigerators and freezers, which have lifespans of almost 20 years. No matter how long a product's lifespan is, every product has one.

The precise lifespan of your product doesn't matter. What matters is that you know what its lifespan is. When you know your product's lifespan, you have a goldmine of opportunity waiting for you. All you have to do is know the approximate lifespan and then find out when people purchased what they're using. The two answers together then indicate when a customer is most likely to need to repurchase.

The secret is to get in touch with the client *before* what he's using actually breaks down, and let him know you have some great new products with greater energy efficiency, space-saving designs and other all-round-better features. Put a reminder on your calendar or tag the customer's file for follow-up in your contact management software. Your call just may help the customer replace that old item a little sooner.

Chances are good that the prospect knows that his product is on its last legs and he's just been putting off making the decision to replace it. Maybe he's been waiting for a good buy or sale to appear in the paper – that doesn't matter. What matters is that he hasn't acted *yet*.

Always make sure strategies such as this one are approved by your manager or are acceptable according to company policy, before you implement them.

If your company allows it, take advantage of a strategy known as the *puppy dog*. How do you sell a little puppy? You let someone take it home for a few days to see how things go. This strategy is extremely powerful. Almost every time, the people – that is, the *prospects* – become so attached to the new puppy that they can't bear to part with it.

If you're a car salesperson, you let a trusted customer try out the latest model of the car you think he'd like, and, before 48 hours are up, the prospect loves the new car and wants to keep it. If nothing else, he's started itching for a new car and needs to get back in touch with you to return the loaner. And you've provided yourself with an itchy customer to serve. Such personalised service is guaranteed to keep customers coming back for more.

In any line of selling, when you allow a prospect to use and become familiar with a new offering and experience the benefits, the customer finds it hugely difficult to give the product back and go back to having no benefits.

If you don't already know the replacement cycle for your line of products, find out what it is. When do people begin getting that itch for something new? All you need to do to find out this kind of information is make a few phone calls to people who currently use your products or services. You can treat this like a survey or market study and simply ask for their help. If they know it won't take long, most people love to help you. Begin by verifying that they're still using the product your records show them owning. Then ask what they used prior to the product or service they bought from you. The only time such research fails is if the product or service that you sold to your customer is your customer's first foray into your market. If it's the second, third or later product or service of this type that they've owned, ask how many years, overall, they've used such products or services for before replacing them.

You can also look at your own records to determine the lifespan of your product or service. For example, if you sell copiers and your customer has used your copiers for 17 years, trading in only 4 times during your association, you know he'll need a new copier after he's owned his present model for about 4 years. When that fourth year rolls around, you may want to ask the client a few questions about his current needs and get permission to send him information about the latest and greatest models. If he won't need another machine for two more years, thank him for his help and make a commitment to stay in touch.

With replacement products, the salesperson who gets to the customer at the right time is often the one who wins. Plan to be that person, and you'll be doing a lot of the winning. The early bird makes the sale.

Using your customer list, past and present

Any business that's been around for at least three years should have a pretty good customer list. If customers haven't been assigned to another salesperson or account manager, then you may want to ask permission to contact clients yourself. If nothing else comes of your contacts, you leave a positive impression of the type of follow-up your company provides. And, hopefully, you update your database along the way. Be sure to get email addresses and website addresses (for business contacts) too.

With the many changes that occur in business these days, managers don't always take the time to complete the basic task of transferring clients to new salespeople when the former salespeople move on. If the company is growing rapidly, some customers may get left in the dust. Why not be the one to pick them up and take care of them? They've already bought your brand or service before, so they're likely to again.

If your company has lived up to its promises, your customers should want to continue to work with such a fine organisation. If they haven't made any purchases lately, it may be simply because no one has asked. Don't leave the door open for a competitor to come in and snatch up valuable customers. Prospect your list of past customers, and you may not only solidify their future business but the business that they'll refer to you as well.

Capitalising on the 'new model' mindset

Various products have inevitable itch cycles. Why do you suppose people itch to get something new? In some cases, it's simply because the product wears out. In others, though, it's because of something more personal, like status. They want to have the latest, greatest, fastest and most efficient products that you can provide. When people have the best and latest products, they appear to be doing well.

Few people really want to have the old model of anything, unless they're collectors and the old model is a true antique or classic. Because most businesses today sell high-tech equipment, peripherals and support products and services, knowing and using this method of prospecting is tantamount to success. Whenever you have a new model, an updated version or even a change in the investment for your product, you have a solid reason to reconnect with the people you've already sold to. All owners of 'life-cycle' products value being updated and informed about the newer, faster version. When you make the correct approach, you can win, and win often.

For example, Bill invested in a top-of-the-line home entertainment system a couple years ago, but now some improvement has been made in the product that wasn't available when he bought it. Don't just call up Bill and say, 'Hey, I've got something even better for you.' That would be both pushy and presumptuous and would very likely have the opposite effect to what you wanted – you may turn Bill off to even hearing what you have to say, because you've just, in effect, criticised his system.

Instead, call Bill and ask him how he's enjoying listening to his favourite music on his home entertainment system. Being sure that he's still happy with what he's got before bringing up anything else is critical. If he has a complaint you didn't know about and you start talking about new products, you can lose Bill as a customer forever.

When you've determined that Bill's happy, say the following:

> Bill, I know how diligent you were in your research before investing in the T-tronics system. Because I value your opinion, would you mind evaluating something else our company is coming out with?

See the difference? You've complimented Bill, acknowledged his intelligence *and* asked for his opinion. You've made him feel important. Of course he'll be happy to look at your new toy now. And if it's truly better than the one he has, he'll probably want to upgrade his system.

If you take the time to know what's going on with your current customers, you'll know exactly when and how to contact them with new products or innovations and increase the volume and number of sales you make to each one. Now that's what we call working smarter.

Reading the news

One of the greatest prospecting tools at your disposal is the printed local news media circulated in almost all towns and cities.

For some businesses especially, local papers can be extremely helpful. For example, if you're in financial services, you can check out the births, deaths and marriages section. Without wanting to be callous, each of those headings may mean a massive impact on the family mentioned, and, financially, they may benefit from advice and guidance. You also find plenty of news items about factories expanding and businesses employing new staff and winning new contracts. Each of these stories allows you to make a connection with the business highlighted and offer your product to suit their changing needs.

Knowing how to read your newspaper for leads only takes a few days of practice. When you get started, you'll be amazed at the number of leads you used to glance over. Here's just a brief list of some of the things people need and want when they go through life changes (all of which you can find in your local newspaper):

- ✔ People having babies need more insurance, bigger homes, bigger cars, delivery services and nappies.

- ✔ Families who are moving in to new homes need furniture or appliances to fit the new home, security systems, new carpets and curtains, homeowners' insurance, gardening services and painkillers (lots of painkillers).

- ✔ New or expanding businesses need equipment, personnel and supplies.

Ben had a client who specialised in home relocation services. She saw a news item that said the BBC was relocating a lot of its production to Manchester from London, and she promptly made enquiries. It took several months and several communication attempts, but eventually she won the preferred relocation agent status and moved eight clients to new homes in her area. A sizeable return on simply one news item!

Take today's local newspaper and read every headline. Circle those with stories that may hold some business prospects for you. Then do what any top salesperson who's striving for excellence would do and *contact* those people. Cut out the article (or print it if you're reading online), make a copy for your records and then send a brief note, saying, 'I saw you in the news. I'm in business in the community and hope to meet you some day in person. I thought you might enjoy having an extra copy of the article to share with friends or relatives.' Be sure to include your business card. People love seeing that they were in the news. And they love having extra copies of the articles to send to friends and relatives who aren't in the area. By providing this little service in a non-threatening way, you can gain a lot of business.

Knowing your service and support people

If you're in touch with the people in other departments of your company, you may be able to discover valuable information that helps you keep the clients you already have (and get more down the road).

For example, someone who works in accounting for your company may know that one of your clients has been late several times in making his monthly investment in your product or service. That's a valuable piece of information for anyone in sales. By reconnecting with that client, you may be able to make other arrangements for him. Perhaps his growth rate isn't as high as he anticipated, and your equipment or service just costs too much for him. Instead of letting information like that get away, help the client cut back on his equipment or make other financial arrangements. He'll never forget you and will become a loyal, long-term customer, referring his friends and business associates to you when they need the product or service you provide. If you let such information go without addressing it, you may lose that person as a customer, just because he's overloaded with unnecessary equipment and is too embarrassed to approach your company about it.

Get in the habit of periodically checking your company's service and repair records. Even better, see whether your company can set up a system so that when a service call comes in, the salesperson is automatically emailed a notice of it. Consider asking the team in your customer service department how many times your clients call with questions about the product or service you've sold them. If your clients are calling frequently, you need to get back in touch with them. Maybe they're in a growth phase, and you can help them acquire new services. Or maybe they're having some challenges with particular equipment. If they got stuck with a lemon, you need to be the one to turn it into lemonade – before they demand a replacement, a refund or your head, and you get squeezed out!

Always strive to provide service above and beyond what the average salesperson would give. You build long-term relationships, trust and referral business in the process.

Talking to anybody

Many businesspeople subscribe to the three-foot rule when it comes to prospecting: anyone who comes within three feet of them is worth talking to about their product, service or business.

Whenever you're in a group of people who possibly match your target prospect, start a conversation. You never know where it might end up. For example, standing in a drinks queue at a business exhibition, you can start a conversation about the length of time you've been waiting, and then ask open questions and engage in conversation. Undoubtedly, within a minute or two the other person will ask 'What do you do?' and you're legitimately into a prospecting arena. You won't always get new business this way, but at the very least you enjoy your day more.

Ben has personally used this strategy at a large event in London. By simply swapping a business card and then emails, he secured a lengthy coaching engagement worth several thousand pounds. Not bad for simply standing in a queue for coffee and saying hello!

Chapter 8

Arranging Appointments That Stick

In This Chapter

▶ Knowing how to get in touch with your prospects

▶ Using the telephone and other communication methods to your best advantage

▶ Discovering how to reach even the difficult-to-reach decision-maker

*I*n virtually every selling situation, if you don't get to speak directly with the person who makes the decision, all your hard work developing your selling skills basically counts for nothing. If you aren't 'live and present' with your clients, you'll never be able to discover their needs or allow them to know and like you sufficiently to spend money with you.

So how do you get directly involved with the people you want to persuade? To get face to face with people or to speak directly with a specific person in a telephone sales environment, you must first sell them on scheduling an appointment with you or, at the very least, agreeing to allow you to pop by and visit. And you must schedule an appointment before you can ever persuade your prospect to own your product, start using your service or consider your idea.

In the real world, however, not all appointments stick. Appointments may not happen as planned, perhaps because something you said wasn't quite clear enough when you made the arrangement, or maybe the decision-maker's availability has changed. In sales, your aim is for 100 per cent of the appointments that you arrange to turn into productive sales appointments where the prospect is actually waiting and keen to see you as planned. So, in this chapter, we let you know exactly how to get an appointment (which, as a sales professional, you call a 'visit' or a 'meeting') with your prospective clients that sticks.

Getting the Basics Right

Your first line of approach when you're contacting a prospective client is simply to call or email and create dialogue. After all, without dialogue, you can't progress any further.

Your goal, whichever way you contact a prospective client, is to get a time set aside so that you can speak clearly and directly about your offering. Everybody expects unsolicited incoming sales calls to be a prelude to them spending money that they haven't planned to spend, so they usually have the mindset: 'It's not worth my time. I'm not really interested.' Thus your first challenge when in a selling cycle is to actually sell the appointment. And that means you must offer benefits to the prospect in your very first contact.

Keep the following tips in mind when you're trying to get a potential client's attention via phone, mail or email:

- ✔ **Always be courteous:** Say 'please' and 'thank you'. Manners cost nothing and they go a long way in creating the correct impression.

- ✔ **Wherever viable, meet the prospect:** Unless you're selling a small ticket item, then you're always best to get face to face. For lower value sales, prospects won't expect a visit but will value a personal phone call.

- ✔ **Get straight to the point with your hottest benefits:** Prospects want to get on with what they're doing, so hit them straight away with powerful reasons that they should give you two minutes on the telephone. If you're returning an incoming call, first establish what source triggered the enquiry and then reiterate the benefits portrayed by that marketing avenue.

- ✔ **Confirm all the details about where and when you'll meet:** Verbal confirmation is a must. Written confirmation is even better.

These instructions may seem too simple at first glance, but many a novice salesperson has become so excited about getting an appointment that she's forgotten some basics and learned the hard way. As an example, you can easily forget to confirm details and write them down, and then your prospect cools slightly if you're struggling to remember information later on.

Reaching Your Prospects by Telephone First

The important thing to keep in mind when you've come up with a list of prospective clients is that not all of those clients will need your product or service. You may have to contact 20 or 30 people to find one who wants just what you have to offer. But every one of those other calls brings you closer to the right person. Professional salespeople remember that a *no* is one step nearer to a *yes* and never allow themselves to see the rejection as anything other than normal. Keep in mind that selling is possibly the only profession in the world where you can be a roaring success when you actually only succeed (by getting a sale) 30 per cent of the time!

To assist you in your first contact with a prospect, here are seven steps that you can work through:

1. **Offer a greeting.**

2. **Introduce yourself and your business.**

3. **Express gratitude and check that it's a convenient time for the telephone call.**

4. **Tell the person the purpose of your call and verify that she's the correct person to be speaking to.**

5. **Present your case and pitch to get an appointment to talk with the person face to face.**

6. **Thank the person while you're on the phone.**

7. **Send a written confirmation letter clearly stating what was agreed and the time, date and place of the scheduled meeting.**

The rest, as they say, is selling.

When you're about to contact your prospective clients, keep three things at the forefront of your mind: your belief in what you're offering, the happiness of your current clients and your desire to serve others. This advice remains the same whether you're selling yourself as an employee, selling your skills as a freelance writer or pitching in for a multi-million pound contract.

Step 1: The greeting

When you call a prospective client for the first time, begin by using the most important thing for anyone to hear: her name. Using a formal approach, such as 'Good morning, Ms James' or 'Good morning. I'm calling for Ms James' is best because it conveys respect.

We recommend the use of *Good morning, Good afternoon* or *Good evening* because it sounds more professional than just saying, 'Hello.' Keep the greeting simple and professional.

Too often, people are tempted to use a person's first name possibly a little too quickly. Only use Bob or Liz, or indeed Robert or Elizabeth, when invited to do so by Mr or Mrs Smith.

Common courtesy goes a long, long way in making initial contacts. If you aren't confident in your skill level in this area then quietly ask a senior colleague what they might recommend. As a simple rule of thumb, we suggest always being completely honest and open. Ben once trained a young salesperson who suffered from nerves and Ben encouraged him to simply state the truth. Thus the young man in question called on every prospect and stated almost immediately: 'I'm not usually in sales, so please bear with me if I get it wrong or sound a little unsure. I'm usually only helping out in the office, but we're so busy they've sent me.' With this approach the prospects immediately relaxed and even helped the young man, who then, in turn, just did his job the way he was trained. He went on to be hugely successful.

Step 2: The introduction

After offering your greeting, introduce yourself and give your company name. If your company name doesn't explain what you do – as it would if your name were, say, Jensen Portrait Studios – then also mention briefly what type of business you're in. The key word here is *briefly*. Ben once asked a salesman what he sold and got a 45-minute response on the features and benefits of owning his very own high-sensitivity weighing device. No, he didn't buy one.

Clearly and succinctly state what you do. Business owners or consumer or corporate buyers get many approaches every week. The recipient of these incoming prospecting calls is wary of 'around the houses' approaches. So don't tell a prospect you're an image specialist, when actually you clean carpets. You say, 'My company specialises in carpet cleaning. A dirty carpet can have a subtle but powerful influence on the image of a company.' Say it straight without leaving a bad impression of a slippery approach.

Step 3: The thankyou and time check

After you've introduced yourself and your business, you need to use your good old-fashioned manners and courtesy to acknowledge that your prospect's time is valuable and thank her for taking your call. This lets her know you consider her to be an important person. Say something like this:

> Thank you for talking with me briefly. I'll only keep you a minute or two. Is it convenient to quickly speak with you now? I'll only be a moment, and then I'll let you get back to the important work you do.

You don't need to gush at your prospects with gratitude, though. Just be professional and businesslike in your manner.

Step 4: The purpose and person verification

When you've expressed your gratitude for your prospect's time, you need to get right to the heart of the matter by letting her know why you're calling and by clarifying that you're speaking to the correct person. Always express your purpose with a question. Something like this may be appropriate:

> Okay, good, so can I ask, when was the last time you had the carpets in your facility steam cleaned to eliminate germs and improve the experience your clients have in your store? And would that be something that you're personally involved with?

If she says the carpets were cleaned only a week ago, you may just need to remain polite and ask for permission to contact her when she needs the service again. (*Hint:* Ask how long ago she had her carpets cleaned, and you'll find out when she'll need them cleaned again.) Thank her for her time. Put a note in your calendar to contact her a couple of weeks before she needs the carpets cleaned again, and move on to your next potential client call.

Another superb method for using the telephone to make good quality appointments is to use a market research approach first. During your market research telephone call you simply say:

> The company I represent has given me an assignment to conduct a quick market research survey of a few local and successful companies such as yours. I've only five or six questions, so won't take more than a moment of your valuable time. We would greatly value your opinion. Would you help me by answering these brief questions?

When you ask for the prospect's help and show that you value her opinion, she's likely to comply. Plus, by informing her that your company is having you do this, you're likely to gain her empathy and co-operation.

The purpose of conducting this brief survey is to get the person on the other end of the line talking. Hopefully, what she tells you will give you the information you need to confirm just how worthy of a visit the prospect is, and then you can make another call on another day to confirm the valuable sales visit.

Keep the purpose of the call to market research – don't slide into selling. Be careful not to just go from one question to the next without really listening to your prospect's answers. She'll know by how you phrase the next question whether her last answer was heard. If she thinks you're just waiting to ask the next question without really bothering about her answer, she'll switch off and terminate the call. So how can you show that you're really listening to what your prospect is saying? Paraphrase her responses before moving on to the next question. When she hears that you cared enough to listen, she'll be more inclined to continue.

The market research call isn't just handy as an 'in' for selling. Say you're selling a service that reduces energy costs and saves money on utilities. You want to find out how much a company consumes. If the company has very low energy and utility consumption, then no matter how good your service is you'd be merely saving a few pence . . . not enough to justify your input or their time. So separating the learning call from the appointment call is extremely effective in saving you time and leading you only to potentially high-value sales prospects.

Step 5: The actual appointment

If you've used the market research call approach, then you're now on the second telephone call. Either way, by now you know that you're speaking with the relevant decision-maker and you're aware as to how qualified she is. Now's the time to make that appointment.

When Ms James agrees to give you a time to meet, give her an option of when, with an alternative choice question such as this:

> Would tomorrow at 10:20 a.m. be good for you, or is Wednesday at 2:40 p.m. better?

This question lets your prospect choose, yet keeps you in control. Whichever option she chooses, she's committing to the appointment, which is exactly what you want.

Notice that this example mentions off times, as opposed to 10 a.m. or 2 p.m., for example. Using off times subtly differentiates you from all the other salespeople who call, and the rarity gets you noticed and the prospect listening.

You're going to need enough time to do your selling job effectively, and so when making the appointment – after she's agreed to meet – say:

> In order to help your company most effectively I'll need approximately one hour. I just want to double-check that it will be convenient to meet for an hour on the Wednesday at 2:40 p.m. that you've opted for?

In a business-to-business environment most people give an hour as standard for a sales visit. If the sales call takes a few minutes less or more, then that's no big deal. But do clarify the expected length of the meeting – you don't want to roll up and just get flowing when the prospect has to leave after 30 minutes. Your time is your most valuable commodity: spend it wisely and check!

Step 6: The over-the-phone thankyou

When you've secured an appointment, you move on to thanking your prospect again, reiterating the time that you've both agreed to and verifying the location of her office (or the place where you'll be meeting). Nothing is worse than showing up late and presenting the excuse of getting lost.

With traffic and travel being somewhat of a lottery, it's also worth asking if the prospect is aware of any roadworks or issues near to her that could impact on your journey. Very often her own staff can be experiencing travel difficulties getting to work and she's aware of these and can steer you safely. Plus, in asking you add to the conversation factor and help speed up the connection between you.

Making sure you don't set yourself up for disappointment

Between 20 and 30 per cent of prospects will cancel meetings for a variety of reasons. If a lot of your appointments cancel before you get there, review your appointment-making process. Usually, you haven't chosen your prospects carefully enough and they weren't that good. Take a look at Chapter 7, which helps you find good prospects.

Or perhaps you didn't explain the reason for your visit well enough and the prospect got muddled about the purpose of the meeting and cried off. Try slowing down a little and explaining more carefully the purpose of your visit, and even inviting a little more conversation on the phone first.

Better to slow down a little on the phone and make more phone calls to get solid appointments than to whizz through the phone bit and find 30 per cent of your driving is a waste of time!

Also check on parking facilities. Not every location has its own parking, and if you're to use a local car park that requires change and is some distance away, then knowing this information in advance can severely reduce stress on the day of the visit.

Schedule other appointments in the prospect's part of town so you're already in the area when the time for the appointment arrives.

Step 7: The confirmation letter

If your appointment is more than two days from when you call, immediately send your prospect a letter confirming the appointment. Email is convenient, but we recommend a physical letter all the same. Many people have issues with mailboxes and technology and can't access them for days, but few people miss a pile of post and even fewer ignore letters when they arrive. A physical letter confirming the time, date and reason for the visit serves to solidify the appointment. In addition, your letterhead paper reminds the prospect about what you do and it allows her to contact you if she needs to before the day in question.

Putting Mail, Email and Face-to-Face Interactions to Work for You

You can contact your prospects in four major ways: by phone (see the previous section), traditional mail, email or face to face. Keep in mind that when you use any of these four methods, you're asking busy professionals or consumers to give up time that they may think can be spent more productively.

Most professional salespeople integrate all four methods into an effective prospecting strategy. For some, one method works better than others. As you gain experience in prospecting, you'll decide which methods work best for you and at which times.

Sending mail

If you choose to use mail as your primary method of prospecting and setting up appointments, choose your targeting carefully. Mailing is a great way to prospect, but mail sent to the wrong list of people is a tremendous waste of your time, money and effort. Being aware of your process – knowing that you're going to follow up the letter with an appointment-making telephone call, for example – means that you have to consider very carefully the content of the mail piece and indeed the volume that you plan to send. Traditional mail sent in smaller numbers and followed up with a telephone call is a superb way to prospect.

Whatever you send in the mail, be absolutely certain that it includes your website address and your email address. Interested people will want to check you out by visiting your website, and this can only help when you telephone to arrange a sales visit.

Using email

You can handle email prospecting in two ways:

- ✔ Working with a bona-fide mail house that specialises in sending email marketing e-shots. This is a superb method as the company usually has clean, targeted lists of opt-in email addresses and they can help produce a visually effective email that grabs attention when received.

- ✔ Search out the email addresses individually of the targeted prospects and send a very specific, customised email.

In either case, you want to make sure that your opening approach email is sexy and exciting! Grab attention and have one or two strong benefits as headline points. Also include a call to action at the bottom so that clients can easily take the next step.

Interacting face-to-face

Face-to-face prospecting for some sales roles – visible products like security shutters or replacement windows, for example – can be *the* best method, especially when selling into a consumer market. Walking from office to office or home to home trying to find decision-makers is physically exhausting, which can be tough. But even worse is the sad fact that you may not get many leads out of all your legwork.

What you will get, though, is a load of information from neighbours and receptionists. They can be powerhouses who help you either eliminate a family or company as prospects or advance your chances of obtaining an appointment for making your presentation with the decision-maker by providing great prequalifying information. Receptionists, secretaries and assistants hold the keys to opening the doors you want to get through. Hence their title in sales jargon is 'gatekeeper'. Too many salespeople think this term is negative in that their job is to keep you out. In reality, it's to let in the right people. You just need to figure out how to demonstrate that you *are* the right person.

Treat receptionists or secretaries with the respect they deserve. Their time is valuable too. If you try to rush past a receptionist or quickly ask to see her boss without first showing concern or interest in her, you may as well not have gone in at all. Introduce yourself, ask the receptionist's name and then try to have a friendly dialogue with her before asking to see the boss. She'll be more inclined to introduce a friend to her boss than she will a pushy salesperson, so try to get her to see you as the former rather than the latter.

Getting to the Elusive Decision-Maker

When you're seeking meetings with prospective clients, what you really want is to get in with the person who has the ability to make decisions about the products and services that are used, otherwise known as the *decision-maker*. In consumer sales, the decision-maker is most often the head of the household (even though one spouse or partner may defer to the choices of the other). In some situations the end user will have the final word, such as a child or parent of the person you believe to be the decision-maker. They may have their hands on the purse strings, but be working to please someone else.

In the case of a purchasing agent or business owner, that person may have so many people contacting her that she's established a hierarchy of people around her who screen calls quite heavily on her behalf. Your task remains the same: get past the shields with charm and professionalism and eventually succeed in getting face-to-face time with the decision-maker.

When you have trouble getting through to the decision-maker, you get the opportunity to be a little creative. Yes, this situation requires more work. But keep in mind that those people who are hardest to get to will be tough on your competition as well. So if you stick it out, get to visit with them and win their business, you'll be on the inside of that same protective wall. And those same support people will keep not you but your *competition* at bay.

Getting past the receptionist

If you're having trouble getting through to a company's decision-maker, begin with the receptionist who answers the phone when you call. If at all possible, get the name of the decision-maker on your first contact. Tell the receptionist that you need her help and ask, 'Who would be in charge of the decision-making process if your company were to need a [whatever your product or service is]?' The receptionist is the person who has to know what each employee's area of responsibility is in order to direct calls properly, so she should be a great help. Then, whenever you make follow-up calls, use the decision-maker's name.

Be sure to ask for the correct pronunciation and spelling of any names the receptionist gives you. Never guess about names or take the chance of writing them down incorrectly; business practices like that are likely to haunt you later. It never hurts to get the receptionist's name as well.

If the receptionist is especially helpful – as receptionists tend to be – take a moment to send a thankyou note to her along with your business card. A little bit of recognition now can prove valuable later on. When you've built a solid relationship with the receptionist, she'll always look forward to hearing from you or seeing you, and future visits will be much warmer.

Using creativity to get you in

Whatever unusual method you choose for getting in touch with the decision-maker, always consider how the other person will receive it. Your goal is to find an inoffensive method for getting people's attention – but your method has to be creative too.

We know of a salesperson who sent a lottery ticket attached to a letter with the headline: 'If this doesn't win, then I have a solution that will solve your sales challenges and make you feel like a lottery winner!' The strategy broke through the barrier in a creative way, and the salesperson succeeded in consistently getting appointments with target prospects.

Another creative way to make a good impression on the decision-maker is to ask her receptionist or assistant who she respects and listens to in her field or what leisure pursuits she enjoys. You can then send her a book or CD, or even tickets to a concert or local event where a favoured artist is appearing.

If the decision-maker's schedule really is strict and all else fails, try to arrange a telephone or online meeting instead of a face-to-face one. You'll have to adjust your presentation to give it just the right impact. But it may be a method worth trying.

Chapter 9

Building Relationships and Gathering Information to Ensure Success

In This Chapter

▶ Getting off on the right foot with a good first impression

▶ Building rapport and getting the prospect to like and trust you

▶ Asking questions to get the information you need

▶ Making successful approaches in a retail environment

*Y*ou've found your prospect, made initial contact and arranged to meet in person or via the telephone. The prospect has shown a certain level of interest in your product or service, and now you're ready to sell to him. The result: you may find that your meeting goes fabulously, or you may struggle to get along with or convince the prospect.

But what if you could improve your relationship-building and fact-finding skills so that you could more often have dream calls and less often leave a meeting downcast? In this chapter, we guide you through handling your meetings with prospects in such a way that you increase your chances of success dramatically. Read on, apply the advice and then watch your sales calls feel easier and your results sky-rocket.

Working on non-verbal communication

In a well-documented study measuring initial impressions, the amount of influence attributed to various parts of the communication was a staggering 93 per cent to non-verbal. Actual words accounted for only 7 per cent! A massive 55 per cent was attributed to body language – the way a person walks, talks and carries herself. The remaining 38 per cent was tone and pitch and speed of the voice, huge indicators in any language of how a person feels. In short, when you're selling, you need your prospect to feel at ease and confident with you, and he'll read you to gauge how he feels. So work on body language and how you speak so that you can more often walk into a *yes*.

Making a Good First Impression at Your Meeting

Your prospective clients make many decisions about you in the first ten seconds after they meet you for the very first time. That's right. Within *ten seconds* you can be either a potential guest at the next family barbecue or someone to be ushered out as soon as possible!

Your job is to come up with a way to help the people who meet you for the first time see that they made a good choice in agreeing to see you.

If you're new to selling or simply a nervous person, take care not to put too much into those first few moments. Concentrate on being as relaxed as possible and always offer a big, warm smile, a handshake and a sincere 'hello'.

Dressing for success

Before you arrive for your appointment or visit with a potential client, consider the way you dress. Your goal is to ensure that your prospects like you and see that you're similar to them. So dress like your clients dress.

Use good judgement and common sense when it comes to the way you dress, and you can't go wrong. If you sell farm equipment and the meeting is on a farm then arriving dressed as a banker in a suit and tie probably won't go down well. Instead, jeans and boots with an overcoat make the client feel at ease and immediately one barrier is removed.

If you're new in sales or new to a particular group of clients, pay attention to what the other successful salespeople at your company wear, and then dress like they do. If your company has a dress code, there's probably a good reason for that – it's probably done some research and determined that clothes in line with the dress code are what customers expect to see. Be sure to abide by it.

If you show up at a meeting with your prospective client wearing something that's a good bit different from what the prospect is wearing, then you must work during the first few minutes of your meeting to find a way to get yourself on an even footing with her. After that, it's too late.

Paying attention to your body language

In addition to the message you communicate to your clients with what you wear, the body language you use expresses something. Your posture, your facial expression, the placement of your hands, the speed, volume and tone of your voice, how much you lick your lips as you talk . . . all these govern first impressions just as much as what you wear.

Being aware of your body language may require some time in front of a mirror or video camera, or you may need to spend time with someone who truly cares about your success and is willing to give you an honest opinion. Dress for work and walk your normal walk. If your normal body language doesn't present an image of success and confidence, watch someone who does and emulate her. Basically, you want to:

✔ Walk with your shoulders comfortably back and your arms freely at your sides (no hands in pockets or stiffly glued to your side!).

✔ Make good eye contact with the people you meet (but don't stare them down!).

✔ Keep your tone of voice confident and fluent. If you're struggling with this, then keep rehearsing until you've got it right.

If you're sincere about your pleasure in meeting people, this behaviour will be automatic.

Getting your potential clients to like and trust you

When you meet people, your main goal is to help them relax with you. No one gets involved in a decision-making process when they're uptight. When selling, always remember that your goal is to be a person whom other people like, trust and want to listen to.

So how can you help your prospective clients like and trust you? Start in those first ten seconds after you meet, and move through five important steps to making a powerful first impression (covered in the following sections in more detail):

1. **Smile warmly.**

2. **Make eye contact.**

3. **Offer a greeting.**

4. **Shake hands.**

5. **Offer your name and get the prospect's name.**

If you handle these steps properly, you'll earn the opportunity to continue building rapport and lead into the next phase of selling.

People are, for the most part, reactive and will respond according to what's given them. So if you expect them to be cordial, open and friendly, they will be. When your body language and opening statements are pleasant, they'll very likely respond in kind.

Step 1: Smile

Life can make you feel less cheery sometimes, but a professional knows that having a little more money can help even in sad times, so putting that smile on and raising the game for work really is the best thing that you can do.

When you first come into contact with a prospective client, smile. (Yes, it's that simple!) A smile radiates warmth, and it's infectious. If you're not smiling, if your smile appears fake or if it looks like it hurts when you do it, your prospect will want to avoid you, and she'll put up a wall of doubt and fear in just a few seconds.

If you're contacting people over the telephone, smiling still counts. Believe it or not, people can hear a smile (or a lack of one) in your voice. You transmit your feelings over the telephone.

Step 2: Make eye contact

When you meet a prospect, look into her eyes. This is a part of body language that builds trust. People tend not to trust those who can't look them in the eye. Think about it: people usually glance away when they're lying to you. So when you don't look your clients in the eye, they may doubt what you're saying.

Although looking your clients in the eyes is very important, be sure not to go to the extreme and lock onto their eyes. Don't scare them off! Getting into a staring contest is dangerous in any selling situation.

Step 3: Say hello (or something like it)

The style of the greeting you offer depends on whom you're calling, but essentially, in this role, when prospecting you'll be calling either unknown targets or 'almost friends' you've met already. Either way, you'll be okay with a standard 'Hello' or possibly a 'Good morning' or 'Good afternoon'.

If you already know your prospect's name, use it with your greeting (for example, 'Good morning, Mr Williams'). If you don't know your prospect's name, don't rush to get it. The caller is aware that you're selling, so establish a bit of rapport *before* asking for your prospect's name!

Step 4: Shake hands

The accepted method of greeting on a sales visit is to shake hands. If you're familiar as friends then an embrace might be good, but don't go hugging a newly met company director – a tad inappropriate!

Not everybody is comfortable with a handshake, so watch body language. If a prospect is evidently reaching out, then proceed confidently, but if she's evidently holding back, then don't push it. A handshake isn't a deal breaker. If she doesn't feel like shaking hands at the beginning, then simply carry on and be a professional and work at her warming to you. Then you can see whether she'll shake your hand as you leave. If you make this a little game, it adds to the enjoyment!

The handshake is appropriate in most instances, but only if you do it properly. If you've ever shaken a hand that feels like a dead fish, you'll understand what we mean. Or, if you've experienced a bone-crushing handshake, you'll also see the importance of having the right kind of handshake.

To convey the highest level of trust, confidence and competence, you need to grasp the whole hand of the other individual and give it a brief but solid squeeze – not too tight, but definitely not loosey-goosey either. Keep it brief. There's nothing more uncomfortable than to have someone keep holding your hand when you're ready to have it back.

If you're meeting a married couple, shaking the hands of both the husband and the wife is appropriate. If they have children with them, shaking the kids' hands is a nice gesture as well, but proceed with caution, because sometimes children are nervous and parents don't want a stranger being over friendly with their children.

Step 5: Offer your name for theirs

The handshake is the most natural time to exchange names. Depending on the situation, you may want to use the formal greeting of, 'Good morning. My name is Robert Smith with Jones & Company.' If the setting is more casual, try something like, 'Hi. My name is Rob and I'm from Jones & Co.'

What's in a name?

If you're being introduced to a group of people, be careful to use the same level of formality with each member. Don't call one person Mrs Johnson but call Mrs Johnson's associate by her first name, Sarah, just because you can't remember Sarah's last name. That's more offensive than having to ask again what Sarah's name is.

A good tip to avoid any issue is to write names down on a notepad along with notes from the meeting. You can double-check spellings and know that you have names correct for any contractual details that you hope to get to later on in the meeting. Plus, you show a supremely professional approach.

If a woman says her name is Judith Carter, use Ms Carter when you first address her. Don't jump to the familiar Judy. You can set the wrong tone inadvertently even though you meant well. Our advice is simply to ask, 'Would you prefer me to call you Ms Carter?' Your prospect will then clearly say something like, 'Oh no, it's Judy', and you'll know exactly how to proceed.

Establishing Rapport with Your Potential Clients

Your clients feel comfortable around you when you know how to establish *rapport* with them, which is what selling situations are all about – establishing common ground. People like to be around other people who are similar to them. Bringing out the similarities you share with your prospects proves that you're just like them: you have a family, you have a job, you have similar values, and, when you're seeking any product other than the one you represent, you work with salespeople too, just like your prospects. You just happen to be more of an expert on the particular product line or service you represent than your prospects are – and you're happy to use your knowledge to their advantage.

Whatever field of sales you're in – whether you sell home improvements to homeowners, or large industrial equipment to construction companies, or high-level software to government departments – you sell to *people*. So you need to reach the person beyond the business suit, and form a personal connection. To do so, you need to connect on a human level – and the best starting point is to relax and be yourself.

If you sense that the other party is concerned as to whether you're on the same page, say something like this:

> Mr Williams, when I'm not helping people get involved with my product, I'm a consumer, just like you, looking for quality products at the best price. What I hope for when I'm shopping is to find someone who can help me understand all the facts about the item I'm interested in so I can make a wise decision. Today, I'd like to earn your confidence in me as an expert on state-of-the-art stereo systems. So feel free to ask any questions you may have.

Don't wince at the thought of using these words – they've been proven to work successfully in lowering barriers people put up when dealing with salespeople. Although no one likes hearing 'scripted' material, it's only scripted if you let it sound that way. In sales, *how* you say something is as important as what you say. Always remember to speak with a sincere concern for your customers. If you're not truly concerned for them, you shouldn't be in this field.

To build rapport with your clients, you have to be truly interested in them. You need to be sincere in wanting to get to know them well enough so you can help them have more, do more and be more. If your clients believe you're being real – speaking from your heart – they'll put their confidence in you much more quickly.

When you see a professional salesman at work, you can think that the process is easy – that little or no resistance to the sale existed. In fact, the salesperson has a range of techniques up his sleeve that he uses smoothly to help achieve the sale. The following sections clue you in on some powerful rapport-building tips and techniques.

Keeping the conversation light

Someone may have referred Mr Johnson to you. If that's the case, mention the mutual acquaintance – that's usually a great starting point. 'Good old Jim' may have an excellent talent, great family or wonderful sense of humour. Those are all nice, non-controversial topics to cover. In other instances you may pick up an accent from another part of the country and that can be an excellent talking point, if you have connections to that area too.

Don't let the conversation part of rapport building become too hard for you. If all else fails, bring up something in the local news. Just make sure it's a non-controversial subject. Try your best not to bring up the weather – if you start off talking about how wet it is as you take off your soaking coat that's acceptable, but more than that and your prospect will know you're struggling for something to talk about or that you're nervous.

Another good tactic is to give your prospect a sincere compliment. *Sincere* is the key word here. Sincerity takes you everywhere; blatant, insincere flattery gets you nowhere. A stale line like 'Mrs Fletcher, you look absolutely terrific' doesn't qualify as sincere.

Here's a good example of light conversation:

> SALESPERSON: Good afternoon, Ms Thompson. I appreciate your time. I was wondering how long the company has been in this location? I know I've seen your sign on the building for many years.
>
> PROSPECT: We've been here 25 years.
>
> SALESPERSON: That's great. And how long have you been with the company?
>
> PROSPECT: I started ten years ago in the area of stock control. For the past five years, I've handled all the purchasing.

Gaining common ground means asking questions to establish a mutual interest. But be careful of wandering off into something that feels like an interview or an interrogation! The aim is just to get the conversation going and make the prospect feel comfortable with you, so be gentle and open and let the chat flow. If the conversation stalls for a moment don't worry – that might merely be her style; it doesn't mean that she doesn't like you.

Acknowledging your prospect's pride

If you happen to be working in a business where you give a lot of in-home presentations, and the people you're presenting to have a nice home, say this:

> I want to tell you that I spend a lot of time in other people's homes, and you should be proud of what you've done here. Your home is lovely.

Look for signs of hobbies or crafts that you can comment on. If a woman is an artist and has her paintings on display, you can say, 'You did that? What a great talent to have.' That way you're not lying if you think the painting is really poor. Painting *is* a great talent – whether or not your prospect has any is in the eye of the beholder. If your prospect has any hobby she's obviously proud of, give her a sincere compliment about it. People always enjoy hearing compliments.

Avoiding controversy

Be cautious that the prospect doesn't tempt you into a conversation about a controversial subject. Some people do that just to test you. Specifically, avoid discussing politics and religion at all costs, unless you've really mastered the art of conversation and can allow the other party to express her feelings without being drawn into a debate as to how you feel.

Here's how to get around any topic that may lead you down the wrong path:

> I'm so busy serving clients, I haven't had time to stay current on that topic. What do you think?

By skilfully sidestepping the subject, you may well have prevented lighting the fuse to a time bomb. Better to appear slightly ignorant now than to get bogged down in an emotional argument and lose a sale later. If the prospect comes back at you with a very strong opinion, you'll know to avoid that sub-ject in future meetings. Or you may feel the need to brush up on it, if she's deeply involved, so you'll have a better under-standing of this person before you build a long-term working relationship with her.

In any business contact, be certain to never, *ever* use any profanity or slang. It doesn't matter if such language is widely used on today's most popular television programmes; it has no place in the business world. You never know the values of the person you're talking with when you first meet her and you don't want to risk offending her. The same goes for off-colour, political, ethnic or sexist jokes. Be sensitive to the values, beliefs and morals of the person sitting or standing across from you.

Keeping pace with your prospect

Taking time to become aware of your normal speed of talking is extremely valuable. And notice the rate of talking of every-one else you encounter. When you become tuned in to it, it happens naturally.

When you're aware of your speaking rate, you need to know how to gently and subtly adjust your tone and speed to match that of the prospect. It's not too difficult – just concentrate on how the person speaks. When you more closely match how the prospect speaks, you'll see that she feels more connected and sales meetings flow magically!

Touching on emotive subjects

You don't want the prospect to remember you as just another player; you want him to have formed an emotional connection to you on a person-to-person basis. Your ability to openly con-verse and share information makes the choice the prospect faces one based upon people, not mere facts. Even the hard-est negotiations are underpinned with feelings about the deal. So you need to get your prospect thinking:

✔ How do you *feel* about backup or support?

✔ How would you *feel* if another supplier let you down?

✔ How would you *feel* if you didn't choose to buy in order to save money, but in the end you lost many times more in lost revenue due to failure?

All these questions and more solicit the feelings behind the decision. To form the emotional connection, you need to get good at unearthing feelings and talking about them.

A great starting point is to talk about subjects that matter to the person in question, *not* the project or deal in question. Subjects such as children, career paths and home lives give you the opportunity to connect – to learn a little about the prospect, and to share a little about yourself. After your prospect shares feelings about other areas of their life, you can ask questions that provoke feelings:

✔ How will the new project affect you if it were to go right . . . maybe promotion?

✔ How about if the project went wrong; how would that hurt you?

✔ What are your fears for the purchase?

✔ If you had all the money in the world, what would you prefer to buy?

Answers to questions like these are gold, but you can only ask them when you've established a level of personal connection and friendship. Work at that and you'll see treasure chests opening before your eyes!

Telling stories

Throughout history messages have been conveyed in story form. Think of the tortoise and the hare, the boy who cried wolf and the ugly duckling. All are enjoyable stories to hear, but they have a point that's easy to grasp. Telling the boy who cried wolf story has more impact than telling someone, 'Don't keep shouting that you're in trouble if you're not!'

Story-telling in the sales arena works the same way. Say you'd like to illustrate just how superb your company's support services are. You could just state, 'Our company offers the best support services.' Not very exciting or convincing; the prospect probably thinks, 'You're bound to say that!' Instead, how about telling a story of a happy customer or a well-known company that recently purchased from you? Try saying, 'That reminds me, let me tell you a story about a recent example of a client of mine. They needed to have a special size of mattress to go with their bed order which, in itself, was not an issue. However, their need was coupled with a delivery deadline of only two weeks, as it was a special surprise gift for a wedding night. Well, under more normal circumstances, a delivery takes eight weeks but, for Mr and Mrs Blythe, we really pulled out the stops to make their special occasion even more special. The full story is here in this brochure, but isn't this the sort of company that you'd prefer to deal with?'

As with all areas, we don't advocate telling anything other than the truth, but search through your company's sales history and chat with colleagues and you'll find stories that you can use to illustrate the benefits of dealing with you. This habit is a powerful one to cultivate.

Winning over the headmaster from hell

Picture the scene: Ben is in his pre-sale warm-up mode while on his way to meet a headmaster for a sales call. He's dressed as a successful young salesperson might dress – fashionable trousers, large tie and long hair (yes, okay, it was a long time ago!) – and is brimming with cheery confidence as he knocks on the door.

But he gets a rude shock when he's ushered into a dark, austere room and introduced to his client. It's blatantly evident that the two men are at opposite ends of many spectrums – age, style, energy, modernity, everything! Talk about potential for mismatch.

Ben searches for some means to build rapport, and finally he spots a photograph on the desk of a young lady at her graduation. He steers the conversation to the pleasure of being a father and how special daughters are. The headmaster eyes Ben with suspicion but allows him to continue. Ben explains that he's a proud single father of a wonderful eight-year-old daughter.

The mood transforms. Instead of seeing Ben as a flash, young nuisance salesman with probably little morality and discipline, the headmaster now warms up. Ben walks away three hours later not only with a sale but with a new friend and a welcome anytime he's passing – especially if he brings his daughter.

Sharing secrets

People like to know secrets. The fact that you've been deemed worthy of knowing means you feel special and valued as someone who's trustworthy enough to keep the secret; plus you feel that knowing the secret gives you an advantage over those who don't know. So secrets are powerful.

How could you use secrets effectively when selling? Well, because selling demands a level of trust; when you share a secret, you're saying, 'I like you and trust you and I want you to have an edge.' Subconsciously, the recipient gets the message and trusts you more.

Just to make ourselves clear, though, we don't advocate telling secrets of the 'restricted company information' type! No! Instead we suggest that, for example, you might share a secret that covers a potential objection, such as finance terms. You might suggest to your prospect that usually finance terms are 36 months, and you already sense that this would make each monthly amount too much for them. So you might lean forward and tell them a secret, such as 'I'm not really supposed to publicise this, but there was a way we used to be able to extend the terms to 60 months. If I could still do that, then your payments would be low enough to manage, but those longer terms were withdrawn last month. Between you and I, though, I know that one of my sales from last month changed into a cash payment, so as long as you don't mention this to anyone else I should be able to replace their arrangement with one for you. You'd have to keep quiet about it, as we aren't actually allowed to do new sales with a 60-month term.'

This type of secret makes a switch in terms acceptable and helps to ease a payment barrier and thus win you a sale. What you say might be a true story, but framing it as a secret helps you to persuade the person to buy.

Understanding that the sale isn't all about you

For many, the word *selling* has selfish connotations. Salespeople have earned a reputation for being chiefly concerned with getting the sale and earning accolades, sometimes at the expense of the prospect. As a result, the public's opinion of a salesperson is not flattering on the whole.

Your job is to break down any preconceptions your prospect has about you due to the fact you're a salesperson. Understanding that the sale isn't all about you is primary to this task. You need to show that the prospect's interests are what matter most. Thus you must be skilled at relaying your concerns about the issues they have that your offering will solve in a manner in which they'll accept as genuine , and not merely as a sly sales technique. With your mannerisms and language style as well as the illustrations that you tell them, you want the prospect to get the message that you only want to do business with them if it's beneficial for both of you.

Try saying:

> We believe that for this to be a good arrangement for both of us, asking a few questions of you in order to establish how we might be a compatible fit as a supplier to you is important. In other words, whilst it might appear that I am selling you the benefits of us being your IT support provider, we only take on board contracts when we've correctly matched the service level required with the service level we know we can safely deliver. We've learned from painful experience that when the levels of service expectations don't exactly match, it creates a lot of friction and irritation for both parties, something we can all do without. So I have a few questions that will help us both see whether working together is a good idea. Would you mind if I briefly run through them?

You're indicating that you're prepared to walk away from the sale if your offering isn't right for the prospect – the very opposite of aggressive, pushy sales. Your prospect will respond warmly to this.

For details of how to ask questions, see the next section.

Fact-finding: Asking the Right Questions

Throughout the relationship-building phase of the selling process, as well as making friends, you have to gather information about the prospect and his company's usage of the services or product that you're there to talk about. Then you can narrow down the best solution for your client, which you present in the next step of the selling cycle – the presentation (see Chapter 10).

A great sales professional invests his time wisely in developing questions that find out exactly what the client expects the product to do for him and then listens very carefully to the answers that are relayed. Then the salesperson tailors his presentation to match exactly what the prospect is looking for, not merely a list of supposed features and benefits.

For example, if your prospect tells you that petrol consumption, or lack of it, is very important to him in buying a new car, before you present the vehicle you think is best for him, you include a question like this:

> Didn't you say that fuel economy was your primary concern?

Such a question starts the *yes* momentum you need to excite the prospect about the product you're planning to present. The *yes* momentum is what every persuader strives for. After you get your prospect agreeing to things, if you simply keep asking the right questions – kind of like following a flow chart – he'll follow where you guide him. Plus, he'll have enough information at the end of your presentation to make a wise decision, which you hope is that he can't live without your product or service.

Questions also create emotional involvement. If you're marketing home security devices, you can ask:

> Wouldn't you feel more confident about entering your home in the evening knowing you would be warned beforehand if there was any danger?

What does that question do? It raises a prickle of alarm on the back of your prospect's neck about the unknown possibilities of walking into an unprotected home. You don't want to frighten anyone into purchasing your product, but you do want to get him picturing himself owning its benefits.

You don't need to ask about every feature that you could possibly present, because when you have a sense of connection your prospect readily shares with you the most important features that he's looking for. In the case of a business-to-business sale you can probably even ask:

> Tell me, Jim, for this to really tick all your boxes, what is it that your company needs right now more than anything else?

You then gently gather the answers and cover each in your presentation.

The following sections offer some questioning techniques to help you with your fact-finding mission.

Asking tie-down questions

The popular *tie-down* questioning style doesn't involve tying clients into their chairs until they say yes. Instead, tie-downs involve making a statement, and then asking for agreement by adding a question to the end of it. Here are some effective tie-downs:

- ✔ **Isn't it?** For example, 'It's a great day for golf, *isn't it?*' When your caller agrees, you set a tee time.

- ✔ **Doesn't it?** For example, 'Jet-skiing at the lake this weekend sounds like fun, *doesn't it?*' When your client agrees, pull out the rental agreement – pronto.

- ✔ **Hasn't he?** For example, 'The previous homeowner has done a great job with the landscaping, *hasn't he?*' When the prospective new homeowner agrees that he likes the landscape, he's just moved one step closer to liking the whole package – house included.

- ✔ **Haven't they?** For example, 'The manufacturers have included every detail about the questions you asked in this proposal, *haven't they?*' Having all the details covered and having the buyer agree that he's covered helps reduce the possibility of stalling when it's time to close.

- ✔ **Don't you?** For example, 'Efficiency of the machine so that it uses less paper is important, *don't you agree?*' When the person agrees, sign him up for your new laser printer and have him choose a date he wants it delivered.

- ✔ **Didn't you?** For example, 'You had a great time the last time you went hiking, *didn't you?*' Then pull out the latest style of boot while your client is in a positive frame of mind about the last trip.

- ✔ **Shouldn't you?** For example, 'With so many choices that you enjoy on the menu, you should come here for dinner more often, *shouldn't you?*' If it was an enjoyable meal, suggest a date for a return visit and book the reservation.

- ✔ **Couldn't you?** For example, 'You could let your spouse have a whole day just to relax and rejuvenate, *couldn't you?*' Get a commitment to a spa package!

The goal of using tie-downs is to get your prospect thinking in the affirmative about the subject you've just tied down. While he's agreeing with you, you can confidently bring up whatever it is you're trying to get a commitment on.

Professional salespeople often use tie-down statements such as this:

> A reputation for prompt, professional service is important, isn't it?

Who can say no to that? The salesperson who asks such a question has begun a cycle of agreement with the prospect who, hopefully, will continue to agree all the way through the selling sequence.

Using the alternate of choice question style

You've certainly seen or heard the *alternate of choice* questioning technique used before, but you probably didn't recognise it as a sales strategy. This strategy involves giving your prospect two *acceptable* suggestions to choose from, where either is essentially an agreement to have what you offer. People most often use the technique for calendar events such as appointments, delivery dates and so on, but you can also use it effectively for choices between models and payment terms. Here are some simple examples:

> ✔ **'I can arrange my schedule so we can visit on Thursday at 3:00 p.m. or would Friday at 11:00 a.m. be better?'** Either answer confirms that you have an appointment.

> ✔ **'This vehicle comes with a choice of engine size – a 2.0 litre or a 2.5 litre. Which would you prefer?'** No matter which vehicle your prospect chooses, he's still chosen to take one of them.

> ✔ **'We have a payment option over 24 months. Or would 60 months be more convenient?'** Whichever option your prospect chooses, you've got commitment on ordering.

You can also use the alternate of choice technique when you want to focus or limit the conversation to certain points. For example, if you're selling playground equipment to a school, you don't want to open up a debate about placement of the equipment when you're preparing a proposal. You just need to know the specifications required for the materials and equipment desired. In that case, you can ask, 'Which do you think would be a better surface under the equipment, wood chips or sand?' You get right to the point of the matter and you give only the two solutions you need addressed.

Trying the involvement question style

In the *involvement* questioning technique you use questions to help your listeners envision themselves *after* they've made a decision to agree with you. If you're marketing office equipment, you can involve your prospect with a question like this:

> Who will be the key contact for us to train on the use of the equipment?

Now you've got him thinking about implementing training *after* he owns the product, not about whether or not he'll own it.

Similarly, if you want to involve someone in business with you, use a question like this:

> What will you and Janet do with the extra income that our business plan says we'll generate in the next year?

Avoiding déjà vu when you ask questions

To save yourself from needlessly repeating questions, make written notes of your prospective client's responses. Referring to your notes to remind yourself what questions you already asked and what the client said his needs were is perfectly okay. Inadvertently asking the same question twice (or more) doesn't inspire confidence in the customer about you or your product. Not only do written notes help you during the presentation, but they also help you to remember what you've already covered when you follow up with the prospect after he's become a regular, happy client. In fact, that's part of how you keep him happy.

Don't forget to ask permission to take notes before you start taking them. Some people get nervous when you start writing down what they tell you. For all you know, they may visualise themselves being grilled in a court of law on what they say to you. If you

think you're with someone like that, give him a pad or piece of paper and a pen (preferably with your company name on it) so that he can take notes too. Being prepared for this situation helps you avoid, or at least handle, uncomfortable situations.

Getting permission to take notes is easy. All you need to say is this: 'Over the years, I've found it very beneficial to make notes during meetings with potential clients. Doing so enables me to do a better job. I wouldn't want to forget anything that might prove to save you money or time as we move forward. So, I hope you won't be offended if, while we chat, I make a few notes.' Putting it that way gives you an opportunity to admit that you're human and that you're also bright enough to have learned how to do your job well. These little sentences help put your clients at ease and build their confidence in you.

Is your listener thinking about whether to get into business with you? Nope. He's just envisioning spending the money he'll earn *after* he goes into business with you. If what he plans to spend the money on is something he wants badly enough, there's a good chance that he'll find himself *having* to go into business with you to satisfy a need he's been feeling without knowing how to fulfil it. Aren't you the good little helper for bringing him just the right business opportunity?

Knowing How to Approach Prospects in a Retail Setting

Selling in a retail environment is really no different from selling in any other environment – you need to get each customer to like you and trust you enough to ask for help, instead of immediately pouncing on your customers with a reflexive, 'May I help you?'

As a customer, you may have heard variations of the 'May I help you?' greeting, including something like this: 'Hi, I'm Bob. What can I do for you today?' What kind of response does Bob hear 99.9 per cent of the time he says those words? 'Oh, nothing. I'm just looking.' If something doesn't work 99.9 per cent of the time, doesn't it make sense to try to come up with a better initial greeting?

If you work in retail sales, here are two important suggestions that will increase your sales and the sales of anyone else in your company you share these suggestions with:

✔ When people enter your establishment, never walk directly toward them.

✔ When you do approach customers, don't rush.

Think about a time as a consumer when you've been approached by a quick-moving, overzealous salesperson, and you had to step back away from her. You don't want that to happen to you. Approach your customers as if you're just walking around the store, not making a beeline to them. Smile. Welcome them, and let your customers know you're there in case they have questions. Then get out of the way and let them look around.

Making the right approach

So what can you say instead of, 'May I help you?' Try saying:

Hello, thanks for coming in. I work here. If you have any questions, please let me know.

What does this greeting do? It projects a warm, welcome feeling rather than an overwhelmed feeling. You've just invited your customer to relax, and when people relax, they're more open to making decisions.

Another greeting you may want to try is this:

> Hello, welcome to Jacksons. I'm very pleased that you had a chance to pop in today. My name is Karen, and I'll be right over here if you have any questions.

Pause momentarily in case the customer does have questions. Then step away.

When you step away from the customer, instead of toward her, you distinguish yourself from all the typical salespeople she's ever encountered – and for most customers that's a very good thing. When you leave customers alone, they walk toward what they want. By observing them from a discreet distance, you know exactly what they came in for. When they finally stop in front of something for a moment, that's when you want to move closer to be ready to answer questions. Don't hang over them like a vulture, though. Just be where they can find you when they look around for help.

Reading the signals your customers project

In any place of business where you have a display area or showroom, let your customers look around before you approach them. Being laid-back is much less threatening and far more professional than rushing over to them with an order pad in hand and a glint of commission in your eyes!

If a customer doesn't look around but remains by one item for a while, then you may walk up and ask a question. Use an involvement question as your opening sentence because she'll have to answer it with more than a *yes* or a *no*. Plus, you'll discover something that will help you keep the conversation going. For example, if the customer is looking at a piece of furniture, ask:

> Will this chair replace an old one, or is it going to be an addition to your furnishings?

When she answers, you'll know why she's interested, and you can then begin guiding her to a good decision.

Make sure that when customers are ready to talk with you, they can find you quickly, but you haven't invaded their space and taken control of their shopping experience.

Chapter 10

Making Winning Presentations

*T*he presentation stage of the selling process is the show – your chance to get your prospective client's senses involved. Although all stages in the selling process are important, the presentation is a supremely key area. You can easily miss the deal if you don't inform the client properly, and conversely, you can miss the deal if you try to inform the client of too much! You need to deliver just what the prospect needs based upon information gleaned by you in the relationship building part of the process (see Chapter 9).

A *presentation* can be as simple as giving out a brochure with a quick explanation or as complex as an elaborate stand at an exhibition where you see attractive displays, video, food and drink and, of course, many members of glamorous-looking staff trying to attract prospects.

In this chapter, we steer you through the potentially frightening territory of the sales presentation (frightening, at least, until you're trained) – everything from finding the power players in the room to giving a presentation over the Internet. We also give you some great tips for avoiding common presentation pitfalls. So before you give a presentation, read on.

You must have your presentation well rehearsed. Memorize anything that you may be required to say. Practise until you can deliver your presentation smoothly yet not sound like you're delivering rote information. How long this takes will depend on your product and your own dedication to getting the job done. Because your presentation engages the clients, you have to be prepared to handle potential breaks in your presentation due to client questions and get smoothly back on track to complete the task.

Getting More Than a Foot in the Door

When you've earned the right to give a prospective client a presentation of your idea, concept, product or service, you're nowhere near done. The decision-maker has chosen you – probably along with several other contestants – and given you the opportunity to present. But you don't know in what timeframe or by what criteria she's planning ahead, and so the potential is a long way from being realised. You need all your skills in gathering the information and building rapport, and you need to be supremely proficient at presenting your reasons that she should maximise her returns and decide in your favour now. That's a big ask!

In any selling situation, understanding the perspective of your contact person is vital. We cover this point at length in Chapter 4.

Every day, salespeople bombard your prospect with over-tures for their business. Your contact person may be a real decision-maker or someone designated to narrow the field to two or three potential suppliers for the real decision-maker to talk with. If you've established a good relationship with your prospect then she may tell you who else is in the field of play. She may even tell you more acute information as to what you need to do to win. But, most likely, you'll have to rely upon hard work to dig out these facts.

Think of this as the opening to all the *Mission: Impossible* films. The first aspect of the mission is to identify the players and what's in it for each of them. This way, should you decide to accept your mission, you'll know who needs more persuading and how to go about doing just that. In the following sections, we provide pointers on how to start your presentation on the right foot.

Finding the power players

Whatever the scenario, presenting to more than one person means that one of the persons involved is more dominant and is the power player. But how can you find out which person has the power?

Always thank and acknowledge the person who invited you to make the presentation and then add your thanks to the others present. Make eye contact with each person as you do so. If you watch very carefully as you do this and as you start your presentation, you find clues as to who's dominant. Analyse which people look at which people. Notice who's stronger in conversation, or feel the energy in a pause and sense who's in control. When you concentrate, you'll spot the power player.

Some power players are the strong, silent type. They don't play the game the way you'd expect and may sit unobtrusively in the back of the room. By watching everyone else's body language, though, you should still be able to recognise that person.

Being quick or being sorry

In today's world of the ten-second TV commercial and the era of instant messaging and the Internet, few people bother any more to develop their ability to concentrate. In fact, the average person has a limited attention span, which means that you must compress the heart of your presentation down to a matter of only a few minutes. You can't afford the luxury of 30 slides that cover everything that the prospect could possibly need. You have to cover the three most salient points for that particular prospect based upon the information gleaned in your relationship-building phase. You have to have everything there, but selectively present only a fraction of it – and of course you do this seamlessly!

To help your prospect focus on your presentation and to help yourself stay on track, state your objectives prior to beginning your presentation. Limit your objectives to three. For example, if your prospect was in printing and you were selling paper and ink supplies, you might say the following:

> Mr and Mrs Bradshaw, today I would like to cover three things. First, I would like to look at your business demands and its fluctuation issues for consumables. Second, I would like to show clearly how costs and storage concerns impact the choice. And finally, I'll look closely at the bigger picture and what might be of importance in two or three years from now. These all have a bearing on what might be the best choice for you in this purchase.

We recommend that the ideal length for a presentation is between 10 and 15 minutes. Go past 15 minutes, and your prospect's mind wanders and her eyelids droop. Besides helping to keep your prospect awake, brevity and conciseness demonstrate concern for her valuable time. She may not realise that she appreciates your concern for her time, but on some level she does appreciate it – and the concern makes a difference.

This 15-minute time constraint may challenge you if your product is, say, a complicated mechanical system. However, the selling is more about the prospect than the machine. Homing in on the prospect's three biggest concerns means that you can easily demonstrate how your offering meets her needs. If you can't present on the product within 15 minutes, then something's wrong with your presentation format. Go and work on your presentation; don't extend the time and risk boring your prospect out of the deal.

The magic 15 minutes don't begin the moment you enter the room or while you're building rapport. The 15-minute period begins when you start to discuss the newly discovered salient points and specifically how your offering will address them.

It also doesn't include the time you invest in answering client questions, overcoming their concerns or closing. It's just the amount of time you should target for the actual product benefit presentation.

Breaking well, and prospering

If you choose to schedule a break, or even if an unplanned break occurs, here's a vital piece of advice you must take to heart: always do a brief recap before starting back into your presentation. A *brief recap* is not just a restatement of the major points that you've covered so far – a quick way to bring everyone back to where you were before the break. It's also about working hard to reinstate the emotional energy and the warmth and connection between you and the prospect, and between the offering and the prospect.

Studies have proven that, after any interruption, it takes you ten minutes to get back to the same level of concentration and emotional involvement you were at before the interruption. Just thinking about all the interruptions you have in a normal day makes you wonder how you ever get anything done, doesn't it?

Knowing How to Present More Effectively

The general guidelines for giving effective presentations are simple. They're the same ones you learned in English class for writing a good essay: tell them what you're going to tell them, tell them and finish by telling them what you've told them. This method serves the same purpose in oral presentations as it does in written ones. It helps the person on the receiving end understand and remember the story you've told him.

The following sections cover helpful guidance for delivering a winning presentation.

Making adjustments according to the prospect's perspective

Know enough about your prospect – going into the presentation – that you can talk with her on her level. What does it mean to talk on someone else's level? Consider this example.

Suppose you're in your 30s, and you're trying to sell a refrigerator to an older couple who want to replace a 20-year-old appliance. What do you say to them? Well, with these prospects you'd probably talk about dependability and the new features that your product displays. You'd talk about the benefits of lower utility bills, increased appliance efficiency, longer food storage time, the outside drink dispenser and so on.

Now cut to a different scene: you're trying to sell the same refrigerator to a newly married couple for their first home. Do you talk to them the same way you did to the older couple who were replacing an old appliance? No, with the younger couple you accentuate the features and benefits that apply to their situation and satisfy their present needs. The features are the same, but the young couple see the benefits in a different light. They may want something less expensive because that's all they can afford. But if you can show them the overall savings of getting a bigger or better fridge now, as opposed to the replacement costs down the road, you'll be farther ahead because they'll be more comfortable making the investment when the decision is rationalised for them.

Also, within a committee or family, you may have decision-makers with different interests. For example, in a business situation where you're presenting to a committee, you may have a finance person, a technical person and an executive in the room. Each has a different perspective. Know who's in the room and speak to each individually.

Presenting at the prospect's pace

When you give a presentation to a prospect, you need to be sensitive enough to recognise the proper demeanour to have with each client. This part of your presentation is similar to what stage actors and actresses do: they play off the attitude and enthusiasm of the audience. If you're too energetic for your audience and speak at too fast a rate, they'll be turned off. Then again, if you're too mild mannered for them and speak too slowly, you may lose them as well.

The ideal approach is to pay attention to the rate and pitch of your prospect's speech and then closely match it. When this happens, on some subconscious level, your prospect gets the message that you're like she is.

Be careful if the other person has an accent different from yours. If you adopt her accent, she'll think you're mocking her. In selling you have to be yourself *and* be like the prospect! A true chameleon approach without losing sincerity . . . a challenge, but one that pays huge dividends in both cash and satisfaction.

Being confident that your prospect will buy from you

Speak as though your prospect already owns what it is you're selling. Don't say, 'If you join our neighbourhood safety awareness group . . .' Instead, say, 'When we meet, you'll enjoy the value of participating in our neighbourhood safety awareness group.' Giving your prospect the ownership of your idea, product or service helps to move her closer to making a decision. This is called *assumptive selling*.

Another example is to talk about what life is like *after* your prospect owns your product, as in, 'After the system is installed, you'll enter your home after work every day knowing that you saved energy without having to turn the thermostat up or down.'

Assumptive selling is not the same as *suggestive selling* – when you order nothing more than a chocolate milkshake but your friendly McDonald's server oh-so-sweetly asks whether she can get you an apple turnover today. With suggestive selling you're being offered something you haven't yet asked for or about. Assumptive selling is operating as if you've made the decision to own a product or service you've expressed an interest in.

Recognising and understanding body language

The study of body language has been around for a long time. In fact, most people are aware of body language, but they don't consciously read it and benefit from it.

Here are just a few examples of the kinds of messages body language communicates (and how to read them):

- ✔ **Leaning forward:** If you lean forward when you're talking to someone, you're showing that you're interested and paying attention. When you recognise that positive sign in other people, you should keep moving forward. In fact, you may be able to pick up the pace of your presentation a bit if your entire audience is leaning forward.

- ✔ **Leaning back or glancing away:** When you lean back or glance away from someone who's talking, that means you're losing interest in what she's saying or that you're uncomfortable with what was just said. What do you do if you recognise this body language in your audience? Pause if you're in the middle of a long monologue, summarise the last couple of points and ask your client a question. Or, if it's a group presentation and you see several of your clients displaying this body language, suggest a short break or a question-and-answer period.

- ✔ **Crossed arms:** If you cross your arms when you're listening to someone, this indicates that you doubt what the other person is saying or that you're not truly interested in hearing what she has to say. When you receive this sign from your audience, move to a point-proving demonstration, chart, graph or diagram. Or, ask a question such as, 'On a scale of one to five with five being very important, how valuable is this point to you?' If it's not valuable, skip ahead in your presentation to the next topic.

Just as important as knowing how to read the language is knowing how to speak it. When you understand positive body language cues, practise them as a part of your presentation. They can be as critical as the words you say. If you want to successfully persuade your prospects, you need to be able to give positive, warm, honesty-projecting gestures, such as the following:

✔ **Sit beside the person you're trying to persuade instead of opposite her.** You're not on an opposing side. You're on your prospect's side.

✔ **Use a pen or pointer to draw attention, at the appropriate times, to your visual aids.** If you wonder about the effectiveness of this technique, watch magicians. They'd never be able to keep their 'magic' if they didn't master the ability to draw your attention to (or away from) what they want.

✔ **Use open-hand gestures and eye contact.** Open-hand gestures (such as exposing your palms or pointing with your whole hand rather than an index finger) and lots of eye contact say that you have nothing to hide.

Don't use the palm out (or pushing) gesture unless you're trying to eliminate a prospect's negative concern. Even then, push to the side, not toward the prospect.

These are just a few of the basics of body language, but the whole field of study on body language can help you so much more. When you begin paying attention, you'll find that many other body language cues become obvious to you. We highly recommend that you research what's available at your local library or online if body language piques your interest.

Not letting distance phase you

When you can't possibly meet in person with your prospective client and you have to conduct business over the telephone or online, you need to be aware of certain strategies to apply.

Phone presentations

Because you can't see your clients when you're on the phone, you may have trouble knowing whether they're being distracted or interrupted. Even though you can't read body language over the phone, you can definitely listen to their voice inflections (just as they'll be listening to yours). You can tell fairly easily whether someone is paying attention by counting the length of pauses between their comments, and the number of *uh-huhs* or *hmms* you hear. Also, pay attention to any background noise on the other end of the line. If you hear barking dogs, doorbells ringing or small children, chances are good that you won't have this person's full attention.

If you're in doubt as to whether your prospects are on the same page with you, ask a question of them. Don't, of course, ask whether they're paying attention. Instead, ask how something you just covered relates to their business or what they think of it. Restate that point or benefit clearly so they're not embarrassed if they really weren't paying attention.

Another strategy to use when you're giving phone presentations is what we call the *pregnant pause*. If you briefly pause during your presentation, the pause makes your prospects wonder what happened and draws their attention to what you'll say next, thus drawing them back to the point at hand.

The product needs to be the star of the presentation – especially if you're not meeting in person. If at all possible, be sure to send a sample product or, at the very least, an attractive visual of it to the client so she'll be seeing what you want her to see during your presentation. An even better option: if your client has Internet access, try to arrange to give your presentation via a Web conferencing service (see the next section), or at the very least, have her log on to your company's website and direct her to where to look, what to click and so on.

Video or web presentations

If you're asked by a prospective client to join her for a presentation via videoconference or through an online service but you're not savvy to these types of communication tools, you'll need to find someone who is and take a quick lesson. They're not too difficult to work with, but the logistics of setting the stage just right can be tricky.

For example, when video-conferencing, you'll probably use a camera attached to your computer. You may even be doing this from home. When you participate in video-conferencing, you need to be aware of what else is in the picture with you. Check your camera and be sure that it doesn't allow your next potential major client to see an inappropriate poster hanging on the wall behind you, or a neglected plant. Better still, adjust your seating in relationship to the camera so that you occupy most of the client's field of view.

Take note of how TV news reporters appear and act on camera. They're in the talking-head type of shot, which is what you'll be in – your head and shoulders will be in the frame, but not much else. News reporters make great eye contact with the camera – they smile into it, smiling with their eyes.

If your presentation online requires you to show slides or other visuals, maintain as much control over how the flow goes as you can. For example, you can control a presentation from your computer while it's being viewed online from someone else's computer. Using any of the web conferencing programmes allows you to share screens and view each other's screens when you want to show a slide, instead of just your face, when talking, and you can switch between whatever view you want whenever you want to. Familiarise yourself with the many programmes available and start using one with immediate effect. This sort of distance selling is only going to grow and become more normalised.

Letting the Product Be the Star

One key in presenting or demonstrating anything is really pretty simple: let the product shine, let it be the star. You're just the host who introduces the key players (your product and your prospect) to each other and then fades into the background to let them get acquainted.

Even though one of the players may be an inanimate object, even an intangible one, you need to think of that object in terms of the future primary relationship between the product and its new owner. And you need to let the possibilities for that relationship develop (with your encouragement, of course) while keeping the entire process under control.

Getting out of the picture

Before the presentation, you as the salesperson are the focus (see the sidebar 'Selling you versus the product'). But during the presentation, the product or service that you offer starts to take the limelight.

Selling you versus the product

For many sales, the prospect is shopping in a competitive arena and you're selling a product that has many close competitors, each having slight variations but pretty much the same in everyday functionality. So the prospect has to make a choice based on more subtle variants. She may be swayed on service issues or pricing and payment issues, but more usually human relationships determine the sale. It is *you* who wins the deal because it is *you* that the customer buys into.

But after you've secured the sale, you pass the prospect over to those whose role it is to manage that account going forward. You have to step sideways and go on to the next prospect to close more sales. So then the sale becomes more about the offering and what it does for the new client. You have to maintain the focus on the offered product or service and the company behind it. In some smaller sales situations you may be selling services that you deliver. Still, the customer bought a solution, and it's this that then takes centre stage.

Even though the product must be the star, never forget that your prospective client needs to always remain the focus of your presentation. Never give so much attention to the product and what it can do that you ignore what it will do for the person sitting there with you – your prospective client.

If you start putting your hands on the product or turning your eyes, back or chair more toward the product than the clients, you risk losing their attention. Better to allow the client to get her hands on the product even if it means she turns her back on you. You remain the director of the presentation, assisting the client in her experience with the product.

Staying in control

Don't let your prospects see what you want them to see until you're ready for them to see it. The product has to be the star, but you need to be the guide and direct when they see it or learn more.

If your demonstration involves the use of a piece of equipment, don't let your prospective client come in and begin punching buttons or demanding answers to a lot of questions – taking control of the presentation away from you. Just tell the prospect that she has great questions and that you'll cover most of them in your presentation. Then ask that she hold her questions until after the demonstration. When she recognises that you've planned something special for her, she'll probably settle down and let you do your thing.

Keeping control can become a challenge when you have several things to display. If your demonstration falls into this category, we recommend that you bring something (like a cloth) to cover your display items, uncovering only those items you're prepared to discuss. Or, if you can, simply leave anything not pertinent to the moment out of the client's line of sight. If you're using a laptop, simply close it so that the screen isn't visible. You must be in control at all times.

Mastering the Art of Visuals

The majority of people learn and understand best when they involve as many of their senses as possible; however, each person usually has one dominant sense. Some people learn best by closing their eyes and listening. Others have a strong need to touch and feel things. Most people, however, gain the best understanding by seeing things. Except for the visually impaired, the sense of sight carries the most weight and influence, so use this to your advantage.

We're sure you've heard the phrase 'seeing is believing'. That phrase comes from the desire of most people to see the proof that something is real, or at least that it can come true. Take a moment to see the difference between *telling* someone about a new product and letting her *see* it, either in picture form or through a product demonstration. Obviously, letting the prospect see it involves more of her senses. And that's where visual aids come into play.

Visual aids should show three things to new clients:

  ✔ **Who you (and your company) are:** Visual aids should identify your company and the industry to which it belongs. The story of your company builds credibility.

  ✔ **What you've done:** If you've managed to attain an amount of recognised credibility then here's where you need to 'big it up' a little. Be careful not to labour the point too much, though. Being proud of your company is one thing; being a bore is another thing altogether.

✔ **What you do for your clients:** This is the part your prospective client is most interested in. This is where you tune into her favourite radio station, WII-FM, 'What's In It For Me?'

The best visual aids include all three of these key points. If they don't, be sure to try to verbally incorporate these points into your presentation. Ask creative questions, such as how something might feel or what the prospect thinks the sweet taste of success might be like. Involve all of the senses with your language and you engage far more of the prospect's brain and make persuasion more likely.

Using the visuals your company supplies

If you represent a company's products or services, you've probably been exposed to their visual aids. These are usually slick, high-quality sheets with graphs, charts, diagrams and photos. You may work for a company that's more high-tech. For example:

✔ You may get computer-generated graphics or Flash animation and you'll most likely have a laptop computer and multimedia projector to use for presenting these images and sales aids.

When you prepare for one of these high-tech presentations, be sure that your prospective client has a white board or screen for you to project your images onto. Presenting your product professionally is tough when all you have to work with for a background is wood panelling or flowered wallpaper.

✔ You may also work with videos for your presentations. Videos often include recorded testimonials from actual customers your prospect can relate to. When your prospect sees someone just like herself who's benefiting from your product or service, the relationship between the prospect and your product grows a little stronger.

Whatever your specific visual aids depict, the important thing to remember is this: your company invested in the creation of your visual aids for a reason. And that reason was not to make your life more complicated by having to carry all this stuff around and keep it updated. Instead, your company did it because many, many years' experience has proven that visual aids are very effective when used properly.

So what's the best way to use visual aids provided by your company? Most likely, it's the way your company recommends. Few companies succeed in business by putting out poor presentation aids and then leaving their salespeople to work out how best to use them. Often companies have engaged the input of many senior professionals and the accumulative knowledge is both well-tuned and powerful. All their suggestions usually have to be approved by a director or manager of the marketing department – someone who will ultimately be held accountable if the brochures, videos or sample products do the job of moving products into the hands of consumers (or if they don't).

If for some reason you don't like or have trouble using the company's visual aids, talk with the people who trained you on how to use them. If their suggestions don't satisfy you, talk with a top salesperson, someone who does use them effectively. You may even want to go on a customer call with that salesperson to watch how she handles things. After you master her suggestions for using the visual aids as well as possible, if you still think you have room for improvement, ask to meet with the people who put them together. They'll probably be glad to offer you constructive suggestions and, hopefully, listen to yours.

Developing your own visual aids

If you have no visual aids to work with, put some thought into what you can develop on your own. Involvement of the senses in attempting to persuade others is critical, so make sure that you involve as many of a prospect's senses as possible.

For example, say you want to sell your family the idea of action and adventure holidays in the mountains and forests when they may usually prefer a beach holiday. You can show a video on all the outdoor adventures available to them; many holiday centres now offer free videos as promotional items in information packages. Or you can get a video on nature in general, with flowing waterfalls, gentle breezes blowing in the trees, canoeing, horseback riding . . . whatever appeals to your audience (in this case, your family). Such a video would involve two senses: sight and hearing. And what's that we smell out front – a campfire? If it really means a lot to you, you may even want to have a little campfire going in the garden while the family watches your video. You can be as creative as you like.

The same strategy applies to formal business sales presentations: the more senses you can involve, the better. Start with developing aids that focus on sight and hearing, such as the ones described in the preceding section – charts, graphs, computer graphics, videos and the like. To strengthen the impact of the visual aids, find ways to get additional sensual involvement (no, we don't mean *that* kind of sensual involvement). You can involve your prospects' sense of touch just by handing them things. Smell and taste are a little tougher, especially if you're selling an intangible object like a service. With intangibles, you may want to paint visual pictures that bring those senses into play. (We discuss product demonstrations and how to talk about intangible goods later in this chapter.)

For example, say you're selling a cleaning service to a working mother. You may not necessarily want to have her smell the cleaning agents you use – but you can talk about how fresh the home will be after your professional crew has completed its duties. You can say, 'Imagine how nice it will feel to come home after a hard day in the office and immediately notice that the air smells fresh and the carpet has been vacuumed and the cushions straightened and you just want to sit down and relax straight away.' And to get a homeowner prospect's senses completely involved, always refer to her residence as her *home* – not her *house*. (A house is made up of lifeless bricks and boards; a home is made up of the people who live there and the events of those people's lives.) Bringing a small box of chocolates as a new-client gift involves the sense of taste in your presentation, even though it doesn't directly apply to your service.

Demonstrating Products to Your Prospective Clients

When you demonstrate a tangible product, you have to be like a magician who simultaneously intrigues and engages the audience. You allow your prospect to see and feel the features that are relevant to her, as discovered in your relationship-building phase, but you also keep her slightly guessing and eager to see whether the product really does deliver what you promise.

Selling is not a *spectator* sport; it's an *involvement* sport.

One of the greatest fears all clients have in selling situations is that they'll trust what the salesperson tells them, buy the product or service that's for sale and then, after they own the product or service, find out that it doesn't meet their expectations or meet their needs. The best demonstrations give people the opportunity to prove to themselves that what the salesperson is telling them is true.

For example, if you sell copiers and you don't invite the prospects to push the buttons, make double-sided copies, change the paper, and open and close the machine, you're not selling, you're showing. You *must* let your prospective clients perform the functions, and become actively involved.

It won't matter to the office manager that you've won all the time trials at your office for making the most complicated copying challenges come out perfectly. Instead, what matters is how simple it is for everyone on your prospect's staff to meet those challenges – and you should build into your demonstration the proof that they can do so. During your demonstration, your prospect and her staff members should be able to make normal copies simply and to find out something about a new feature that's going to make their job easier. Your key contact person should see exactly what all the warning lights are on the machine and what to do about each one, or at least feel confident that when she can't fix an issue someone at your company is always there to help out.

Here's another example: if you're selling computer software, then simply stand or sit at your client's shoulder while giving her instructions on how she can do whatever it is she just asked about. Make sure the client's hands are on the keyboard and mouse. That way, she has a positive experience with the product. What's really happening is that the client is learning something new and building her confidence in her own ability to use the software. She's doing it, not merely seeing it being done, and that makes a world of difference because she knows that she can do it and won't be in big trouble post-sale, after you've left!

Presenting Intangible Goods

If the item you're selling is intangible – insurance, financial services, banking services, education and so on – your presentation will differ from that of salespeople offering tangible items. When a potential client can't see, touch, hear, taste or smell what you're selling, you need to develop ways of keeping her attention during your presentation.

Fortunately, many companies employ software that can provide immediate analyses of individual needs. For example, if you sell financial services, you may be able to enter Mary and Simon's details into a program that works out their needs for life insurance cover and other related financial products. Playing with the numbers in various scenarios can be fun and definitely keeps them involved. Indeed, the program is powerful because people trust what a computer says – if the computer says you don't have enough life insurance cover, then it must be right! This type of approach will almost certainly result in larger sales if used correctly.

If you don't have anything other than paper (brochures, flyers, proposals and so on) to work with, there are specific strategies to consider:

> ✔ Don't hand your prospects anything to read until you want them to read it. Their attention will be on the printed piece, not on what you're saying about its contents.

✔ If no comparison chart is available that shows how your products or services stack up against the competition, create one. You want to be certain that any information your client gathers is perceived correctly (as in comparing apples to apples).

When talking about intangible services, you have to work at creating mental pictures in the minds of your potential clients. You don't have anything physical to show them, but you can create images in their minds of how much better their lives will be after they own what you're offering. For example, they'll have greater health if starting a new exercise programme or joining a gym. Get them thinking about feeling better, stronger and more energised. Help them *feel* the satisfaction of having their clothes fit better and *hear* the compliments they'll receive from others. For insurance, focus on the peace of mind they'll have knowing they're properly protected. If you're selling retirement programmes, help them *envision* what their future lifestyle can be like through the commitment they're making now. Constantly take what the intangible *is* and help them see what they can *be*, *do* or *have* when they own it.

Avoiding Nightmare Presentations

If we were to tell you all the horror stories we've heard about failed sales presentations, we'd need a week to cover them all! The unfortunate thing is that those same salespeople could have avoided the problems they came across, if they'd taken a few simple precautions. But, fortunately for you, hearing so many of these horror stories has helped us develop effective suggestions for avoiding your own demonstration *faux pas*. In the following sections, we cover just a few things you may not think of, but all of them should become a vital part of your pre-presentation checklist.

Finding the power sockets and knowing you can reach them

If your demonstration requires the use of electrical power, find out in advance exactly where the available electrical outlets are whether you'll need an extension cable to reach them. If you're running the show on your computer battery, check and double-check that it's fully charged prior to your presentation – and bring a spare, fully charged battery with you, just in case.

A businesswoman Ben knows invested hours in preparing her computer-generated demonstration with high-quality graphics, customised charts, graphs and diagrams. Her only problem: the power cord she brought to her presentation was too short. She had to place all her equipment right next to a wall that was about 20 feet from her audience. As a result, she lost vital eye contact and other rapport-building closeness with her audience, and probably the sale too – all because she brought the wrong extension lead.

Being sure your visual aids are in order

If you use printed material and paper or similar sales aids, please make sure that they aren't tatty! There's nothing worse than sitting down to present in a professional situation and then pulling out second-rate materials. Food stains and bent corners on your presentation materials give the impression that you don't care about details. And if you work as part of a larger team, never rule out the possibility of well-meaning but off-putting practical jokes – where the joker has swapped a slide or two for some embarrassing content swap or has removed a needed piece of literature. These things happen, so be prepared and double-check in plenty of time.

Never use your materials immediately after someone else has been through them. Misplacement of contents is rarely intentional, but it does happen.

Testing everything ahead of time

You may have a very dependable demonstration model of your computer software. In fact, it could be one you've used for several weeks or months without any challenges. But on the day of your big presentation, Murphy's Law may strike. You remember Mr Murphy. He's the poor bloke who deduced the most prevalent law in the known universe: if anything can go wrong, it will. Having a bad cable for your equipment or your computer can wreak havoc on the best-laid plans. Not having Wi-Fi available or having a weak Internet signal in the location where you're meeting is always a possibility. So always arrive early enough to test your equipment on-site. And test it early enough that, if you find something isn't working, you can adjust for it.

Personalising as much as you can

Don't you love it when someone gives you a generic presentation that you just know she's given, word-for-word, to at least 40 other people before? We didn't think so. No one does. By making the extra effort to customise your materials, you appear competent and knowledgeable about your customer's specific needs. And that's just the kind of person she's looking for.

Remember that all humans are by nature selfish creatures and mostly interested in their own issues. Making the presentation around your prospect's issues and adding personal touches, like using your prospect's name on slides, goes a long, long way to winning her over.

Don't customise by skipping over materials in your generic, full-blown presentation. People will feel slighted by the absence of this information. Instead, remove pages or delete slides you won't need. Page past graphics on your computer screen that are unnecessary. If you can't delete them, go ahead and show them. Just make sure you offer a brief explanation that you know those particular graphics don't apply to your present audience's needs and that you won't waste their valuable time going over them in detail.

Bringing a protective pad

If you're scheduled to make a presentation in someone else's office, don't take a chance that any of your equipment will mark her furniture. To prevent damages, always check the bottom of your equipment before placing anything on a potential customer's furniture, and, if in doubt, have a protective cloth to wrap over something. Rough edges can easily leave scratch marks.

Chapter 11

Handling Client Objections

. . . .

In This Chapter

▶ Understanding that hesitation is not the same as 'no'

▶ Handling concerns with a few basic strategies

▶ Making sure you don't offend your prospects when you address their concerns

▶ Getting prescription-strength objection relief through six proven steps

. . . .

*U*nless you sell balloons at a fairground, few customers will contact you, make an impulse purchase and go away without any questions. What really happens is that customers have concerns. Almost every single person when purchasing something will have concerns as to whether purchasing the item in question from the person in question at the time in question is the smartest move.

Little doubts and fears creep up on potential clients when they feel the urge to invest in your product or service or to commit to your idea. The concerns that arise when a potential client feels moved to make any commitment that involves his time or money are completely natural.

Unfortunately, most people in sales feel that hesitation means that their potential client is thinking about not buying. The seasoned professional, however, knows that this hesitation is a natural and needed part of the process. Your client's hesitation can simply be a sign that he wants to slow down the selling process so he can absorb all the information you're giving him. Or hesitation can mean that the client needs *more* information before he feels comfortable making a decision. In such a case, the client objects in order to show you that you need to back up and resell him on a certain point. When a potential client hesitates or gives you a stall, just think, 'He's asking for more information.' *No* means not yet, tell me more, give me another reason to say yes.

If you get nervous or afraid when you hear an objection and start closing your briefcase and preparing to leave, then you're leaving empty-handed. And if you try to overcome your client's objection and he doesn't like the way you handle it, you're going to be heading for the door anyway, and he'll have it open before you get there! So why not experiment with ways to address your client's concerns or handle his objections? The worst that can happen is that you won't get what you want and you'll be free to move on to the next likely candidate. The best that can happen is that your client sees how competently you handled his concern and that his concern wasn't strong enough to keep him from going ahead with your offering.

In selling you're going to encounter objections or concerns about buying almost every time, and to succeed in your career you need to master them. So in this chapter, we show you how to address concerns and make the sale.

Understanding What Clients Are Really Saying

Prospective clients give you three important pieces of information when they voice objections or raise concerns during your presentation:

- ✔ **They're interested, but they don't want to be thought of as an easy sale:** If you've properly qualified the prospect (see Chapter 9 for more information), you know what he has now, what he enjoys most about it, what he would alter and that he's the decision-maker. Armed with that knowledge, if you're confident the prospect would benefit from your offering, chances are he's interested, but he just doesn't want you to think of him as an easy sale. In that case, you want to slow down the pace, encourage questions and generally get him relaxed and chatting before you ask him to make a decision.

- ✔ **They may be interested, but they aren't 100 per cent clear about what's in it for them:** If your prospect is

already asking lots of questions and looks somewhat per-
plexed or doubtful, he's interested, but he just doesn't
have a clear enough picture of what's in it for him. This
situation is especially common when the prospect
doesn't have previous experience with a similar product.
To respond to this kind of prospect, you have to work
harder at the relationship building part of selling and
cover the features and benefits in a more specific way
that is personal to them.

✔ **They may not be interested, but they can be if you educate them properly:** Creating interest can be as simple as
helping the prospect discover an element of the product
or service that helps him. If you've done your prospecting correctly, then lack of interest is usually a lack of correct understanding.

All three situations tell you one thing: the prospect needs
more information. By backing up and clarifying exactly what it
is the prospect is objecting to, you find out just which direction to take for your next step.

When the fish aren't biting, change your bait

Most persuaders find it hard to influence people who voice no objections and raise no questions. In other
words, the most difficult people to
persuade are like dead fish: their
eyes wiggle every now and then,
but they don't respond. You need a
response to work with.

In selling situations, you carry the
presentation forward by directing
and redirecting your course of questions and information based on the
feedback your prospect gives you. If
he tells you nothing, the communication often stalls. When that happens,
you have to guess which direction
to follow next – and guessing is very

bad because when you guess, you're
no longer in control. Guessing is like
casting your line with no bait on it.

The people who don't get verbally or
physically involved in your presentation probably have no intention of
going ahead with your proposition.
Those who *do* bring up challenges
for you to address are, at the very
least, interested. If they're really
tough to convince, they'll probably
become your best customers when
you finally do convince them. So the
next time you hear an objection, be
glad. Getting objections and getting
past them are necessary steps in the
selling cycle.

Distinguishing conditions from objections

If your customer's objection is 'I just can't afford it' and you're selling a luxury item, chances are pretty good that you've just heard a condition, not an objection. And there's a big difference between the two.

A *condition* is not an excuse or a stall. It's a valid reason that the prospect can't agree to what you're proposing. If you're trying to exchange your offering for your potential customer's money, and the customer genuinely has no money and has no credit, just thank him for his time, get permission to stay in touch should things change in the future and move on.

For example, if you're selling to a consumer market and the prospect you're with doesn't own his own home, has County Court Judgments and can't get credit, then chances are it's going to be extremely challenging to sell to him and you'd be better served using your time elsewhere. That lack of options for funding is a condition, not the same as the prospect saying 'I can't afford it' in the same breath as talking about his plans for an extension and his winter cruise! In this case, the prospect can find the money if he wants to badly enough, and your job as a sales professional is to persuade him.

Addressing Your Prospects' Concerns with Some Simple Strategies

Objections from prospects are just part of the business of selling. What's important is that you know how to handle them. Fortunately, you can use some key strategies to address your prospects' objections so that they come away with more information *and* more respect for you and your product. In this section, we show you how.

Bypassing your prospects' concerns completely

If you know your prospect wants and needs the product or service you're offering, but he feels a natural inclination to object, you can often bypass the objection altogether.

Simply say, 'That's a good point, Mr Smith. I believe it will be addressed to your satisfaction by the end of my presentation. May I make a note of it and come back to it later?' If he gives you permission, he'll be paying attention to the rest of your presentation for a satisfactory answer. Or he may see enough benefit during the balance of the presentation that the value outweighs his concern and he doesn't raise it again.

If you're new to persuading, don't ignore any objection without testing the waters to see how big a concern it truly is. Sometimes just acknowledging the concern is enough. Your prospect will be satisfied that you're really listening, and then he'll move ahead.

'No' may simply be a way for the prospect to say, 'Not *this* way.' If that's the case, you just need to adjust what you're saying and take another path to the same destination.

For most people, buying is an uncomfortable process because they're not flush with spare money. People have an inbuilt programme that tries to save them from their fate of spending what they don't have – they react reflexively to keep their money safe. Your role as a professional is to help the prospect through the fear. When the prospect starts to see that you're immune to the fear reflex, he settles down and listens and starts to take ownership comfortably.

Helping your prospects see that they're trading up

If your prospective client has money, credit or both, but he just doesn't want to part with it now, you haven't convinced him that he'd be better off with the product than he would be with his money. This is where you need to work on building the value of the benefits of your product or service.

If an investment you're offering requires the person's time, 'No time' is not a valid condition, it's an objection. Everyone has the same 24 hours in every day. How people use them is their choice. If you want someone to invest his time with you, you have to show him enough benefits for him to *want* to spend his time on your offering instead of on what he's already planned.

Raising the objection before they do

If you know that your prospect is likely to voice a particular concern, beat him to it. Too often a salesperson allows an objection to be raised and then deals with it 'head on' in a confrontational manner. Avoid this at all costs. The best strategy is to flush out the objection before the prospect does and deal with it in an indirect manner. Deliberately speak about commonly raised objections and explain in your presentation why they're not actually issues.

For example, if you know your product costs more than others on the market, you can be fairly certain that your prospect will be concerned about that cost. But you can beat the prospect to that objection by explaining upfront that your product requires a higher investment because it contains only the highest-quality ingredients. And those high-quality ingredients make people feel better, last longer or perform in a superior manner. Those benefits are worth bragging about *before* your prospect gets busy laying bricks for that wall of defence against the investment. So you may say something like this:

> You know, I've learned something over the years. People look for three things when they spend money: the finest quality, the best service and, of course, the lowest price. I've also found that no company can offer all three. They can't offer the finest quality and the best service for the lowest price. And, I'm curious, for your long-term happiness, which of the three would you be most willing to give up? Fine quality? Excellent service? Or low price?

This prospect is going to have a tough time coming back at you and saying, 'Well, poor quality and rubbish service are okay as long as they're cheap.'

Make a list of all of the commonly expressed objections. Then prepare stories and illustrations that flush out the objections, whatever the prospect comes up with.

As an example, if you're aware that your company's reputation for speed isn't so great and a direct competitor can deliver in 6 weeks as opposed to your 12, simply state:

> We know that our competitors have a quicker delivery on most of their initial orders. However, we also know that many competitors have a horrible secondary delay, when too often the delivery is incorrect and results in more discomfort as the issues are sorted out. On the other hand, our bespoke service and thorough survey approach eliminates mistakes and the stress that they cause – a happier outcome that our customers are prepared to wait just a little longer for. All in all, a 12-week, solid, professional delivery works best for most clients, doesn't it?

Concerns range across different areas, such as money, delivery, product features and after-sales service. Whatever the reason, give a positive spin. Then simply ask a question along the lines of, 'What are your thoughts, then, Sally?' The prospect will usually come back at you with an honest comment, and from there you can find a way around the objection.

Testimonials and case studies are hugely powerful to illustrate each of the major benefits of your offering. If you have local and/or recognisable folks endorsing your offering, your voice carries a lot of extra weight. Let your prospect read the testimonials for himself, such as by looking at your company's website prior to your presentation. Send the prospect an email with your web address and a few suggestions of areas within your site he may find helpful.

Knowing the Do's and Don'ts of Objection Handling

Before you get too deep into dealing with your prospect's concerns, you need to be aware of some basic do's and don'ts of this important step in selling. In this section, we fill you in on a couple of each that will guide you through any selling situation.

Do acknowledge the legitimacy of the concern

Dismissing your prospect's concerns as unimportant can cause those objections to get completely blown out of proportion. In many cases a simple 'I see' or 'I understand' is acknowledgment enough. In other cases, you may do well to say, 'Let me make a note of that so we can discuss it in depth after we cover the benefits you've indicated you need most.' Do actually make a note: jotting down the concern validates the concern and shows professionalism on your part. Whatever you do, at least acknowledge the concern.

Do get the clients to answer their own concerns

The most important 'do' of addressing concerns is: get the other person to answer his own objection. That advice may sound tricky to follow, but here's why it's so important. You're trying to persuade your prospect, so he'll have reservations about anything you do or say. Why? Because anything you say must be good for you too. Until the prospect realises that you're acting in his best interest, he'll doubt you.

When *you* say something, the prospect tends to doubt it. When *he* says it, he believes it to be true. And *that's* why you want to get your prospect to answer his own objections – because he's much more likely to believe *himself* than he is to believe *you*. All you need to do is provide the information that answers his concern and let him draw his own conclusions. You let him persuade himself.

You may need to nudge him a little by asking a question to get him to state the desired answer: 'How do you see that feature impacting your company's level of efficiency, Jim?' It's much more powerful when he answers than if you just say, 'That feature will increase your company's efficiency by 20 per cent.' See the difference? Take advantage of the strategy, and you'll close more sales because your clients will be convincing themselves.

This technique often works well when you're working in a domestic environment. When one partner objects to something, don't respond immediately. *Average* persuaders are quick to defend their offering. But there's a better way: sit tight. Many times, one partner jumps in with the next comment, and you have a 50/50 chance that the originally silent partner will answer the objection for you. If the second partner agrees with his partner's objection, then you know you'll have to work a little harder to overcome it. The point is that these two people already have a positive relationship (you hope) and trust each other's judgement. Being quiet while they think it through can cause the objection to evaporate into thin air right before your eyes.

When something important to you is hanging in the balance, being patient is difficult. During such moments, seconds feel like hours, and you can quickly become very uncomfortable. However you manage it, you must maintain your silent approach and allow prospects to sort out their own opinions. Allow the scenario to unfold and gently nudge the partner in your favour to nudge the other party. Easy!

What you never want to do when you're waiting for a response is look at your watch or at a clock in the room. Even a slight glance at a timepiece can distract the prospects, because they're already looking at you, waiting for your next move. So practise this step until you're comfortable with it.

Don't argue with your client

Although not arguing with your client may seem obvious, when you're negotiating with someone, emotions can take over and things can get out of hand. Arguing against or fighting an objection or concern raises a barrier between you and the person you're trying to persuade. You're trying to persuade him of something, not go ten rounds with him. If you keep the perspective that objections are simply requests for further information, you shouldn't have much of a challenge with this advice.

Outsmart your client's last objection

Objections and concerns show up at all times, even when selling yourself. Ben remembers a time a few years ago when he applied for a job selling industrial air-compressor equipment, but was then quite poorly on the day of the interview and couldn't make it. He did, of course, phone to apologise, but he felt sure the company thought he had made an excuse.

Not to be outdone, he waited until he was fully recovered and then rang the company back to reschedule his interview. He was passed from a secretary to the sales manager, who basically said that he had missed his chance and he was on the verge of hiring someone else. Immediately, Ben said to the manager that if he was on the verge of hiring someone else, that meant he hadn't yet done so. Ben told the manager, 'I'll give you the chance to make a better decision and hire the best by coming along this afternoon.' The manager – far senior to Ben – laughed at the cheeky confidence. Following an interview that afternoon, Ben got the job, thanks to taking a smarter approach.

Don't minimise a concern

To the person you're persuading, every point he raises is valid. Remember to put yourself in his shoes. How would you react to someone who acts as though your concerns are stupid or unimportant? Simply point out the benefits of your offering and reassure him that his concerns are covered and that his choice in purchasing is a solid one. Then he'll silently agree, and you have your sale.

Handling Objections in Six Easy Steps

In the following sections, we give you six steps for handling objections or addressing concerns that almost always work in your favour. If you practise and apply the following steps properly, they'll take you a long way toward achieving your goal of selling to others, even when they raise objections or concerns. (They also work pretty well to diffuse unusually tense situations, so take heed.)

Before you begin the six-step process, take note of the following general pointers on objections:

> ✔ Sometimes you'll hear more than one objection or concern from a prospect. If you start running through all six steps with each objection you hear, you can spend a lifetime trying to persuade them. Experience helps you tell which concerns you need to address and which you may be able to bypass (see the section 'Bypassing your prospects' concerns completely', earlier in this chapter).

> ✔ If prospects raise a concern or objection during a group presentation, and you have to do a bit of research and get back to them, be certain you have the contact information (specifically, an email address) for each person in the group. Never rely on one person to relay vital information in the manner that you know to be best for moving the selling process forward. Send the exact same email message to each person and let them all see that they're part of the group email. If each person receives the message individually, they could all wonder what else you may have shared with the others.

> ✔ Include the link to your company's website for each member of the group to peruse. Often in a committee, decision-making situation, only one or two members get the whole package of information. They then break it down for the balance of the decision-makers. This may be the way the *company* wants the process handled, but what *you* want is to get as much information as possible equally distributed.

Step 1: Hear them out

When someone trusts you enough to tell you what's bothering him, do him the courtesy of listening. Don't be quick to address every phrase he utters. Give him time; encourage him to tell you the whole story behind his concern. If you don't get the whole story, you won't know what to do or say to change his feelings. Don't interrupt either; you may jump in and answer the wrong concern.

Step 2: Feed it back

By rephrasing what your client's concerns are, you're, in effect, asking for even more information. You want to be absolutely certain that he's aired all his concerns and that no others are lurking ready to crop up later. You're saying to him, 'Go ahead. Lay it all on me. Get it off your chest.' In doing this, you're asking him to trust you.

Step 3: Question it

This step is where subtlety and tact come into play. If a potential client objects to the amount of space your product will take up, don't say, 'What's wrong with it?' Instead, gently ask, 'Would you feel more comfortable with a smaller model?' Or, 'Is that the only thing that's holding you back?' If it is, he'll tell you why. Maybe he's simply shy and keen not to offend you, but you need to draw him out. Then gently build on his confidence and show him that getting an upgraded photocopier machine to increase office admin production is a wiser move than worrying about a small increase in the floor space taken.

Step 4: Answer it

When you're confident that you have the whole story behind your client's concern, you can answer that concern with confidence. If the prospect's concern is cost, you can engage in the following dialogue:

> SALESPERSON: I can certainly appreciate your feelings. At first glance, it's easy to feel that you're spending a lot of extra money. However, I know that when you're still using this machine reliably in six or seven years then, like many of our clients, you'll be pleased that you made the added investment. Indeed, your additional £1,000 is actually only approximately £150 a year! Does that sound more like an investment worth making?
>
> PROSPECT: Yes, it does.

SALESPERSON: So, in fact, you're using this machine for 50 weeks each year, which means only a little over £3 a week. Given what you now know about our reliability and your increased production capacity, would you really want to lose out over something as nominal as £3 a week?

PROSPECT: Well, when you put it that way, it does sound a little silly.

And you've just got the prospect to answer his own concern.

Step 5: Confirm your answer

When you've answered the objection, confirming that your prospect heard and accepted your answer is important. If you don't complete this step, the prospect will very likely raise that concern again.

The client must answer a straight question to agree that the issue is dealt with. For example, ask: 'So, Holly, does that answer your concerns with regard to the slightly higher initial cost? Do you agree it would be a worthy additional investment?' If Holly agrees, then you have a deal.

Sometimes you still have work to do on money issues. However, usually this happens when the prospect needs higher authorisation to spend a larger sum of money. Then you must at least agree 'subject to higher authority sign-off'.

Step 6: By the way . . .

By the way are three of the most useful words in any attempt to persuade or convince another person. You use the phrase to change gears – to move on to the next topic. Don't just keep talking. Take a conscious, purposeful step back into your presentation and then say, 'By the way, Holly, did I show you our latest automated stapling facility on the newer range of photocopiers?' At this point you resume selling the new machine, and when she follows you into the dialogue, you know she's happy.

The lady doth protest too much

If prospects bombard you with objections, you may want to ask a few questions to get them to express their *real* objection. If people protest too much, they're either not interested and don't have the guts to tell you so, or they're hiding the real reason they aren't going ahead. For some people, liking your offering but being unable to afford it is hard to admit. So instead of admitting that they're strapped, they come up with a hundred other reasons why your product, service or idea isn't right for them. Eventually, you may need to say something like this:

Mrs Johnson, obviously you have quite a few concerns about our product. May I ask, what will you base your final decision on, the overall benefits to your family or the financial aspects of this transaction?

This way you're asking, as is your right, for the real objection to your product or service, while still being nice, warm and friendly (and the most common final objection is the money). *Remember:* You can't move beyond this step in the selling cycle until you identify and handle that real final objection.

Chapter 12

Winning the Business and Closing the Sale

....

In This Chapter

▶ Asking for what you want at the right time

▶ Finding out whether your prospect is ready to make a buying decision

▶ Using skill and empathy to help your prospects overcome their hesitation

....

losing is the exciting part of sales, the moment when you tie it all together, the moment when you finally taste sweet success and can start to dream of how you'll spend the bonus cheque. If you've adopted this book's philosophy of selling, you know that, in effect, you work on closing the sale from the moment you first contact any prospect. Closing the sale starts at the beginning of the transaction, when you first make contact with your prospect. You close them on meeting with you. You close for the date, time and location of your meeting. You close them on qualifying, on handling objections, on presentations or on any other area of the sales process covered in Part III of this book.

In this chapter, we take you through the final stage of the closing process and give you a series of superb techniques that we encourage you to adopt as habits. No one closes every sale, but just think how much better you can become when you put your best effort into it. A perfect ending needs a perfect beginning.

Knowing When to Ask for the Order

The crucial question in any selling situation is this: When should you close the sale? A certain electricity is in the air when the prospect is ready to go ahead with the close. Here are some positive buying signs to watch for:

- ✔ **The prospect has been moving along at a smooth pace and suddenly she slows the pace right down:** She's making her final analysis or rationalising the decision.

- ✔ **She speeds up the pace:** She's excited to move ahead.

- ✔ **The prospect suddenly starts asking lots of questions:** She asks questions only about things that interest her.

- ✔ **She asks questions about general terms of purchase after she settles on one particular model:** Some people immediately start asking questions about initial investment, delivery and so on. They feel safe doing this because they know you can't sell them everything. But if they ask these questions after you know exactly what they want, it's a good sign.

If you've noticed any of these positive signs, test the waters. If you think that your prospect is ready to close the sale, ask a confirmation question to make sure you're reading her buying signs correctly: 'Helen, can you see yourself using this new cookware as you have the family around for a celebration dinner?' When you ask this question (from which you expect an answer confirming that the prospect wants to go ahead with the purchase), one of two things happens:

- ✔ The prospect gives you a yes or an answer that indirectly confirms her desire to go ahead with the sale.

- ✔ The prospect gives you an objection or asks for more information to enable her to make a decision.

Don't start talking before she answers. You want to be sure to get either a confirmation to go ahead or an objection. If you get the former, you can go ahead with the close (see the next section for more about confirmation questions). If you get the latter, you need to answer the prospect's questions and address her concerns (see Chapter 11 for more information).

Recognising That Sometimes All You Need to Do Is Ask

Salespeople are often uncomfortable if they have to go beyond putting their offering out there. Too often, especially when new to selling or influenced by those who themselves are poor at selling, many people think that simply being present, with wares to sell, results in sales happening! Nope. Sales happen when you're deliberate about them. You have to ask and ask and ask again. You can't lose confidence at the first *no*. Expect to ask several times and expect your rewards to come when you're persistent.

Research shows that the main reason that people don't buy is that salespeople neglect to actually ask them to buy. You can contact a prospect, demonstrate a product or service and answer her questions, but if you don't actually ask her to make a commitment, she won't!

When you ask your prospect for the close, what you're doing is using a question to confirm what the prospect wants. This type of question is called a *confirmation question*. In the following sections, we give you several ways to confirm your prospect's level of interest.

The bottom line with this most bottom of all lines in selling is this: if you want the sale, sooner or later you need to ask for it. Don't ever let the fact that you didn't ask someone to make a buying decision be the reason a prospect doesn't go along with you.

Taking your client's buying temperature with basic questions

One way to determine whether your prospective client is ready to make a decision involves basic 'testing' questions. They come in a variety of styles, such as yes/no questions and open-ended questions. The style you choose to use depends on how you feel about each situation. With yes/no questions, you just test whether your prospective client is ready for the next step in the selling process. Use open-ended questions if you feel you need more information or clarification from the prospective client about what she's thinking at this point in the sale. With these types of questions, your goal is to get her to open up to you about her level of interest or what may still be nagging at her or holding her back. For example:

> Jane, do you see why we're so excited about what this new model is doing for our clients?

If Jane isn't excited, you still have more selling to do. Any hesitation on Jane's part after you ask this question tells you that you've missed something. It may be wise to do a brief benefit summary of all the points Jane has agreed to up to this point to reaffirm her excitement. Pay close attention to her reaction to the benefits you mention. She may need further clarification on something. It'll show in her demeanour.

Here's another example of a 'testing' question:

> Jack, tell me, how are you feeling about all of this so far?

Listen carefully not only to what Jack says but how he says it. You'll hear uncertainty in his answer as he tells you where he's currently standing about making a decision.

Asking assumptive questions

Sometimes salespeople wait so long to ask for the sale that the right time to ask passes them by. To get past this timing challenge, figure out how to take a prospect's buying temperature (see the earlier section 'Knowing When to Ask for the Order' for more about timing your close). You do this by asking a question like the following (this strategy is commonly referred to as the *trial close*):

> Not to be assumptive, but if everything we've discussed here makes sense, how soon would you want to begin benefitting from your new computer system?

Soften this type of question by beginning with 'Not to be assumptive, but . . .' or 'Out of interest, James . . .'. Either way you gently lead into a direct, 'Would you like to buy it now, based on what you've seen so far?' This approach is extremely powerful because it isn't offensive but gives you a very clear answer. Usually, the answer is a *no*, followed by a series of reasons that you can slowly chip away at until the prospect has nothing to pin a *no* to.

Giving your prospect alternatives

The *alternate advance* involves giving your prospect two choices – but either one advances the sale. This way, no matter which option your prospect chooses, the sale moves forward because the prospect isn't given the option of saying no. Giving your prospect positive choices helps her focus better on what would be best for her – and that's what you really want, isn't it?

> SALESPERSON: Mr Hall, which delivery date would be best for you: the 8th or the 13th?
>
> MR HALL: I'd need to have it in my warehouse by the 10th.

What's happened in this exchange? As long as the salesperson can meet that delivery date, she owns it. If Mr Hall is uncertain, he'll raise an objection here or try to change the subject.

Here's another example of the alternate advance:

> SALESPERSON: Hina, would you be the one trained on the use of the new system, or would you want someone else to be involved?

When Hina tells the salesperson whom to train, the salesperson knows that she's going ahead with the sale.

Jumping to an erroneous conclusion

The *erroneous conclusion* is an intentional error you make to test how serious the prospect is about going ahead with the sale. If the prospect doesn't correct you, you may have missed some information along the way (perhaps during qualifying) that would have told you she wasn't serious. If she does correct you, her buying temperature is heating up. In this kind of test, all you want to do is take your prospect's buying temperature to see whether it's warm enough to go ahead.

For example, if a salesperson is selling a new conservatory to John and Cathy in their home, and during her demonstration Cathy tells John, 'Darling, my mother is coming in July. If we decide what we want today, we need to have it finished by then,' many salespeople would ignore that remark or regard it as an interruption. But the champion salesperson hears that comment and logs it mentally. Later, when it comes time to close, the salesperson may smile at the wife and have the following exchange, using an erroneous conclusion:

> SALESPERSON: I can see that you're kind of excited about this addition. Now, your mother is coming in August, isn't she?
>
> CATHY: No, in July.
>
> SALESPERSON: So the first week in June would be the best time to get started?
>
> CATHY: Yes.
>
> SALESPERSON: Let me make a note of that.

The salesperson *knew* that Cathy's mother was coming in July, but she asked whether her mother was coming in August, because she knew Cathy would correct her if she was serious about getting the work done. Then, when Cathy offers the correct answer, the salesperson can neatly lead into a conversation regarding timeframes and completion dates and the sale is agreed by virtue of the fact that they're discussing dates.

The purpose of this method isn't to tell a lie or trick the customer – we'd never recommend that. It's simply a test for you to determine whether the prospect is sincere in moving ahead. After all, the prospect wouldn't correct you if she weren't interested. But if you're at all uncomfortable with this method, don't use it. A secondary warning here is not to use this method more than once in a sales presentation or your potential client may begin to doubt that you know what you're doing.

Feeding back with the porcupine method

If someone tossed a prickly porcupine at you right now, what would you do? Instinctively, you'd probably either jump out of its way or catch it and quickly toss it back, kind of like a game of hot potato. You can use a method of questioning called the *porcupine method* in much the same way. When your prospect asks you a question, you just ask another question about that question.

Here's an example of the porcupine method in action at a car dealership. A young woman is walking through a garage looking at convertibles. Suddenly, she stops, points at a car and says, 'This is the convertible I'm interested in. Do you have it in red?' The average salesperson would answer her by saying, 'If we don't have it in red, I can call around and get one for you in a hurry.' When a salesperson gives an answer like that, she's losing a huge opportunity to confirm a buying choice and move a step or two nearer to the prospect owning the car. By far the better strategy is to answer the question with a sideways stall and another question fired back.

Unlike the average salesperson, the champion salesperson would answer the customer's question this way:

> SALESPERSON: I'm not sure actually. I'll have to check and maybe ask a few other group dealers. But if I could get you a red vehicle, which shade of red did you want to buy?

How is the customer going to respond to the salesperson's question? She's already said that she's interested in the convertible and she wants it in red, so she'll most likely choose one colour or the other, and the salesperson can note that on her paperwork. The salesperson is now one step closer to getting the customer's autograph on that dotted line and having her drive away happily in her new red-hot red convertible.

The real power in selling is in pulling with questions.

Overcoming Your Prospect's Hesitations and Fears

When you're closing sales, you may come across situations in which closing isn't quite as simple as the example we provide in the previous section – situations in which your prospects stall or hide behind a wall of fear. So in the following sections, we show you exactly how you can help the prospect work through that block so that she has no more objections or concerns . . . and you can close the sale.

If you listen carefully and watch closely you'll see signals that give you a clearer picture of how your prospect is feeling. There must be congruency: the message from body language must match the words, which must also match the feelings portrayed when the prospect speaks. If you see fear or hesitancy, even if not in the words, show the prospect that you're understanding of her fears and allow her space to explain. Usually, by giving her a comfort zone, she opens up and you can easily get around what wasn't really a blockage.

Empathy is understanding another person's feelings, thoughts and motives – and it's extremely important in the world of selling. When you have empathy for your prospect, you put yourself in her shoes. You know and feel what your prospect is feeling – which means you know exactly how to proceed based on the information the prospect has given you. Until you develop empathy for your customers, you probably won't make it in selling. Your prospects need to sense that you understand and care about helping them solve their problems, not think that you're just out looking for a sale. As a professional salesperson, you must truly believe that you can satisfy the prospect's needs. You must see the benefits, features and limitations of your product or service from your prospect's view; you must weigh things on the prospect's scale of values, not your own; and you must realise what is important to the prospect. Your prospect must always be the star of the show.

Getting past 'I want to think about it' to a concrete final objection

By far the most common stall used by prospects is 'I want to think about it'. It's a tricky one unless handled correctly.

Imagine Heather and Jonny are considering buying a static holiday caravan together in which to take family holidays whilst the children they plan to have are young. After looking

at various display caravans and speaking with the sales consultants for a couple of hours on a couple of visits, Jonny
says, 'I want to think it over.' The salesperson has a £5,000
sales incentive offer up her sleeve that Jonny and Heather
don't know about. She proceeds as follows:

> SALESPERSON: [running through a list of specifics to
> uncover the source of the reluctance]. Heather, Jonny –
> obviously, you wouldn't take the time to think it over
> unless you were seriously interested, would you? Jonny,
> can I just ask you directly, because I know that you're an
> honest man and I feel that we've got along well, are you
> considering some of the factors about the caravan itself,
> like its size, the number of bedrooms, the balcony and
> view. . .? What are your thoughts with reference to the
> location of the holiday park or the specific plot on the
> park?

> JONNY: No, all of those things are fine, actually. We just
> need to have a chat, privately.

> SALESPERSON: Ok, so I hear what you're saying then.
> You're basically happy with the location of the holiday
> park, the position on the park, and the size and layout of
> the holiday caravan, so I guess that what you are saying is
> that it's the nitty-gritty of the money and the expenses of
> actually occupying it and making it yours that you need to
> think about?

> JONNY: Well, yes. You see, we might have to replace the
> car because it's been barely managing for a while now,
> and it's just a case of us sitting down and making sure
> that we can afford the caravan too.

> SALESPERSON: Jonny, I've seen a lot of couples like your-
> self over my years here and I totally understand your situ-
> ation. What sort of budget, loosely, do you think that you
> might have to spend on the car? I mean, how much of an
> extra burden are we talking about?

> JONNY: Well, we haven't decided yet. Probably about
> £3,000 to £4,000.

> SALESPERSON: Okay, let me ask you a straight question:
> if you didn't have the cost of the car to worry about,
> would you then feel you could afford the house and want
> to buy it?

> JONNY: Well, yes.

SALESPERSON: Well, I'm allowed a very small incentive budget to help customers take advantage of our holiday park homes. To be honest, I haven't had to use it on the last couple of sales, and so I have approximately £5,000 in my budget. It's Friday, it's been a good month and I know that the developer wants to finish off the sales on this holiday park and move on. If I asked him and could allocate all of the unspent allowance to your selected caravan and position, it would cover the car costs. How do you fancy a new holiday caravan and a new car to boot?

Very often a 'I want to think about it' is genuine and you need skill and persistence to ease out the real objection. But when you apply a little creativity, you can spin the objection into a sale there and then. It's this type of winning strategy and technique that makes selling such a fun game.

Responding to 'It costs too much'

When you isolate a money objection as the obstacle to final agreement, one particular technique is ideal: reducing the amount to a *difference*. Using this strategy, you take the large investment cost and deduct the expected costs or competitor offer costs and break it down into a smaller difference amount.

To show you this technique at work, we continue the example of Heather and Jonny from the preceding section:

HEATHER: I just feel that this holiday caravan costs too much.

SALESPERSON: [ever in search of specific obstacles to *yes*] I know how you feel! Blimey, everything these days seems to cost too much, doesn't it! I spend a fortune just getting to work, so I know how you feel. But genuinely, how much 'too much' do you feel it is?

Salespeople tend to look at the total investment when they hear 'It costs too much', but this tendency usually spells trouble. Instead of addressing the total cost, go for the difference. If your prospect plans to spend £20,000 for a car, and the car she's looking at is £22,000, the problem isn't £22,000, it's £2,000.

Going back to our example:

> HEATHER: We really wanted to spend around £19,000, and I don't feel that we can go as high as £25,000.
>
> SALESPERSON: So, what we're really talking about is £6,000, aren't we?
>
> JONNY: £6,000. Right. That's exactly what we're concerned about.

Now the salesperson has got Jonny and Heather to admit that the real problem they're having is over the £6,000 difference between what they'd planned to spend and what they are being asked to spend. It's much easier to make a smaller amount feel acceptable, so reduce the amount to a difference amount. And now the sales professional is ready to move to the story in the following section, where she shows them just how little money that really is.

Reducing an expense to the ridiculous

When you know exactly what amount of money your prospects are concerned about, you can help them see how to handle the amount and still have what they really want – the product or service – at the same time by reducing the expense they're faced with to a ridiculously low amount. Start by handing them your calculator. Giving them a calculator is a good way to get them involved as you work out the finances. Here are Jonny and Heather again:

> SALESPERSON: [asking what Heather already knows] Heather, do you think it would be safe to assume that this would be your holiday home and you could be happy visiting here for many years, assuming everything else was right?
>
> HEATHER: Yeah, probably. I think it would be a great place to holiday as we raise the kids.
>
> SALESPERSON: Okay, so let's just say that you're going to holiday in this beautiful caravan for 10 years. Would you say that's about right?

HEATHER: Ten years . . . yeah, that'd be about right.

SALESPERSON: Let's divide that £6,000 by 10 years, okay? We get £600 per year, don't we?

JONNY: Yes, if you say so. I'll check!

SALESPERSON: And would you say that you'd actually be in the holiday home roughly 10 weeks of the year, bearing in mind your other commitments and things ?

JONNY: That sounds about right.

SALESPERSON: Dividing our £ 600 per year by 10 weeks, that makes the difference in the investment £60 per week. So now we have 7 days in each of those weeks, and when we divide £60 by 7, what do we get?

HEATHER: [catching an early glimpse of the ridiculous] £8.57.

The salesperson has got Jonny and Heather to see that they're really upset over just £8.57 per day. Pretty ridiculous, isn't it?

Making the indirect comparison

When you make an indirect comparison, you help your prospects rationalise having the product, service or idea you're offering simply by sacrificing, for now, some small luxury that they'd certainly give up in order to have a much larger gain. Here's how the salesperson in the previous example uses this strategy with Heather and Jonny:

SALESPERSON: [giving them something to compare it to] Jonny, do you and Heather ever go into town for a coffee or enjoy a coffee most days when at work?

JONNY: Yeah, we like to do that most days.

SALESPERSON: How much are coffees these days?

HEATHER: Around £3 each.

SALESPERSON: Heather, Jonny, wouldn't you agree that the benefits and the enjoyment you'll get out of this wonderful home are worth £8.57 a day? Seriously, for little more than the price of a cup of coffee each, would you say no to this wonderful new holiday home?

JONNY: When you look at it that way, I guess it doesn't seem to be such a significant amount.

SALESPERSON: Then we've agreed, haven't we? Now, let's get to work to get you into this *beautiful holiday home* by the *holidays* so you and your family can begin *building memories* right away.

Notice the words that **are** italicised? These keywords create pleasant pictures in the prospects' minds. For the sake of this example, assume that Jonny and Heather said they wanted to be in the holiday caravan by 1st June. That gives the salesperson the licence to talk about the approaching summer holidays in the new holiday home, a time of year that almost always creates warm feelings in buyers.

Use a calculator when you crunch numbers

Champion salespeople always use a calculator and know their formulas and figures so that they can quickly provide any numerical information that their prospect may request.

A prospect who sees you punch numbers into your calculator – or one who runs the figures herself – probably won't question the figures. But if you start furiously scratching numbers on paper with a pencil, the prospect gets uncomfortable sitting and watching you. Even worse, if you rattle figures off the top of your head, your prospect may doubt you. Instead of paying attention to your presentation, she'll be looking over your shoulder to double-check your sums.

Not using a calculator raises doubts about your mathematical abilities. Plus, your prospect may wonder, 'If she's this careless with figures, where else will she be careless?' You don't want to do anything at this stage of the relationship to make your prospect start wondering whether she should be working with you at all. You want her entirely focused on the purchase at hand as you show her how she really can afford the product she wants so badly.

Is closing good for your customer?

Are closing questions, assumptive statements and sales-time stories in the best interests of your customers? Based on our experience, the answer is an unequivocal *yes*. We've done a lot of selling and we always take our customers' interests to heart. We know that they'll get the truth from us, as well as great service. But we can't guarantee them truth in selling and excellent service if they go to somebody else.

All along, from early days in selling up until today, we've tried to help every consumer have a positive image of the sales industry. We knew that positive image would be there if we gave customers a professional service, and we've always been driven to provide it. That's why we've worked harder than many of our associates to consummate sales that we knew were in the best interests of our customers. This obviously would not include selling them anything they didn't want. However, if all things were right, we would do

everything possible to help our customers get over the barriers of fear and procrastination. We felt it was our obligation.

Remember: If you properly qualify people (as we describe in Chapter 9), you'll know whether they truly have a need or desire for your product or service. If their lives will be better because they own your offering, you should do your best to persuade them into having it.

Think about it: drawing on your own experience, have you appreciated the professionals who've helped you make buying decisions? Have you been happy enough to recommend those people to others? Of course you have! We all have. To become a champion salesperson, you should set a goal to become someone people will not hesitate to recommend. Become someone people seek out as an expert in your field. And then everyone – you and your customers – wins.

Citing a similar situation

What better way to ease your prospects' fears than offering a story of another couple who had all the same concerns and indecisions, but who still decided to buy and now are glad they did? Here's an example of a story you can relate to your clients, based on their fears and hesitations:

Graham, Beth, I know you're hesitant about the financial commitment of buying a holiday home when you have your first baby on the way. You know, I had another family looking for the perfect caravan just about a year ago. We searched and searched, and they just couldn't decide on the right caravan or the right position.

One day we looked at a beautiful new caravan and they got very excited about it. I asked them if they thought that this was the style that was suitable for them, and they agreed that it was a great design of caravan for extensive holiday usage. I also asked if they wanted to begin the process of owning that great van. Bob thought we should go ahead, but Jill was afraid that the home might be a bit larger than they really needed. She thought they could get by in a smaller van, and she wasn't sure that she wanted to move before their baby came.

Well, they decided to go ahead and were amazed at how much space the baby things took up. After they holidayed for their first time, Bob and Jill were so glad that they'd decided to invest in the bigger holiday home when they did.

Now, you'd like to be all settled in at your new van before your baby comes, wouldn't you?

Make notes about the stories you have to tell about your other satisfied clients, and then use these stories when new prospects experience the same situation, as will inevitably happen.

Noting a competitive edge

If you're faced with a prospect who doesn't want to make a decision about your product, service or idea, you can tell a competitive-edge story to help her along. These stories don't need to be elaborate, and they're not meant to talk your prospects into anything they don't want or need. The stories just remind prospects (mainly ones who are in business, as opposed to individuals) that they have competitors. So if you're not telling them anything they don't already know, what's the appeal in competitive edge stories? In a word, *survival.*

A little competitive-edge story like this, for example, works well:

> Mr Ramirez, remember that many of your competitors are facing the same challenges today that you are. Isn't it interesting that, when an entire industry is fighting the same forces, some companies do a better job of meeting those challenges than others? My entire objective here today has been to help provide you with a competitive edge. Gaining a competitive edge, no matter how large or small, makes good business sense, doesn't it?

Prospects are all alike in one regard: they need help making decisions. Think about it. How many things have you been talked into owning that you really didn't want? Probably not very many. Few people get talked into buying something they don't really want. If it's a major purchase, you usually have a hard time selling your prospects on it, even if they *do* want it.

Problems arise when unscrupulous salespeople lie about what a product is and what it will do. Through deceit, these salespeople violate the buyer's trust and the buyer ends up owning something other than what she thought she was getting. The jails are full of salespeople who've done things like this. They let greed get in the way of their service to customers. Such an approach to selling is the direct opposite of the kind of selling we advocate. If you put customer service ahead of money, you *always* come out on top.

Chapter 13

Getting Referrals from Your Present Clients

*F*or many seasoned salespeople, referrals are a major source of new business. Clients who come to you from an existing client's recommendation are usually more inclined than cold-call clients to want to own your product, service or idea. Why? Because they already have positive feelings about you and your offering – and the source of their positive feelings is someone they already know and trust.

Referred prospects have much higher potency than cold leads and they often close at higher volumes and margins too. Yet most salespeople don't enjoy as full a flow of referred leads as they would like. Too often people believe that referrals just happen and that you can't influence them or increase the volume of them. That's just not true.

In this chapter, we share with you a proven and highly effective method of generating a constant flow of good-quality referral enquiries. The system may not work 100 per cent of the time, but even if it works only 50 per cent of the time, you generate many more selling situations than you're getting now, with clients who look forward to finding out about you and your offering.

Never take a referral for granted. As with any other sales technique, method isn't the only factor to consider when you try to get referrals. Salespeople must show referrals the same positive attitude, the same high energy level, the same respectful manner and the same quality presentation that they show to cold calls. Referrals are only *partially* sold on you or your product. The important thing is that they're willing to give you the chance to convince them of how they'll benefit from your offering.

If you're successful at convincing them, referrals will just keep on coming. Before you know it, you'll create an endless chain of happily involved clients who are more than willing to contribute to your success. Remember, when you make a referred client happy, you've impressed two people – the referred client and the person who did the referring. All this happiness converts to even more leads for you because you did the job right.

Understanding Where, How and When Referrals Arise

The closing rate on referral leads can be as high as 50 to 60 per cent, and the price and margins of these sales are usually high too, so they prove to be a very lucrative income stream. You can't afford not to know how to identify and obtain such a substantial increase in your sales potential. So in this section we give you a good overview that helps you recognise referrals when you see them.

In addition to using our proven system to gather referral enquiries for yourself, stay on the lookout for enquiries for your business contacts. If you develop a listening ear and keep your eyes open to each and every situation, then you'll find loads of enquiries that you can pass on to other contacts. In turn, by establishing a reputation for giving to others, you enjoy a frequent flow of enquiries for you.

Figuring out where to get referrals

Referrals are all around. The key is to upgrade your radar and not miss the signals. Especially important are some areas where the chances of referrals appearing increase. The following sections describe several great sources of referrals.

From family and friends

Perhaps the easiest and most accessible referrals are those that your family and friends can give you. But do wait a while after joining your new job before boldly inviting those you know and love to purchase from you. Product or service issues may exist that you haven't yet discovered, and if these become apparent post-sale to those close to you, the sale could spoil friendships and upset family situations.

When you're totally blown away by the fantastic service and product offering that you sell and know that it's of benefit, then encourage as much activity among people you know as possible. If your offering is as good as you believe, your friends and family will thank you for being so diligent.

Through networking

Networking at business conferences, clubs, professional organisations, religious gatherings and informal events is a way to increase your number of referrals. Getting referrals can be as simple as mentioning to others what you do or something exciting that's happened during your busy week of selling. When you're excited, other people will be too. People are attracted to energetic conversation and happy dispositions – so be a people magnet.

If you're having a particularly great week, share it with the world. Let them enjoy the positive vibe created by your success! Don't brag. Just allow yourself to be exuberant about your accomplishments. Exuberance is contagious and referral opportunities will naturally appear in conversations.

From happy customers

Make sure that your products and service are beyond reproach, because negative news spreads like a wild fire. Slip up just once, even just a little bit, and visiting clients can become awkward and your referral flow dries up.

For example, avoid promising the moon and the stars within a two-day delivery period, unless you can also wave Harry Potter's magic wand and make it happen. It's so easy to get carried away and tell your client what he wants to hear even when you know your information is inaccurate. In the long run, not only will you lose the disillusioned client, but you can also kiss goodbye all the wonderful referral opportunities he could have steered your way.

Satisfied clients tell at least three people about their experience with you. Dissatisfied clients tell at least 11 people. Negative stories generate more sympathy than positive stories do. So don't allow the flames of discontent to spread far when a challenge arises. Honesty and integrity must be first and foremost in your mind if you intend to succeed in business and in life.

If you leave your customer's office with a sale but no referrals, you have unfinished business to attend to – kind of like having a great dinner but leaving before dessert. Happy customers love to talk to the people they know about their new purchases, and so you need to develop the habit of enabling this to happen for them – and allowing the benefits to come your way too! So, before you leave your client's office, ask them who else they know that would like to benefit, as they have, from what you've provided, and then allow them to enjoy the feeling of being an 'introducer' when you contact the names your client has given to you.

From other salespeople in your field

As you progress in your sales career – especially if you remain or work consistently around a set geographical area or within a specific sector of industry – you become familiar with other salespeople in that arena. Thinking of these sales colleagues as a possible source for referral business is a profitable attitude. For instance, if you're in the healthcare field and you know a sales representative who's extremely successful selling surgical supply equipment and you're selling diagnostic testing equipment, that salesperson may be able to provide referrals or at least be willing to swap referrals with you.

If your relationship with other salespeople is based on mutual respect, you'll find that other salespeople pass leads to you when you meet or talk, whether you have a formal arrangement to do so or not.

Of course, returning the favour is only common courtesy. It's not unusual for salespeople at car dealerships or insurance agencies to recommend another salesperson who's better suited to meet a particular customer's needs. Professionals who have the needs of the client at heart, and know they would do the client a disservice by handling those needs ineffectively, work this way. They know the value of giving good customer service to their fellow salespeople and they know that what goes around, comes around.

Through public-speaking engagements and teaching opportunities

Public-speaking engagements and teaching opportunities are great for referral business, especially if you're the professional chosen to give the presentation or to teach. When this happens, you're automatically considered the expert in your field. But to earn the reputation you've been awarded, you'd better be prepared and handle your presentation well.

We recommend participating in these situations only if you can carry it off effectively. Too many people get carried away with the moment of stardom and forget that they're there to build their business, not to audition for a new starring role as a TV presenter.

Usually, gathering referrals is simply a case of asking. For example, at a conference we attended, a speaker provided cards on which participants wrote their names and names of others to contact who would also benefit from attending the conference. Each referral was put on a different card along with comments on why the participants believed that their referrals would enjoy and learn from the conference. The speaker encouraged us to fill out as many cards as we liked. We then put the cards into a large barrel. Each day of the conference, a member of the speaker's entourage pulled a card from the barrel to see who would win weekend getaways, free admission to advanced seminars, audio or video recordings, or books that were being sold at the conference. At the end of the conference, the speaker had the makings of another conference. What a system!

Knowing how and when to get referrals

Getting referrals is simple! You get referrals by asking for them. You'd be surprised how many salespeople feel awkward asking for referrals, and so too they don't ask the question. They avoid the referral part of the selling situation altogether – and in the process cost themselves and their companies big bucks.

Alternatively, some salespeople try to get referrals by asking their clients, 'Can you think of anyone else who may be interested?' And the clients can think of no one who may benefit from the salesperson's offering. Such a salesperson concludes that asking for referral business didn't really work for him.

In reality, it wasn't that it was impossible for these two groups of salespeople to get referrals. Instead, it was impossible to get referrals using the methods they were using. Instead of analysing their methods and trying something different, they stopped asking for referrals altogether.

Good referral business comes from clients with whom you have good relationships. This doesn't necessarily mean that they own your offering. For example, you may have built a good relationship with a past or potential customer who, for some reason, is unable to own your product at this time. If you've kept in close contact and done a good job in building rapport with the customer, though, he more than likely would be willing to steer you toward a business associate who can benefit from your product or service. All you have to do is ask.

Be cautious about asking for referrals before you've closed the sale with your present potential client. Asking before you have his autograph on your paperwork or his credit card approved is like putting the cart before the horse. It appears that you're no longer interested in the client, just in what he can do for you. And that's not a part of professional selling.

There is one specific time when your chances of getting referrals are better than most: just after you've successfully closed a sale and the customer is excited about owning your offering. At that moment, the client is usually more than happy to give you referrals – names of other people who need what the client now owns. Just after the sale is a time when enthusiasm is high and resistance is low.

But don't just plunge in and say, 'Do you know anyone else who may want my whatchamacallit?' If you ask that way, your client probably won't be able to come up with a name. He's too distracted by his new purchase. You have to *prepare* him in the art of giving good referrals. We cover this important topic in the next section.

Getting Referrals in Five Powerful Steps

This section's easy, five-step process to obtaining referrals will give you so much more success in developing your referral business that you'll make it an automatic part of every selling situation. Begin by setting a goal for how many referrals you want from each contact. Start with a goal of just one referral, and work your way up to a place where you know the steps so well and they flow so naturally that you get at least three referrals with every contact you make. Some practitioners of this process are getting as many as five or ten referrals from every client by implementing this simple strategy.

Memorise these five steps to getting referrals. The better you know them, the better you'll mine the rich stream of referrals that's just waiting for you in your current clientèle:

1. **Help your client remember why he bought from you.**

2. **Help your client think of specific people he knows.**

3. **Make a note of the referrals' names.**

4. **Ask qualifying questions and get contact information.**

5. **Ask your client to call the referral and set up the meeting.**

We cover each step in more detail in the following sections, examining this referral system so you can make it an integral part of your successful selling plan.

Step 1: Help your client remember why he bought from you

To successfully gather referrals from a past client, help him remember why he bought your offering in the first place. The existing customer bought your offering because he was attached to it and chose to wait no longer for it. He bought from you because he was in a certain emotional place. Now you need to re-stimulate that emotional state.

Think about a professional chef who absolutely loves cooking. You ask him to imagine he's in his kitchen cooking his favourite dish. Watch as he describes how carefully he selects and measures out ingredients. Listen intently as he involves all of his senses to recreate the culinary delight in his mind and relay the process to you verbally. That's the kind of emotional involvement you want to trigger in your client's mind.

When you guide the client mentally back into a situation like this, where they are re-discovering those really pleasant emotions that using your product or service has given them, you enable them to connect on an emotional level with the offering. When this happens, the desire to pass on that good feeling is strong – and referrals flow.

Step 2: Help your client think of specific people he knows

Guide your client to think of people he knows and cares about who may be interested in your offering. Ask questions with specific direction: 'Who looks after your company's IT demands?' or, 'What's the name of the person who keeps your garden so beautiful and neat?' Steer the customer towards a named contact that fits with the ideal customer type for your offering. Then keep asking the same questions in other areas where your clients use another supplier who might benefit from your product or service too – and then you have a nice list of referrals. Works every time!

Step 3: Make a note of the referrals' names

After your client has thought of specific people he knows, take out a piece of paper, or maybe some of your own business cards, and write down the names of those referrals. Keep the cards out so you can jot down the information your client gives you.

Step 4: Ask qualifying questions and get contact information

While your client is busy answering questions about the referrals, jot down notes to help you remember specific things about them. The notes and information that you glean now help make the newly referred contact warm to you and hugely increase the sale likelihood. In addition, you want to ascertain early on in this process whether the new prospect is suitable, and your questions and subsequent notes help you see whether the lead is qualified.

Never assume that what your client tells you about the referral's needs is 100 per cent true. He may not know all the answers to your questions and guess at some of them. And never tell the referral that your client told you all this information about him. Just have your notes handy to use as you qualify him further during your contact.

Step 5: Ask your client to call the referral and set up the meeting

This step is where most novice salespeople balk. They won't even try it. But keep in mind that this step in the process has an absolutely enormous impact on the strength of the future sales call. If you can get your customer to telephone your new referred prospect, then you allow the prospect to ask questions and dig information out. And if the referred appointment still agrees to a visit after your existing client has telephoned, then you're almost walking into a sale!

Setting Up Meetings with Referrals

When you call someone and you already have an 'in' with that person's close personal friend or respected business associate, you have common ground. You also have the benefit of knowing some pertinent information that may be relevant to getting the appointment.

Before you call such a referral, review the information you wrote in your notes and decide how you'll set the stage for this selling situation. If you properly qualified the referral, you know enough about him to ask just a few additional questions to get him interested in your offering and want to meet with you.

Through testimonials from your mutual business associate or friend, you can tell the referred lead what your client (and his friend) thought was most attractive or appealing about your offering. Chances are good that your referral will be just as interested in those same special features as his friend or associate was.

Aiming to Get Referrals Even When the Going Gets Tough

Just like you won't get a sale every time, you won't get a referral meeting every time. But always try to get referrals, even when you don't persuade or convince the prospect to get involved with your product or service. Now may not be the right time for that prospect, but that doesn't mean that he doesn't know anyone else who may be ripe for getting involved with the product, service or idea you represent.

Getting a meeting with a referral may require some time and persistent follow-up. People who are referred to you don't have a relationship with you. So you need to build that relationship by keeping your face and name in their minds and in front of their faces all the time.

Often, the ability to get the referral appointment depends on the success of your follow-up programme – if, of course, you use one at all. It's disheartening to go through all the work to get referrals, only to lose them because you lack an organised follow-up system.

In Chapter 14, I show you how getting referrals and setting up meetings are closely linked with practising proper and creative follow-up methods. When you follow up on those who offered the referrals, they're happy to refer you again when the situation arises. When you follow up on the referrals themselves, you give yourself greater opportunities to increase your profitability. How? By improving your closing rates through cultivating an effective referral business. Remember that 60 per cent closing rate I mentioned at the beginning of this chapter?

You may not get a meeting with every referral. But then you don't need to in order for referrals to become a highly productive way for you to find new business. Selling is a numbers game. Everyone you meet is likely to know someone else who may benefit from your product or service.

Because referred leads are stronger and richer pickings than any colder enquiry, aim to make referrals account for 20 to 30 per cent of your business. This way you ensure that you're always in touch with your satisfied clients and that new clients are left satisfied and never disgruntled, because the income potential is too great to let this slip.

Part IV
Growing Your Business

'My friends on the dock helped me
with the slogan.'

In this part...

*H*aving adopted many of the ideas of the preceding parts and applied them, you're really winning. Now, in this section, you build upon the skills and endeavours covered in the preceding chapters and benefit from shared ideas about following up and maintaining relationships with clients. This knowledge will see your success progress towards a higher production and maturity level. You also consider managing your motivations and your progress with goals and how you might fit them into time frames so that they become real and achieved instead of mere dreams.

Chapter 14

Following Up and Keeping in Touch

. . . .

In This Chapter

▶ Understanding who requires a follow-up (and when)

▶ Knowing what clients want from a follow-up

▶ Using follow-up methods successfully

▶ Getting results by sending simple thankyou notes

▶ Making the most of any follow-up

. . . .

*P*ractising consistent and persistent follow-up is proven to be one of the most important factors in successful selling. That's why developing an organised, systematic approach to follow-up is a must if you're serious about developing your sales career.

In simple language, *following up* after meeting someone is a reflection of your evaluation of that contact. Is the person a likely sales prospect one day? Could she introduce you to a flow of sales prospects? Might she one day be a useful contact for either direct sales or introduction to sales or maybe key influencers? You decide. . . .

With advances in technology, some professional salespeople are practising highly structured, thorough follow-up methods and enjoying fabulous rewards as a result of their diligence. If you want to compete with the big boys and girls in the world of sales, you must make follow-up an important part of your regular selling routine. In this chapter, we let you know with whom you should follow up and when. We describe what type and level of service clients expect from your follow-ups and give examples of effective follow-up methods. We also fill you in on the importance of sending thankyou notes and let you know how to get the best results from your follow-ups.

Be a follow-up fanatic! Even if you haven't found the most creative or memorable way to follow up, practising follow-up with zeal is better than doing nothing at all. Allow yourself a few mistakes and plenty of time to organise and maintain your chosen follow-up schedule. Expect *gradual* increases in the number of *yeses* you get. Be diligent about follow-up with your prospects, your customers and yourself. And above all, think of follow-up as your way to travel the path of sales success.

Knowing When (And with Whom) to Follow Up

The kind of follow-up you do depends on the kind of person you're following up with. The following four groups of people are the foundation of your business. Keeping in touch with them will build your future:

- ✔ **Referral contacts from existing happy clients:** There's no point in asking for referrals (see Chapter 13) if you don't follow up with the referrals you get. Referrals are a great source of business. Studies show that experienced salespeople spend half of the time selling a referred, qualified lead than they spend selling a non-referred, non-qualified lead – with a much higher closing rate. *Remember:* A referral isn't a guaranteed sale. But contacting a referral is definitely easier than starting from scratch.

- ✔ **Current clients:** Frequent communication with an existing client base, using such mediums as a newsletter, is a very productive form of following up. A good source of sales is to stay close and remind clients when it's time to consider updating the product you sold them, and to keep them informed as to relevant market or technology changes.

✔ **Difficult-to-reach prospective clients:** Some prospects are hard to reach, so you need to follow up with them several times before finally getting an appointment. In the initial stages your follow-up might be a telephone call or an email. As a professional, you demonstrate persistence and the prospect knows that you're chasing her without feeling pestered. **Remember:** Those salespeople who are persistent are rewarded. Some clients may not be as difficult to reach as they are difficult to close. You need a plan for following up with people who expressed an interest in your product but, for whatever reason, couldn't make the buying decision yet.

✔ **People in your network:** They may not be clients, but people you meet and speak with a few times each year. They may be other professional business contacts you've interacted with at past exhibitions, for example, or contacts from a social function whom you enjoyed meeting and you can see value in maintaining the connection. If you haven't met with them physically for a while, then following up by other methods is a powerful way to keep the relationship alive. As with all areas of follow-up, you differentiate both style and frequency according to which network you know the person from – so a follow-up with a contact from an organised business networking group differs to a follow-up with a contact from your local health club.

Even the briefest contact or smallest sale can lead to a whole new list of potential referrals for new business if you stay in touch and maintain a warm connection. Treat everyone you contact as if they control 1,000 new leads for your product or service. This is important no matter how your current selling career is going or what's happening in the economy. You can't sell if you're not talking to people.

Paying Attention to What Your Clients Want from Follow-Ups

To adopt effective methods of follow-up (see the following section), you need to know the concerns that clients have about the level of service they expect and the frequency of your follow-up. After all, you'll only be able to serve your clients well when you know what they want. Here's a list of clients' most pressing concerns about the selling and servicing of their accounts:

✔ Receiving a call that a salesperson promised to make

✔ Knowing contact numbers and the best available times to keep in touch with the sales and service people

✔ Being able to reach someone whenever the need arises

✔ Having the ability to talk to someone in authority

✔ Knowing that the salesperson and the salesperson's company appreciate their business

✔ Spending minimal time on hold in order to speak to a real person

✔ Being kept informed of ways to keep costs down and productivity up

✔ Being informed promptly of potential challenges and getting any problems resolved quickly

✔ Receiving acknowledgment of recognised challenges and accountability for errors

✔ Being addressed politely and receiving personal attention

✔ Being given realistic and honest information as it applies to delivery or problem-solving issues

By making follow-up and service a regular part of your day, you can efficiently address all these client concerns and maintain an edge over your competitor, who may not be as determined to follow up as you are.

Recognising How to Follow Up

If you want your clients or prospects to remember you and your offering, you must offer them a memorable experience. If you see follow-up as boring, tedious repetition, you can expect your clients to feel the same way: bored and tired of your constant contacts. So make sure that your methods of follow-up – and the messages you give through them – provide valuable information and add up to a rewarding and memorable experience for your clients. The following sections describe the most common follow-up methods.

 A key question to ask every client and potential client is this: 'How do you prefer that I keep in touch with you?' Your goal with follow-up is not to work on a schedule that suits you, but to meet their needs in whatever format they desire.

In person

Depending upon what you sell, it may be appropriate for you to occasionally pop by and visit with your clients in person. In almost all instances, the adage 'People buy people' is true and so *you* are what they buy! Thus it follows that some of *you* is what the client needs after the sale. To optimise sales potential, by gathering constant referrals and by being there at the right time for add-on sales and upgrades, you have to be close enough to be thought of in that moment. And regular, friendly calls are the best way for you to grow your business.

An example is if you sell office or warehouse equipment. It's nice for the clients to talk to you face to face and beneficial for you to see your products in action. Seeing how real people use your products helps you better understand their needs. For instance, maybe you got your clients involved in a particular product because of what they told you during the qualification process that we describe in Chapter 9; however, when you see how they're using the product, you can offer additional suggestions for increased productivity or ways to cut costs with the product that they hadn't realised.

If your clients prefer in-person contact, ask whether it's okay for you to pop by when you're in the area or whether they prefer you to set a specific time to visit. Some people don't care when you stop by as long as you *do* stop by.

This strategy applies to both business and consumer sales. If you help homeowners create their ideal garden environment, such as a pool, landscaping, built-in barbecue and so on, meeting with them at home may be prudent. You want to see how they're enjoying the result, what questions they may have or to pass along other ideas for enhancing their experience even more.

Phone

Telephone follow-up is perhaps the most common, most economical and most difficult method of follow-up. People can avoid your calls by using screening devices such as answering machines, secretaries or voice mail. Even if the people you're calling aren't trying to avoid you, they may be very busy and what you're offering may not be the most important thing in *their* day – even though it is to you.

If you have to leave a message because the person you're calling doesn't answer, then state clearly who you are, the company you're calling from and the prime reason that you're calling. For example, to an existing client you may say:

> Hello, a quick message for Gary. My name is Ben Kench from Donewell Engineering Ltd, and I'm calling to arrange a brief client visit at some stage in the next couple of weeks. I wonder if you could call me back on 01234 567890, please. Thanks, I look forward to speaking with you.

Or for a referral you may say:

> Hello, my name is Ben Kench from Donewell Engineering Ltd. I'm briefly calling following a meeting with a mutual friend of ours, Barry Brown from Colour Press Ltd. I'd love to come and meet you personally, especially in light of Barry's comments. Could you call me back, please, on 01234 567890. If it helps, a good time to call would be between 8 a.m. and 10 a.m. I look forward to chatting soon. Thanks.

Direct mail

Direct mail is a common method of follow-up, but your mailings don't have to be ordinary. Even if you're sending out a grouped follow-up mailing, you can still personalise your follow-up to make it memorable for the person you're contacting. For example:

- ✔ You may want to include *special offers* with your mailings – offers that benefit customers when they respond specifically to that mailing. They may include a special promotional discount on your offering or a coupon to use the services included in your mailed package. Sometimes a mailing includes nothing but a coupon bearing the client's name or company name. With the modern digital print and mail merge facility, this is now extremely achievable and has a huge impact. The client feels like she's getting a cheque in the mail.

 If you use this method of follow-up, invite the client to call you personally to spend her cheque and suggest that you'll see how far you can stretch it. Your customer feels valued, and you can expect a warm welcome when you do make contact, plus you've lots of potential for keeping or receiving her business.

- ✔ Another personal touch you can give to direct mailings is the 'I saw this and thought of you' type approach. This mail piece may not have anything to do with your personal offering, but it lets your clients know that you're thinking of them. Look out for an interesting and relevant press release relating to your client's field of expertise or maybe a news story in the local or national press and cut it out or copy it and send it onward. Sending the release may be of no direct, immediate benefit to you. But it informs your customers that you're thinking about them and is very powerful in terms of relationship and business generation.

 The more spontaneous your 'I saw this and thought of you' approach is, the more effective it will be. Instead of having your secretary type a formal cover letter, just jot a little handwritten note and attach it to the mailed material. Your note can be as simple as a few lines to let the client know that you were thinking about him.

Networking to find more ways to follow up

Top-producing salespeople have found ways to follow up that are both effective and creative. It may not be too effective to ask your competitors for their methods of follow-up. But other salespeople in your company may be doing creative things that they'd be more than willing to share with you.

At your next sales meeting, make a point of discussing different methods of follow-up, especially with proven top performers. This is called *networking*, even though you're doing it right at home within your own ranks of salespeople. And don't forget to follow up your discussion on follow-up by taking some follow-up action!

Before you toss all those collected business cards from all those business meetings into the circular file or tuck them away in a file you'll never see again, take the time to go through the cards and write a note about how much you enjoyed the person's input or conversation at the business meeting. If you've been thorough enough to jot down a word or two on the back of each card to remind you of your conversation, you'll have something specific to address when you do your networking follow-up.

You'd be surprised how many people have a positive response to this type of follow-up. Many even go out of their way to contact you with future needs! If you follow up shortly after you attend the business breakfast or networking event, you'll more easily recall what everybody said. Keep a copy of your correspondence attached to that colleague's card so you can remember her when she calls.

Email

Email is a wonderful tool to use for follow-up if your client uses it regularly. Make the email subject line grab attention and encourage the reading of the message.

Many people drown under the weight of their email inbox. So when following up with an email, be considerate of the recipient's time demands and don't send lengthy messages – short and sweet is best! Your message style should reflect the typical speedy way in which most people deal with inbox mail, so summarise what the message is about within the first two sentences. If relevant, include a hyperlink that takes the reader to an exact article on your website so that they can choose to go directly there or not without reading lots of text from you.

By the way, it never hurts to include in the email an offer to serve the client's needs should a question arise. Always, always keep yourself open to hearing from your clients.

This strategy also applies to consumers. Let's say you helped a client acquire a new office furniture pack that she's assembled and installed in her home. Now, your company offers accessories, such as filing units, shelving or picture frames for personalising the work environment. You have a valid reason to contact the client with the opportunity. You can include a link right in your message to where the client can take advantage of the products. In this case, you're following up and potentially selling another product all at once.

One of the major advantages of using email as a follow-up is that many email programs have a feature that sends you a message when the recipient reads your email. That way you know the client received your message.

Mobile messaging

Many people run all the details of their business and personal lives from their mobile phones. They may be on the go a lot and not have immediate computer access all the time. Whereas some folks receive their email messages on their mobile phones, others don't. As a professional salesperson, you need to be flexible. As we mention earlier in this chapter, a key question to ask every client and potential client is this: 'How do you prefer that I keep in touch with you?' If their lives revolve around their mobile phones, the answer may be 'by text'.

Sending messages via text is a great tool for people who are busy and want only basic information, but want it *now*. If your clients prefer to be contacted that way, invest a little time in learning some basic text shortcuts and etiquette. And always be brief when sending this type of message. Texting is a very good discipline because it forces you to make your message to the point. For example, you may say verbally to a client, 'I have a number of potential diary times during which we could meet. How about I arrange my schedule to meet with you at 1 p.m., or possibly a bit later at 3 p.m. if that's better for you?' But the text can simply say, 'I can meet at 1 or 3. Which do you prefer?' When your client is happy to communicate with you via text, that signals that you don't need lengthy, more formal communication.

If you have a message of exceptional importance to deliver, begin by using the method the client prefers, but consider following up that message with a different format. For example, if your client prefers you contact her via telephone and you end up leaving a voice mail message, also send the message via email or text to increase the likelihood of it being received.

As well as text messaging, you can contact people via social media platforms such as LinkedIn, Twitter and Facebook, if the client prefers.

Remembering the Importance of Thankyou Notes and Gifts

Everybody likes to be appreciated, and we think you'll agree that there's precious little recognition and appreciation in this world. So use your follow-up system and include a message delivery to simply let your customers and prospects know that you appreciate them. The deceptively modest thankyou note or greetings card is both simple and effective. In the following sections, we describe appropriate times for sending thankyou notes and explain when you can move beyond notes and send thankyou gifts.

Knowing when you can send a thankyou note

We've made it easy for you to get started with the thankyou note habit. Here are some instances in which thankyou messages or cards are appropriate, followed by an example of exact words that we've used effectively:

- ✔ **For in-person contact:** 'Thank you for taking time to meet/talk with me today. I know that time is your most precious resource and so I genuinely value the time you gave to me. If I can be of service to you at any stage in the future then it will be my pleasure. Once again, thank you, and have a great week.'

- ✔ **After a demonstration or presentation:** 'Thank you for giving me the opportunity today to discuss and present our offering to you. I sincerely appreciate the fact that you gave your time and I look forward to a potentially long and mutually rewarding relationship.'

- ✔ **After a purchase:** 'Thank you for your business. I fully recognise that in today's world you have many choices and options, and I am proud and grateful that you have chosen me/us. I will always do my very best to help you and to show you that your choice was indeed a wise one.'

- ✔ **For a referral:** 'Thank you for your kind referral. I will diligently follow up on the enquiry. And you can rest assured that anyone you refer to me will receive the highest degree of professional service.'

- ✔ **To anyone who gives you service:** 'Thank you for your continued and professional service. Genuinely, it is a pleasure to be your client. If my company or I can serve you in any way, please do not hesitate to call.'

As you can see, you have many reasons to say, 'Thank you.' A thankyou note or two to the right person at the right time can go a long way toward building your success. How? Suppose receptionists or assistants who think they don't get enough recognition *do* get recognition from you. Will they remember? Of course, they will. Will they feel good about you? Yes. Will they be more receptive to your calls and questions? Probably. *Remember:* You can never go wrong by thanking someone.

Take advantage of technology to help you start and stay on top of a thankyou note process. Websites such as www.funkypigeon.com or www.moonpig.com allow you to send cards that you customise with your own photos and your own handwriting font, and to include gifts.

Going beyond notes with thankyou gifts

There may be instances for which a thankyou note doesn't seem to be enough and you want to send a gift. For example, if someone has gone *way* out of her way to help you, and if you think she deserves a little gift or an extra-special thankyou, and if a thankyou is appropriate, then by all means send that person a thankyou right away.

So now you may be wondering this: what are some appropriate gift ideas? If a customer likes classical music, consider sending her a set of tickets to a symphony performance. You may want to send movie tickets to a secretary or assistant. You can thank clients with a round of golf at their favourite course, or give the secretary and her guest a gift certificate for lunch to show your gratitude for her extra effort to arrange the appointment that you worked on for a month.

 In some businesses, sending gifts isn't appropriate due to rules or regulations in those industries. Gifts can be perceived as an inducement or bribe. However, in almost any instance where you already have a 'friendship', then a gift to a friend is perfectly acceptable, especially when the gift is more social and non-exclusive, such as invitations to corporate or sporting events.

 Many gifts to clients are tax-deductible to your business. Ask your accountant about this. Your thankyou gift can be even *more* beneficial for you.

Maximising Results from Your Follow-Ups

Maximising results is a great goal to have in handling any contact, not just a follow-up. To do so requires efficiency, a well-laid plan and good records. In this section, we cover just those aspects of follow-up so you can get the best results from your effort.

The power of thank you

As a young and eager salesman, Ben was fortunate enough to be schooled in the habit of giving thankyou gifts. The company he worked for insisted that each salesperson send a client flowers automatically after every sale and pay the cost for the gift. New customers were always thankful, and Ben is sure the flowers rescued many sales where customers were having second thoughts a day or so later. Indeed, as a reminder of the power of thank you, Ben still has a thankyou card from a customer who was delighted by his thankyou gift.

To this day, after a seminar or any client engagement, Ben writes thankyou notes to the people he's had the pleasure to speak with, and all his sales and business development programmes include a section on saying thank you.

Imposing order

Follow-up sounds so simple when somebody advises you to send a letter or to just pick up the phone and make a call, but establishing an effective follow-up system involves much more than that. An effective follow-up plan requires you to master and implement the Rule of Seven, a rule of selling that can increase your sales volume many times over: to make the sale, you should contact prospects a minimum of seven times within a 12-month period with an expectation that the magic happens on the seventh occasion!

If you're new to sales, you need to work extra-hard at creating personal discipline and a process to provide prompt follow-up to referrals, prospective clients, loyal customers who now own your offering, networking possibilities and just about everybody you come into contact with during a normal business day (as if there is such a thing as a normal business day!).

For your follow-up to be effective, and because follow-up is a constant in the selling process, you must organise your follow-up time and programme to ensure that your business stays productive. If you have a lot of people to keep track of, use a sales customer relationship management software program designed to store the maximum amount of information in the minimum amount of space. If you're employed, your employer has probably already invested in this type of program, so spend a few extra hours getting to know it. By setting up a database specially designed for follow-up, you can save time and energy that you can then devote to face-to-face selling. Some of the most popular software programs include Sage ACT! (www.act.com) and GoldMine (www.goldmine.com). Other methods are Internet-driven services, such as Salesforce.com (www.salesforce.com).

If you already use a program, invest some time in working out how to maximise the scheduling or sequencing of the mail features. If you don't have one currently, be certain to get a system similar to these recommended ones and to ensure that these features are easy to manage in any program you decide to use. (Check out Chapter 6 for more information on taking advantage of technology.)

Whichever way you choose to organise your time and the follow-up information you collect, your method should enable you to systematically and periodically keep in touch with all your contacts.

As you schedule your follow-up time, keep your customers informed of the best ways to communicate with you. Be flexible and offer a range of communication channels. Let your customers know your work schedule (as far as possible), and they'll appreciate being able to reach you when you say you'll be available. Do make sure that you're accessible at the times you tell them to contact you! Keeping your announced office hours is just another way to let your clients see how efficiently you run your business and, likewise, how efficiently you would (or do) service their needs. (Flip to Chapter 15 for more pointers on planning your time efficiently.)

Avoiding becoming a nuisance

Whether you receive a *yes* or a *no* from people to whom you present your product or service, you should include them all in your follow-up programme. In the following sections, we explain when and how often to contact people in your follow-up programme and describe actions to take when someone still says no to your product or service after follow-up.

Knowing when and how often to make contact

With your clients, you want to stay in touch fairly often, depending upon the product or service they acquired. If they're purchasing office supplies from you, you may need to be in touch every two or three weeks. According to consumption rates, however, a capital purchase, such as machinery in a factory, may warrant a call every couple of months to ensure that function and production issues are always smooth.

With prospects, you need to get in touch often. You could offer a monthly newsletter that they subscribe to. Then they can unsubscribe at any time should they feel that the frequency is too heavy or their needs change.

 Don't say, 'How often shall I contact you?' because then your client or prospect may answer with, 'Don't call us. We'll call you.' Instead, suggest it this way, 'With your permission, I'd like to give you a call in about 30 days just to see how well the product is meeting your needs and to find out whether you have any questions. Would that be all right with you?' She may suggest you call sooner or that she'll have a better idea of how things are working out in 45 days. You can gauge your nuisance factor based on her response.

 Keep your follow-up succinct, and do it at times most convenient for your prospects' schedules. Interruptions are sometimes unavoidable, but when too many interruptions occur, give your customers the opportunity to get back with you at a time better suited to their busy schedules.

Treading carefully with someone who says no after follow-up

If you're following up a non-buying prospect and you're calling after a series of sales visits that weren't successful, be careful to ensure that you leave with no bitter taste remaining. If you know that her answer wasn't based on your poor performance, you may still be able to get a referral from her or do future business with her when her situation changes.

Be polite! Find out when she expects her situation to change and ask her permission to call back again. She may be receptive to hearing what you have to say a few short months down the road when she's ready to own your offering. If you leave her with a positive feeling and continue to build rapport through gentle follow-up, then she may well come back to you one day or pass referrals to you.

If your customer admits that she's bought from your competitor, don't you think you need to discover why she chose your competitor over you? If this situation arises, don't get angry with your prospective client. Instead, make her feel important by asking her whether you can take up just a few more moments of her time to get her advice on how you can improve your sales skills or your product or service, and then add her to your usual follow-up process.

If you're diligent in following up with customers who choose not to own your offering, you may just sneak them away from your competitor the next time they get the itch to own. By keeping in touch with them even better than the salesperson with whom they chose to do business, you make the customer wish that she'd done business with you. Let her see your organisation, and care for her well-being through your effective follow-up – and when she needs a new-and-improved version of what she now owns, she'll probably think of you first.

Being disappointed and letting your clients know you're sorry not to have the opportunity to do business with them is okay. Let them know that you're not giving up and that you still hope to win their trust. And for the customers you obtained because of your effective follow-up, remain just as consistent and persistent in the service you provide. Make sure they know that you're concerned about meeting their needs and that you put their needs before your own.

Keeping track of your successes

With technological advances being what they are, you have to hand an extraordinary array of excellent business tools that allow you to record and recall any information. Use these systems to keep thorough notes on all your follow-ups and the success you have with your current follow-up methods.

The more information you record, the more you see patterns and so the more likely you are to repeat the experience in the future.

 If you manage your record-keeping correctly and use a system that allows for information reporting, then you quickly see what works well and how you can best advance your sales career.

Sticking with the follow-up programme

How well your prospects respond to your follow-up depends entirely on the effectiveness and efficiency of the method of follow-up you use. If you follow up quickly and regularly (and with a bit of flair), you can expect high percentages of response from your prospects.

Don't get discouraged if some prospects don't respond at all. Sometimes, no matter how good your follow-up is, you get zip, zero, zilch for your efforts. But numbers hold truths, so watch your results constantly. If they're sliding downwards, be prepared to change your approach methods in order to start winning again.

 Knowing which methods work best for you and which types of clients respond to one method of follow-up as opposed to another can take time. So be patient. Don't give up if, after your first few attempts at follow-up, you get disappointing results. Instead, keep seeking ways to improve your follow-up programme. Contact other professional salespeople who are willing to listen, look at your follow-up programme and offer advice. Good follow-up techniques can sometimes take as long to master as good selling techniques. It doesn't happen overnight.

Chapter 15

Managing Your Time Efficiently

*T*ime is your most valuable resource, and, until you realise that, you'll always be wondering where your time goes. It's more valuable than money and more important to master than selling skills themselves. The greatest challenge with time is that there isn't a source to gain more of it. Everyone has the same number of seconds, minutes and hours in a day. You can always get more money. You can even learn more and better selling skills. But you can't get more time.

Speak with sales leaders everywhere about their greatest challenge, and the overwhelming response will be 'having too little time'. When you have more time to do the things you *need* to do, you can usually generate more income to do the things you *want* to do. Indeed, as renowned sales trainer and leader Zig Ziglar says, 'When you do what you need to do when you need to do it, you will soon have the time to do what you want to do when you want to do it.'

In this chapter, we give you some great tips for staying on top of your time so that you have more time to do the things you want to do, instead of only being able to do the things you need to do. (For more great tips on managing time, turn to *Time Management For Dummies* by Clare Evans (Wiley).)

Investing Your Time Rather Than Spending It

Foolishly, average salespeople often spend their time doing unproductive work – and then they wonder where their day went, why they accomplished so little and why they never seem to have time for the fun stuff they'd really like to do. The key word here is *spend:* they *spent* their time instead of *investing* it. And that makes all the difference.

The words *spending* and *investing* connote very different ideas. When you spend money, depending upon what it's spent on, you may think of the loss of that money rather than the benefits you'll enjoy from what you got in exchange for it. On the other hand, the word *invest* signifies a payment from which you'll derive a return; you don't focus on the momentary loss of money, but rather on the gain of the product or service that you'll receive. Similarly, when you spend your time instead of investing it, you focus on lost time rather than on personal gain.

If you've never put a true value to your time before, do it now. To determine what your time is worth, take your hourly rate and follow this simple equation:

Gross Income ÷ Total Annual Working Hours = Hourly Rate

To help you see the value of this equation, suppose that your annual income is £30,000, and you work 40 hours a week for 50 weeks a year (allowing 2 weeks off for holidays). That means that the value of each hour in your working week is £15. In simple 'lost commission' sales, if you spend just one hour each day of each working week on unproductive activity, you spend £3,750 a year on nothing. And that's exactly what you have to show for your wasted time too – nothing. When you choose not to manage your time, you may end up wasting ten per cent of your annual income or more. And this amount doesn't even account for all the future business you lost because you spent time instead of investing it.

Managing yourself to get a handle on your time

Time management is really all about managing yourself. Don't believe us? Stop and think about it for a minute. When did you last control time? Can you stop time or even slow it down? No way. Can you negotiate with time? If you've figured out how, then you should be writing a book instead of reading one. No one has more time to invest than you do, and you don't have any more time than anyone else, yet some people succeed more often than others, and they do it without controlling time. They do it by disciplining themselves to make the most of every minute.

If such famous names as Edward Jenner, Louis Pasteur, Mahatma Gandhi and Martin Luther King could change the world and our lives today and they still had only 24 hours in each day to do it, then surely we can exercise just a little more self-control and manage to improve our lot? Complaining about not having enough time in light of these examples really is a bit feeble. You just need to kick yourself a little and get focused!

For example, a way to sensibly and effectively manage yourself is to cluster your meetings. By organising your appointments by geographical area, you can save a lot of travel time – and if your travel time is primarily within major cities, you may want to schedule it so you don't get stuck in rush-hour traffic. Also, taking side streets and back roads may lead you to new opportunities if you keep your eyes open and remain aware of your surroundings.

Tip: If you can't put your fingers on the contact information for all your clients within a matter of minutes, consider investing some time in good contact management software. With today's technology, the only reason a client or prospective client's information won't be at your fingertips is because you didn't invest the time to input it correctly as soon as you received it. Entering the information only takes a few minutes, and then it's there for ever. (Always remember to make backup copies of your important data!)

If you think that people who practise time-management strategies are fanatical workaholics who leave no time for personal relaxation, you're mistaken. Just the opposite is the case. In operating more efficiently, they create *more* time for personal endeavours. Invest time in planning your time, and you'll think of dozens of ways to manage yourself more efficiently.

In sales or persuasion situations, you often don't see immediate financial pay-off from the time you invest. The selling business requires patience and wise money management practices as well.

When you invest time in the people you're trying to persuade, thinking of the potential returns when the deal comes off is normal. We don't know of any new salesperson who doesn't take out his calculator and work out the commission he gets on a sale as soon as he's out of sight of the client. However, some sales cycles are long and you must remain focused on the end goal. Sometimes your pay day comes weeks or even months after your initial approach, and throughout that sales cycle you need to manage your investment of time effectively because a 'risk' is still there that you invest time and the sale still doesn't go ahead. The longer the period between selling and pay-off, the harder it is to stay focused on investing your time wisely.

Avoiding 'Fluffy Time' by Planning Thoroughly

We need to warn you right now about a killer disease within the sales and business world – fluffy time!

Simply put, too many people find that at the end of the day they look back and see nothing but a blur. The day has gone by and they haven't simply sat there and done nothing, yet they have nothing much to show for their efforts.

Fluffy time is time 'fluffed' on things that sort of crept up on you. For example, you open your emails 'just to check' and then an hour later realise that you're still immersed in replies. Or you plan to get an early start at work, but then you can't decide what to wear. Or you forget some paperwork and have to go back for it. Or you go to the office with a clear idea of what you have to do, but when you get there you're sucked in to the 'what's going on' atmosphere and your work slips.

To avoid fluffy time, you must plan your work. The true professional is constantly watching for fluffy time and exercises discipline during working hours; for this reason, he'll be the 'lucky one' who stumbles upon the best enquiries.

In a page-per-day diary – notebook or computerised – section up everything you need to do in time slots. By making a record of your plan, you stay on track a lot more easily. It's a fact: taking the time to plan your days saves as much as 20 to 30 times the amount of time that you expend in the planning process.

When you plan your time, divide the things on your 'to do' list in order of importance:

- ✔ **Urgent activities:** These are the tasks you must complete today.

- ✔ **Important activities:** These tasks are ones that are close to immediate, but not quite. You probably need to complete them this week instead of today, for example.

- ✔ **Secondary activities:** These tasks don't need to be completed by a specific deadline. You can work them in when you have a spare moment.

- ✔ **Emergencies:** Although they're rare, you need to build time into your schedule to handle emergencies so you're not left hanging when they happen.

In the following sections, we go into more detail on each of these three categories.

Urgent activities

Urgent activities are *only* those activities that you must complete today. If you clutter your mind with things that should be secondary activities (the things you don't have to do today), you can end up neglecting your immediate activities or not giving them the full, focused attention they require.

Ask yourself these questions to determine the immediacy of your activities and prioritise them by either the amount of relief you'll feel in getting them done or the amount of goodwill or income they'll generate:

- ✔ If I can achieve only three or four activities today, which ones should they be? What if I can only accomplish one?

- ✔ Which activities will yield the largest rewards?

    ✔ If I don't do this activity, what might be the consequences?

    ✔ Which of these activities can I delegate to someone else?

Have your immediate activities in front of you at all times. If you can't see what you need to accomplish today because you've buried your immediate activities under other less-important work, those activities can get lost in the shuffle – and you can lose sight of your goals.

Use your smartphone or computer to set reminders (don't ignore the reminders!), and remember to synchronise your computer and smartphone diaries. If the task is a large one, break it down into smaller pieces so you can accomplish those pieces and get them off that list. Accomplishing those smaller pieces of the project leaves you with a very satisfying feeling – and when you're feeling good, you're more productive. For more on using technology, head to Chapter 6.

Important activities

Identifying your non-urgent but important activities is usually a challenge. Many tasks at first appear to scream at you to be done, and you can be in danger of categorising them all as urgent. However, you can class many tasks as important but not urgent when you ask the questions we provide in the preceding section.

For example, say you have to prepare a quotation for a client you saw yesterday. He said he was away on a seminar for a week and so as long as the quotation was on his desk when he returned that was fine. But you have a heavy week planned and fear that if you don't do the quote now, you'll end up having a last-minute rush.

So is the task urgent or important? Well, you can't classify it as urgent when the urgency is really only as a result of your future planning choices. Urgent is when the client says, 'I need this quotation by tomorrow noon for sign-off at the board meeting.'

Define an urgent task as one that has a deadline that you can't miss. Tasks with no deadline but that you must do are important, and you do these tasks after the urgent ones.

Staying on top of your paperwork

Paperwork, which includes computer-generated or online reports that your company may require, can crop up in any task. Some paperwork, as with the task, is urgent. But plenty of administrative tasks are important and not urgent.

We recommend that you create regular admin slots in your diary. Depending on your personality, your best bet for dealing with paperwork may be to do it either during the last hour of the day or during a regular weekly slot. Whenever you choose, remember that although administration is important, it can't actually make a sale for you. So don't do admin work during prime selling time – unless of course it falls into the urgent category.

Another key factor in becoming more efficient – touch it once! Don't get into the habit of constantly picking something up and putting it down again to be dealt with later. Deal with that paperwork now – either do it, ditch it or delegate it.

Handle your paperwork efficiently and you have a clear desk and good time management, which equate to more sales.

By following this type of thinking process, you save yourself a lot of mental pressure. Clarity ascertained from sharp, honest questioning means that you don't miss deadlines and don't get stressed over non-urgent activities.

Secondary activities

Identifying which tasks fall into the 'secondary' category is difficult. You may think everything needs your attention, because if you have it in front of you and in your mind then it must be important, surely? But such thinking simply isn't true. Other people pass many unimportant activities to you to take care of – activities that have a funny habit of working themselves out if you just ignore them for a while. So you can relieve 'to do' list pressure by categorising tasks that you don't own and that aren't important as secondary activities.

We're not suggesting that you simply forget about tasks and hope that they go away. But when you can't find a clear reason to do a task, put it aside. If a task reappears then you can categorise it as important and slot it into your diary. For example, you might feel that you must create a presentation and document for a forthcoming event that you've proposed you jointly run with a non-competitive service provider. It might be a project that excites you and it probably does warrant the investment of your time to prepare it as professionally as possible. However, until your selected partner equally commits to the event, spending your own time on presentation creation would possibly be unwarranted. So, by removing it from your list and ignoring it you aren't mismanaging your time. Only bring the task back onto your must-do list when your partner says 'yes' and starts to plan the presentation as a definite event.

Emergencies

Planning your time efficiently can prevent some emergencies from happening in the first place, but you should always have an alternative approach to your most important activities just in case an emergency arises.

For example, an emergency might arise in an instance when a prospect – a potentially new and large account customer – calls you and asks you to do a presentation tomorrow! However, this situation would not have been an emergency if you'd already prepared at least an outline of the proposed presentation in advance as part of your planning-to-win-the-business approach.

However, urgent activities do still arise unexpectedly from time to time, and you need a strategy for dealing with these. Sometimes you have to drop a task that you were in the middle of doing and come back to it later, and other times you have to postpone a planned activity. You need to explain to people that an emergency situation has meant that you didn't complete their task.

Don't cry wolf. Never fudge not having done something by faking an emergency. Honesty is always the best policy, and you never want to use up your goodwill credit on fake situations in case a real emergency happens one day!

Accounting for Your Time

Just as you separate work tasks into three categories, you need to separate your personal life into three areas in order to effectively organise your time. You need to

- ✔ Investigate your yesterday
- ✔ Analyse your today
- ✔ Discover your tomorrow

We show you how to do just that in the sections that follow.

Investigating your past

Keep a diary for everything that you do – especially your selling activities. Each day record what you did, where you went, the people you met and what you gained from each activity. Record details as accurately as you can time-wise and make notes that record expectations (why you chose to do that activity in the first place) and outcomes (what you gained as a result of the time invested).

Above all, be honest when you record the time you spend on each activity. If you cheat, you're only cheating yourself.

At the end of each week review the diary and ask yourself whether you got what you had hoped for that week. Our guess is that you'll see:

- ✔ Fluffy time (see the earlier section 'Avoiding "Fluffy Time" by Planning Thoroughly')
- ✔ Time you could have used better
- ✔ Some effective selling time

Notice where you're wasting time, how you might bundle some tasks together to be more efficient and people who may be time thieves.

Analysing your today

If you use the word *productivity* when you refer to time planning, time planning won't be such a mystery to you.

People constantly come up to Ben at events and state that they just can't seem to get all their tasks done. They have an endless list of actions and not enough time. Ben suggests setting a goal of hitting sales targets and then asking for each task: 'Is what I'm doing now (or about to do) clearly helping me towards achieving my goal?' Usually, after a few seconds of thinking and possibly trying to justify the action, the truth is apparent and you decide on the correct action. Indeed, after more than 30 years of teaching sales and business growth, Ben still asks the same question each day and uses this simple rule as a rudder for direction.

Some salespeople spend all their time getting organised or learning new 'tools', such as software, and generally getting ready for persuasion situations that never come about. To them, getting organised itself has become the game, but that's the wrong approach. Yes, buying a smart device to assist efficiency is a good idea, but these tasks are just a small part of a very big picture. Time planning actually starts with goals. Why? Because setting goals is the only way you can tell what the most productive tasks are at any given moment. (If you need help setting goals, turn to Chapter 18.)

When you're planning for the upcoming day, ask yourself the following questions:

- ✔ Did I accomplish all my high-priority items today?

- ✔ Did I reach or surpass my goals for today?

- ✔ Did I invest as much time in actually selling as I planned?

- ✔ Did I contact every prospect on my list for today? If not, why not? What prevented me from getting to that prospect?

- ✔ How much time did I spend prospecting for new clients?

- ✔ How much time did I waste chatting with co-workers or clients?

- ✔ What is the most productive thing I did today?

- ✔ What is the least productive thing I did today?

✔ Of the things I consider a waste of time, could I have avoided or eliminated any of them?

✔ How much time did I spend doing something that will profit me? Can I devote more time to that activity tomorrow?

✔ Was today a productive day for me? Was it productive for my company?

✔ Did I take care of all the paperwork I needed to take care of today?

✔ How many of today's activities have helped me achieve my goals?

✔ How much time today did I allot to my family? Did I spend this time with them? Was it quality time, or was I just at the same place they were, at the same time?

✔ What can I do to improve the quality of time I devote to my family?

✔ Did I plan for, and take some time to work on, my emotional or physical health?

✔ If I could live today over, what would I change?

✔ What did I do today that I feel really good about?

✔ Did I send thankyou notes to the people I dealt with today?

✔ What or who wasted the greatest amount of my time?

The answers to these questions help you see what you're doing right and let you know what you can improve upon tomorrow.

Discovering your tomorrow

Assume that your goals and priorities are in line (turn to Chapter 18 if they're not). You know what you want and how you want to get there. Your goals are all in writing, and your priorities are set. Your daily time-planning should start at night before you go to bed. Go through your diary and lay out the day to come. Get a handle on your top six priorities for the next day, as well as which people you will see or call. Then add any personal areas you need to cover the next day. Writing down or entering the next day's top six priorities shouldn't take more than 10 to 15 minutes if you do it in a nice, quiet spot. When you've mapped out the next day, forget it and go to bed – you'll sleep better with a clear head after planning thoroughly.

At the beginning of the day you've just mapped out, the most productive thing possible may be a 20-minute workout or breakfast with the family, or working in the garden, or any of a thousand other things that may be important to you and part of your goals and priorities. You have many choices throughout your day. Only you know whether what you're doing is the most productive thing in relation to the goals and aspirations you want to achieve.

One thing that's critical is your self-discipline: your management of you actually doing the things that you have planned. Planning is half of the battle – but only half. To win you must follow through with action.

Don't try to plan for every minute of the day. Instead, start by planning just 75 per cent of your total work time. That way, you allow for interruptions, delays and unexpected emergencies. As your work-day planning improves, you can increase to planning 90 per cent of your day. But never plan for 100 per cent – if you do, you won't leave room for the unexpected, and you'll just frustrate yourself when you can't accomplish your designated goals.

Achieving balance

Take a look at five areas of your life: family, health, finances, hobbies and your spirit. Why focus on so many areas outside of your career? Because when you're excited, motivated and feeling good, you persuade better. If you let yourself become just a sales machine with no time for anything else, you burn out. You may also create problems in your personal relationships. And your health most likely suffers. Besides all that, you have no fun, you start feeling sorry for yourself and your career goes down the drain.

Sometimes the most productive thing you can do may be to meet your spouse for lunch and thank him for supporting your goals and putting up with your long hours. Or to go see your child at a school event and enjoy his childhood. Or to do a physical workout to help ensure your good health and high energy. Or to plant roses if planting roses invigorates you.

Remain flexible. Not much is black and white in the world of selling; there are many grey areas. By staying flexible, you can maintain your equilibrium and move on to greater things.

One of the best ways to increase your productivity and your income is to maintain a balance in your life. Address all areas of your needs, including family, leisure time, learning time and health maintenance time. Winners win by keeping themselves in balance – physically and psychologically.

Organising Your Workspace

One of the main causes of wasted time and lost income in business is a disorganised office space. Believe it or not, clearing your desk also helps to clear your mind. When your mind is clear, you're more able to focus on one task at a time. And all you can accomplish is one thing at a time anyway, so why try to do more?

So where do you start? Try the tips in the following sections.

Keep only immediate activities on your desk

Keep everything but your most pressing tasks out of sight. And keep everything you need for accomplishing the immediate tasks somewhere nearby (in a place you'll remember), so you don't waste time running here and there looking for what you need.

Be proactive with your time

If you suffer innumerable interruptions, close your door. If you don't have a door, try earplugs or a headset to isolate yourself.

You must exercise self-discipline, and refuse to allow time thieves to interrupt. Say no to a chat and avoid those who want to drain your time.

Develop your ability to focus on your work. Let your co-workers or family know that sometimes they simply can't interrupt you. Don't answer your telephone – let voice mail be your receptionist for a while. Try checking voice mail and email only four times each day, rather than allowing interruptions to come at you willy-nilly.

Handle phone calls wisely

If the phone isn't a necessary tool of your immediate business, remove it from your desk. Put it on a table behind you or even on the floor if you must – but get it out of your sight.

Not every phone call is an emergency. When the other party gets off the subject, or when the other party stays on the subject but is long-winded, try these techniques:

✔ **If you initiate the call, tell the person, 'I have three things to cover with you':** If he starts to get sidetracked, you have the right to bring him back to one of your three topics.

✔ **If the other party initiates the call and you don't have a lot of time to give him, let him know his call is important, but that you were just heading out the door:** Unless he's an irate customer who has a total stoppage of an assembly line because of your equipment, most people are willing to accept a call-back. If the caller can't wait, it's an emergency and you have to handle it on the spot.

✔ **Call a long-winded person just before lunchtime or just before he goes home for the day:** If that's not possible, start your call by saying, 'I'm really pressed for time, but I just wanted to let you know something,' or, 'I'm on my way to an appointment, but I wanted to touch base with you.'

If you don't take control in non-emergency phone call situations, you'll forever be at the mercy of others.

Avoiding the Most Common Time Traps

You probably know some people who've made time wasting an art form. They've mastered the ability to fall into every time trap they encounter. Not surprisingly, these folks aren't the people who get things done, help the most people or earn the biggest incomes in selling. If you want to get more yeses in your life, knowing – and avoiding – the following common time traps is a great place to start.

Desperately seeking what shouldn't be lost

A sure way to waste valuable time is to keep looking for something you desperately need because you were careless when you 'put it away'. Looking for lost items is the single biggest time waster for everyone. How many hours have you wasted looking for the scrap of paper on which you wrote an important phone number or for the folder with all the referrals that your new client gave you? How about your sunglasses or your car keys? Ring any bells? Those few minutes here and there can really add up, so designate a specific place for every item you use regularly, and then make sure you always use it. If you always hang your keys on a hook by the door, you won't spend precious time searching for them.

Failing to do the job right the first time

Because of the demands salespeople place on themselves, they tend to rush through their paperwork and their planning of presentations without carefully checking or rechecking details. Get out of that habit right away. If you don't have time to do it right the first time, how will you find time to do it again? Consider how much less time you need to do something right the first time than you need if you have to go back and do it over. Don't risk angering others with costly delays or mistakes caused by carelessly written paperwork. Champions double-check everything for accuracy and clarity.

Procrastinating

Procrastination can kill your career. Don't feel alone on this one; everyone procrastinates. Most people procrastinate because of fear. They fear making a mistake, so instead they do nothing. The trouble with doing nothing, though, is that you produce nothing. Better to act and learn and improve next time.

If a client phones to report a problem with the product or service he acquired from a salesperson, what do most salespeople do? They try to put off facing the challenge until tomorrow. By then, though, when they do call to apologise and solve the problem, the client may be furious and vow never to do business with the salesperson's company again. So the salesperson has to work doubly hard and spend even more time with the client, just to diffuse his anger.

Always call an angry client immediately. The longer you wait, the more the anger worsens.

Making unnecessarily long phone calls

The telephone can be your greatest ally or your greatest enemy, especially when it comes to time management. Here are some ideas to help you deal with wasted time on the phone:

- ✔ Control incoming calls and set aside specific time each day to make phone calls.

- ✔ Set a time limit for your calls.

- ✔ Write down your objective for the phone call and focus on it.

- ✔ Have all your materials and information within reach before you pick up the phone.

- ✔ Find polite but effective exit lines to help you get off the phone without interrupting the other person or abruptly ending the conversation. For example, try saying, 'Barbara, just one more thing before I have to go . . .'.

- ✔ Invest in a high-quality headset which allows you to keep both hands free so you can attend to details while you're on the phone.

If you think of the phone as a business tool, not unlike your computer, you can form new habits for using it that keep you out of that common time trap.

Holding unnecessary or unnecessarily long meetings

Attending too many non-productive meetings can be a major time waster. If you're in management and you think you waste a great deal of your time in meetings, maybe you should re-evaluate how often you need to meet with your people and what you need to accomplish when you do get together. Is a daily or weekly meeting really necessary? Or can more effective communications within the company eliminate the need for such meetings? Too often management as well as staff don't properly calculate the cost of the time of those involved in meetings. Don't hold a £1,000 meeting to solve a £50 problem.

For highly productive meetings, create an agenda and encourage brevity by not making everyone too comfortable! Stand-up meetings and no coffee and biscuits go a long way towards achieving this goal.

Attending lengthy client lunches

As with the phone, when you're out for lunch with clients, you need to develop ways to let them know that you've finished your business for today and that you must move on. You can also take control at the beginning of the appointment for a noon lunch by stating clearly that you must leave by 1.30 p.m.

Engaging in negative thinking

Negative thoughts that produce negative talk are another big waste of time for salespeople. If you dwell on life's negatives, what do you think you can accomplish? We're positive (ahem) that you'll accomplish very little. Push negative thoughts from your mind. No one who is a negative thinker ever becomes a success in selling.

Instead of focusing on things you don't like, think about the positive things you *can* do. And by all means surround yourself with positive thinkers – their positive energy will rub off on you.

Not using driving time wisely

Most people in professional selling spend a lot of time in their cars driving from appointment to appointment. The average salesperson drives 25,000 miles a year for his job. That works out at about 15 to 20 hours each week – about the same amount of time as doing a basic college course!

Why not use that driving time and listen to audio programmes that can help you become more successful? You can use driving time to listen to programmes on sales training, motivation, self-esteem, financial planning, small business strategies or even learning a foreign language.

Neglecting to confirm appointments

We find it amazing that so many people don't confirm meetings before they leave the office or their previous client, and then use 'lost appointments' as some sort of excuse for their poor performance. Why do salespeople fail to confirm appointments? The old standby: fear. Some salespeople fear that, if they call, the person may say, 'Never mind.' Such salespeople would rather drive all the way to a client's office and have the receptionist tell them that the person they were supposed to meet got called out of town for the day. How silly is that?

A quick phone call before you leave may not only save you valuable selling time, but also tells the prospect that you're a professional with something valuable to say. If you handle it properly, your brief call to confirm may keep your appointment from being the one that gets cancelled if your customer needs to change his schedule. When you call to confirm a new appointment, try saying something like this:

> Hi, Jayne. I've just quickly called to double-check on some logistics in preparation for our meeting this afternoon at 2 p.m. I know that these days parking can be a real challenge – can you tell me, where's best place to park and will I need a pocketful of change?

Never say, 'I'm just calling to confirm that our meeting is still convenient.' This can too easily give the prospect a chance to back out. Although you don't want to waste time meeting with people who aren't interested, and so sometimes a cancelled appointment is in fact a blessing, the person may feel that he's not interested because he hasn't yet had the benefit of a demonstration to spark that interest. You need to see him to do your job. Even if the decision-maker does have to cancel, you have him on the phone and so can immediately schedule another appointment. If for some reason you can't get through to the person you have the appointment with, tell the person taking the message that you're on your way and you'll be on time.

Always take the time to confirm your appointments. The time you save is well worth the time you invest, because you free up your time to prospect for new business or to take care of something else on your list.

Watching television mindlessly

Our experience with high achievers shows that they don't waste time watching television. TV watching is probably the single least-productive activity in modern life. We're not going to preach to you about the mindlessness of most of what's on TV these days, but we will say that if you're serious about career success, then you can learn lots of things that will progress your career during that three or more hours each night that TV steals.

What part of the word *no* can't you say?

Many people just can't say no when others want a chunk of their time. But you're better off saying no to someone and getting the job done than saying yes and not getting the job done. Sometimes you're not even the most capable person to do the job. Professionals recognise their limitations and delegate requests for work that's outside their scope to colleagues who are more capable and more likely to complete the job efficiently. If you explain, with warmth and care, the fact that others are better suited to getting the job done properly, the people who ask will appreciate your honesty and your ability to refer them to someone trustworthy to do the job. As you become more successful, your time becomes more valuable, making it all the more important for you to learn when (and how) to say no.

Only you know how much you really watch, so the next time an hour in front of the TV turns into three, stop and ask yourself what else you could have been doing with your time instead.

Handling Physical Interruptions

You should always expect to spend part of your day working with people, supporting your co-workers or helping the company problem-solve. But you also need to allow yourself some *solo time*, both at work and in your personal life. Solo time is time for whatever you need to do. It can be your time for emotional and physical health in your private life, as well as your most productive work time.

During your solo work time, if someone asks, 'Do you have a minute?' just answer, 'Not right now. Can it wait until this afternoon?' By that time, most people who were looking for your help will have solved the problem themselves, or they will have realised that their problem wasn't all that important anyway.

Here are some tips for handling physical interruptions to your solo time:

- ✔ **Rearrange your office so that your desk is out of the line of sight of people who walk down the corridor:** If people don't see you as they're walking down the hall, they're less likely to stop to chat.

- ✔ **Remove extra chairs from your office:** Position any necessary chairs as far away from your desk as possible. This way, people won't be tempted to sit down for long periods of time.

- ✔ **Place a large clock where you and any visitors can see it clearly:** A clock helps you – and your visitors – keep track of how much of your time they're taking up.

- ✔ **Don't look up when someone walks into your office:** This habit is hard to get into, but if you appear to be extremely busy and the potential interruption is nothing serious, most people will simply walk away. This advice may sound cold, but if you can't get your work done, your inefficiency will cause your clients to receive less service, which means you earn a lower income.

To get started on minimising interruptions, keep an interruption log just for one day. In it, record the following:

- ✔ Who interrupted you
- ✔ What time he came and left
- ✔ How much time you wasted
- ✔ What you can do about it

If the same person is interrupting you all the time or the same type of challenge is continually presenting itself, taking a bit of time to train that person or to institute a new procedure can save you a lot of time in the long run.

When an occasional crisis comes up, deal with it quickly and then go right back to your original schedule. You don't have to become antisocial around the office but you may be surprised at how much more efficient you can be when you start taking back stray minutes here and there. Time flies . . . and you never hear the rustle of its gossamer wings.

Chapter 16

Partnering Your Way to Success

*N*o (wo)man is an island – you can't succeed all by your-self. All people need to involve others in their business lives at some point or another, and when it comes to the world of selling, you can partner with people in several different ways. In this chapter, we describe partnerships called *joint ventures* and *affiliate programmes*, but before you dive in, we explain the importance of knowing what you want from a partnership in the first place.

It's just as easy to be taken advantage of in business matters as it is in personal dealings. The advantage of working with others on business matters, however, is that most business-people expect the details of any partnership to be put in writing; that way, everyone knows what they're getting into and how they're going to get out of it if the need arises. As a matter of principle, especially in creating strategic alliances, always make a formal contract and then stick to the agreement.

Knowing What You Want Before You Partner with Anyone

Having a clear idea of what you want in terms of outcome is important before you arrange any partnership. Here are some questions to ask yourself if you're considering seeking out others to assist you in your sales ventures:

✔ What can I offer the other person? (If an arrangement is to be successful, it must benefit the other party as much as you, so be prepared to give equally.)

✔ What's in it for me?

✔ How would having a business partner help grow my business faster?

✔ What capacity would I expect a partner to fulfil?

✔ What qualities are important to me in a partner?

✔ What type of revenue share am I willing to offer?

✔ How many weeks/months do I want to try this partnership?

✔ How will I end a partnership relationship when the time comes?

Arranging Joint Ventures

Joint venture opportunities are a type of partnership where you can test the waters with a partner to see whether you can truly be of benefit to each other. In simple terms, a *joint venture* is where each company promotes the other company's wares to their own client base.

Finding and setting up a joint venture takes time and effort, but doing so can prove to be very beneficial. You begin by seeking out the right partners with the help of the pointers in the following sections.

Knowing where you're aiming

If you already market a beneficial product or service, then establishing a suitable partner is sometimes as simple as talking to the customers that you already sell to in order to learn what else they're spending their monies on. An ideal joint venture partnership is where you share the same type of client base and yet offer non-competing products or services.

For example, if you sell property to individuals and families, who else approaches that same market? Financial services and especially mortgage brokers are obvious ones, but how about furniture companies, garden design companies or even other home improvements, such as conservatory suppliers? All those people work with families and homeowners in a certain geographic area. If they already have a solid base of satisfied clients, these other companies may be interested in helping you get your foot in the door in exchange for you doing the same for them with your existing clients. Rather than just swapping leads, ask the other parties to send an email or other form of sales promotion to their contacts for you. If they can include their glowing endorsement of you and your product as well, all the better.

Your offer must truly be a good match for the partner's client lists. Your goal is to make money or acquire leads, but in the process you want to make the other party look good to its clients.

In addition, think about businesses that offer non-competing products and may enjoy the opportunity to access your client list. For example, if you sell lawn mowers, some of your clients may have a need for occasional help with their landscaping. Find a quality landscaper who you can endorse to your clients and would be willing to give you a referral fee or a percentage of the revenue that your efforts generate.

If you don't own the company you work for, or if you distribute products for another company as a dealer or representative, find out whether you can legally or ethically enter into a joint venture. Some companies treat their client contacts as private, and you may be in breach of your employment agreement with them if you start offering other products to their customers.

Determining who has what you need

You already know what your clients want and need. Think about a compatible product or service that might make a nice addition to your offering or fulfil a need that your clients have mentioned to you. Consider your ideal clients and think about what else they invest their hard-earned income on. For example, if you're a hair stylist, consider partnering with an image consultant. If you sell computer systems, hook up with some software clients or office furniture companies.

Each party in a strategic alliance is primarily thinking of the potential threat to her. The potential partner has spent years growing her business and developing a great reputation. The prime issue is risk. What if you don't deliver as you say? What if her client base and, in turn, her reputation suffers, so damaging her future business? You must satisfy these fears. Find a way for the potential partner to be a client and actually experience the service you offer first hand. Indeed, you need to experience the partner's service as well. Only once both parties are totally happy to pass on to their clients the other's service is a joint venture really going to be productive.

Profiting from cross-promotion

Joint ventures can be wonderful two-way streets. You promote the other party's wares to your own client base, and vice versa. This is called *cross-promotion*. No money changes hands in the setting up of the arrangement; you don't actively collect on your partner's behalf and no subsequent payments need to be made: you process all sales generated by marketing to someone else's list, and she processes all of her sales generated by your list.

Setting parameters on what you'll consider offering to your clients is important. Your client base has taken a lot of time and money and patience to create. The last thing you want to do is damage that healthy reputation by endorsing a product or supplier that either doesn't match your clients' criteria or doesn't deliver and angers those who do purchase.

When you start seeing all the opportunities to generate additional income with different types of partnerships, don't get so excited that you commit to sending out a whole bunch of offers to your clients. Not only do you risk being a pest, but you risk losing their business. Some companies send out offers to their lists every week; some send them out more frequently. Others don't even consider doing it more than once a quarter. Believe us when we say that if you're sending offers that your clients don't want or sending other offers too frequently, they'll let you know – possibly by taking their business elsewhere.

After you find a compatible joint venture partner, you need to determine the style of venture. The following sections take you through the options.

Going for a simple cross-promotion joint venture

The most common joint venture arrangement involves a chosen partner making a discounted offer of its product to your clients and your company being responsible for distribution of the marketing offer message. The partner's promotional copy usually includes a sentence like this: 'Because of our relationship with Acme Print and Design, we've made a special offer to you as a privileged client of theirs.' The result, hopefully, is that some of your client base purchases what's on offer and the partner makes added sales. The partner then returns the favour, and you have a chance to make added sales from your partner's client base.

In this type of simple arrangement, if any of your clients purchase, they do so directly from the partner, and so the 'host' pays no commissions to the partner. Instead, as a fair show of gratitude, the partner company sends out to their client list and their client's purchase directly from you.

The potential concerns are twofold:

- ✔ Your promotion for another partner generates clients for her and she wins in revenue. But when the tables turn and the partner sends your offering to her client base, you get no sales.

- ✔ Clients on your list might purchase and then not be entirely happy with the purchase. As a result, you become tainted in their eyes and possibly lose them as a client.

So you must match carefully with a partner who shares the same target audience and verify the partner's credibility and reliability.

Setting up a shared-revenue joint venture

With cross-promotions in which you share revenue, you give a lot of attention to the money side of the agreement. If the arrangement is a revenue-generation exercise for both parties, then you have a considerable requirement for tracking all sales and for accounting processes.

The revenue share between partners is usually based on the net sale, meaning you get a share of the profit after the partner has taken out all relative costs (cost of creating the products offered, costs of mailing or administration after the sale and so on). Many joint venture partners offer a simple 50/50 split after hard costs are covered. Typically, the split may look something like this:

Product retail investment (made by your clients)	£250
Hard cost	–£50
Net Revenue	£200
50% of balance each to you and partner	£100

In this case, you'd earn £100 for each product sold to a client on your list.

In some cases, the lion's share goes to the party doing the bulk of the work. If you're simply sending an email to your list on behalf of another company, you may get a smaller commission because the other party has spent time and money on creation of the sales email and the website that the email points the recipient towards. Similarly, if you're doing all the work of setting up special web pages, hosting a call centre or handling the fulfilment and tracking of orders, you may get a larger portion of the commission.

Some companies take the lesser share just to entice you to work with them. Frequently, in this type of arrangement, the goal is not about making the initial sale to your clients, but, rather, to capture your clients as their own and upsell them something else later. Again, how this works varies. Some

companies offer you a continuing revenue share from anything the client you brought them purchases from them for all
eternity. Others give you a large revenue share upfront and
nothing on the back end. Whatever the proposed opportunity,
just make sure it'll be worth your while or worth your client's
valuable time before you agree to it.

Benefiting from Affiliate Programmes

An *affiliate programme* is a form of joint venture based around
Internet-based client bases. In simple terms, you deliberately
point your client base towards another partner by using
emails and websites. If done effectively, affiliate programmes
can generate significant revenue for all parties involved.

If you have either a website with decent traffic or a list of clients you think would respond well to a certain product offering, look into some affiliate programmes. Being involved in an
affiliate programme means you're set up to earn commissions
on any sales you generate for someone else. If it's your company that hosts the affiliate programme, you pay others to
generate sales for you. It's a win-win situation either way.

Your involvement in an affiliate programme can be as simple
as making a recommendation to others about a certain product and providing them with a specific link to that product
that tracks their purchases back to you. In some cases, you
only need to place a button-style ad or the company's logo
on your website or in your email messages to participate in
the affiliate programme. It's sort of a by-the-way promotion,
rather than a direct one. You earn a commission for any sales
generated through your link.

Possibly the greatest benefit of this type of arrangement
is that software takes care of the work and you can make
money just by sending an email or adding a logo. If you're
an employee in a sales environment, encourage the marketing department to look into affiliate marketing and to seek to
bring offers and partners to the table that can increase your
client base.

Part V
You Can't Win 'Em All: Keeping the Faith in Sales

In this part...

*I*n this section you gain some insights into the career path that you've chosen and ways in which you can maintain your forward momentum when things don't go your way. Changing tastes and economic climates arise from time to time, and the types of sales that you make will possibly change, too.

Selling is a first-class profession in which you can enjoy superb success – more so than in many other jobs – but it demands constant focus and faith. This Part is to help you stay focused as you ride through these challenges and to help you improve your skills and manage your way towards that success.

Chapter 17

Staying Focused and Positive

*Y*ou're *bound* to experience rejection – it's as inevitable as death and taxes. Equally, you'll experience successful times and times that are hard when the rewards are tougher to capture. That's sales! What will separate you from all those who let themselves get sidetracked by rejection and lean times is your attitude.

So what's the best weapon to use when fighting those inadequate feelings created by failure and rejection? *Enthusiasm!* That one little word, a word you've heard so many times, can make the difference between being a highly successful champion in sales and an ineffective struggler. If you're just going through the motions of selling but doing so with little or no enthusiasm for the job, this will discourage all who might possibly buy from you. And so your poor attitude and low enthusiasm are reflected in your disappointing pay cheque on payday.

External factors such as the economy and family issues can be extremely difficult to handle at times, and all salespeople have days when enthusiasm and energy are elusive. But real winners understand that reflecting their low inner state onto the outer world of prospects does them no favours at all. How you handle yourself during challenging times directly determines your success in sales. So in this chapter, we look at what motivates people and what you can do to increase your own levels of enthusiasm in your selling career and beyond.

Finding Out What Motivates You

Why do you do what you do? Philosophers, psychologists and psychiatrists have had a field day with that question for hundreds of years. And they've come up with a shortlist of the most common reasons people give for doing whatever it is they do. Review the following sections so you can determine what your primary motivator is, and then use that knowledge to spur yourself on to even greater success.

Money

Many professional salespeople admit to being motivated to sell because they enjoy lighting up the faces of the people they help to benefit from their offering. Only the brashest and most outspoken, however, say that money motivates them to sell.

We're not going to lay down a right or wrong here. If money does it for you, that's okay. Give yourself permission right now to admit that money is a big motivator – as long as the money you make is in direct proportion to the service you give your clients. If that's not the case (if you're raking in the dough but providing poor service), your money will soon disappear – as will your motivation to strive toward greater achievements in sales.

Money can be one of your motivators, or even your primary motivator, but it can't be the be-all and end-all of your sales transactions. Many top producers look at the amount of money they make as a reflection of the excellent service and high sales standards they develop over the years in their industries. When champion salespeople notice a decline in income, they look to improve service and product knowledge, instead of wasting time being depressed about how a drop in income could have happened to them.

Security

Many people say they work to have security. Wise indeed, because security relates to protecting and supporting families and living comfortably in retirement years. However, security can be a false motivator because life doesn't come with guarantees.

 You're only as secure as your ability to handle insecurity. No matter who you are, you've never been totally secure. We don't care how successful you are, you've experienced fear and want that challenged your security somewhere along the way. It isn't being free of these feelings that contributes to security, but rather how you deal with the insecurities and fear that confront you.

The key to getting what you want may be the willingness to give up what you have. If you'll never take a chance to further your career, you may as well get out of sales right now because taking risks is what selling is all about. If you can't give up what you have, then keep it; but resign yourself to the knowledge that you'll never go much farther up the ladder of success.

 Most famous and powerful people who've acquired a great deal of security have also lost as much (if not more) than they've made. What sets these people apart from the average worker is that they were willing to take the chance in order to become all that they could be, whereas the average worker isn't willing to take the necessary risks.

 Great salespeople follow the same pattern. Be willing to give up what you have for what you can attain. Be a risk taker. Circumstances, people, industries and even countries might change, but within you is the ability to succeed, and when you have this knowledge, you're always secure.

Achievement

Everyone wants to achieve something. Some people strive only for modest goals, whereas others shoot for the stars – but all want to achieve more. In fact, few people are born who wander aimlessly through life without, at the very least, the desire to achieve the basic needs of food and shelter.

All people believe that they should get what they deserve, and, unfortunately, many of them feel they're deserving of greatness, whether they work for it or not. In those moments when you're brutally honest with yourself, you probably realise that the results you're getting are equal to the effort you expend.

Achievement isn't always measured monetarily. In sales, achievement is measured by sales targets (meeting or beating them) and being given larger territories or levels of responsibility, such as being asked to train or mentor others. In your personal life, you can measure achievement by the influence and power you wield or by the humanitarian efforts you give to those in need. Achievement means different things to different people – but it's usually a great motivator.

Recognition

For most people, the need for recognition begins in childhood. Think about it: when you were five or six years old, you probably stood on your head, acted mini dramas for your parents or did other 'look at me' type things that adults thought were adorable, just so you'd get attention. In adult life, for many that need or desire to be noticed and recognised is still very strong. Salespeople receive recognition when they win sales contests or annual sales awards. There's nothing like standing on the stage at the annual company meeting and listening to the applause of your peers and the other company team members because you did something spectacular for the company.

Acceptance from others

Acceptance from others, especially those whom we hold in esteem, is a common and powerful motivator. Relying on acceptance from others for motivation, though, can be a dangerous thing. The day you rise above the masses as a top producer is the same day that others stop trying to climb up to your level and instead try to pull you down. The old adage 'It's lonely at the top' is true.

The acceptance you seek often backfires. If you push higher than all around you, the other salespeople who don't try as hard see that they could have done better. And instead of using that as a lever to motivate themselves, they try to absolve their guilt by pulling you down or minimising your achievements. If acceptance from others is a key driver for you, try to understand what it is you want others to accept in you. Best of all, work on self-acceptance (see the next section).

 Try to surround yourself with positive people who support you in your efforts toward a successful career. Why not make it your philosophy to keep company with people who have similar goals and desires as yours? Seek acceptance from people you know are good for you and stay away from negative people: they only pull your opportunities down the tubes with them.

Self-acceptance

When you accept yourself and you're happy with the person you are, you experience a freedom you may never have thought possible. Achieving self-acceptance is critical to overall success in both sales and in life. When you have it, you're free to do things your own way or not to do them at all. You're free to enjoy life and all the wonders it has to offer. You're free of the damaging effects of rejection and failure. After you achieve this motivator, there's no going back. You are your own person. You know what you want and how to get it, and you go after it with all of your heart.

The very picture of motivation

Pictures are powerful motivators. For many years now Ben has thoroughly appreciated what works as motivation for him. Although recognition on stage and acclaim from clients who've been helped is powerful, real motivation comes from only one source – his children. He keeps pictures of them in his wallet, and each day he looks at them and imagines the smiles on their faces when they see and hear what he's done.

You may prefer a picture of your dream car or country home or sunshine villa, in your wallet, stuck on your wall or set as your computer's screensaver. Whatever you choose, focus on it and before long your picture will become reality.

Most people measure their success by how much money they have, so, self-acceptance for them comes as a result of making money. When you truly accept yourself, you can do what you *want* to do and not what you think you *should* do. You realise that actually money is of very little importance overall. Life is much sweeter when you accept yourself – and wonderful things and people seem to gravitate towards you.

Knowing What De-motivates You

If motivators are what make people move forward toward successful sales careers and de-motivators cause them to stop dead in their tracks or even go backward, why doesn't everyone just do the things that motivate them? Believe it or not, the answer is because the average human being is more de-motivated than motivated. Negativity is kind of like gravity – a powerful force that can hold you back and requires tremendous effort to overcome.

Just as you need to know what motivates you to succeed, you also need to recognise the danger signals that will bring your career to a halt. Here are four of the most powerful de-motivators that stop people from achieving.

Loss of security

A big de-motivator for many people is the fear of losing their security – financially or otherwise. Some people are nervous about being in a commission-only arrangement in sales where if they don't sell, they don't get paid. Others simply see security in a salary and fear anything that isn't fixed. The truth, however, is that nothing is certain and even salaried employment can vanish at a moment's notice.

Security is only internal. If you're committed and dedicated enough to push to learn and thus you enjoy success, then you will always be secure, because everyone wants to hire someone who succeeds! Job security is earned, not a right.

Self-doubt

Self-doubt is a big de-motivator in selling. You may hear the odd negative comment from family and friends and wonder whether you're in the right job when other people you know are in 'safer' occupations. Their job is really no safer, but it's definitely less rewarding when compared with the endless bonuses and income gains you can make as you become more professional and competent as a salesperson.

Most beginners in sales busy themselves with the unnecessary question of 'What did I do wrong?' when they don't succeed in their selling attempts. The difference between champions and novices is that champions ask themselves a different question: 'What did I do *right*?' When the champion examines what was right about the sale, he can easily keep doing what was right over and over again. The champion in sales has realised that the only way you ever learn what to do right in selling is by doing it wrong, keeping your enthusiasm, figuring out what to do and overcoming that pain. Just keep on keeping on!

The only way to overcome fears is to face them. As bestselling author Susan Jeffers says, 'Feel the fear and do it anyway.' Look doubts in the eye and stare them down by doing the exact opposite of what they make you feel like doing. Don't give in to your self-doubts. Develop strong habits, such as well-honed sales skills, post-sales analyses and keeping good notes for yourself.

Home life issues

Personal de-motivation can occur when your home life faces emotional challenges. A sad fact is that many people experience a marriage breakup, a health scare, difficult times with children or wider family issues. No-one is immune, and all of these things can become painful distractions from the task of selling. You must accept these times and aim to do as best you can in the circumstances.

However, in today's world, money helps with most things! The best strategy for emotionally surviving hard times is to focus slightly harder on your career and income and to stay clear-headed. At least if your income enables you to keep everything together in other aspects of your life, then you'll be able to see light at the end of the tunnel. Remembering this can help you get through the tough times.

Fear of failure

A great many people are so afraid of failing that they just quit trying. If ever there was a recipe for not failing, then it's to never attempt anything in the first place! Of course, you won't experience any successes either, so you throw out the baby with the bathwater if you let this de-motivator get the better of you. If you never meet the client, you never close the sale.

We recommend that you live by this principle: do what you fear the most – and you control your fear.

If you're filled with dread at the thought of phoning for appointments, for example, then you're going to need to face the fear and deal with it if you truly want to succeed in sales. Besides, almost anything you do that you once feared doing turns out to be much easier than you thought. By just facing what you fear you're pretty certain to eradicate obstacles and go on to enjoy a happy and successful career path.

Change

Change is a fierce opponent of progress. You've probably often heard statements such as these: 'We've always done it this way', 'You'll get used to it – it's just my way of doing things' or 'We prefer to stay with the standard procedure'. Workers really don't favour the old ways, though; they merely don't fancy changing, because something new represents challenges and short-term discomforts.

As an example, the hardest thing for most salespeople to do is to prospect. (Wouldn't it be so much nicer if you simply opened the door or sat next to the telephone and enquiring buyers flooded your way? Dream on!) But if you can push yourself to make your calls, then you're on the road to sales success.

By the way, doing what you don't want to do is what you're paid the most to do. You really have to *want* to change. Being satisfied with yourself today is still crucial, but if you want more tomorrow, then you must be willing to put up with the pain of change. According to Dr Maxwell Maltz, former plastic surgeon and developer of psycho-cybernetics, it takes 21 days to effect change. So you'll need about 21 days of concentrating and studying the material in this book for this material to become a part of you. No pain, no gain.

The champion salesperson's anti-failure formula

What's the first word you picked up from your mother and father when you were a baby? *No*. Ah, those were the days, weren't they? And why do you suppose *no* was the first word you learned? Because your parents wanted to protect you from painful experiences.

But all you knew as a child was that *no* kept you from getting what you wanted. So, as you grew older and kept hearing *no*, you didn't give up quite as easily as when you were a baby. You caught on to this persuasion stuff early on when you realised that *no* doesn't necessarily mean 'No! Absolutely not! Never! No way!' and you tried to cajole your parents to see things differently – even if it involved holding your breath and turning several lovely shades of blue.

The same thing happens in your selling career. When you begin in sales and you hear *no*, you think it's the end of the discussion. Some salespeople relate stories from early in their careers about how they never got completely through their prepared presentation because the moment the client said *no* the salespeople slid out the door quicker than a rat up a drainpipe.

As they matured in sales, though, their stories changed. *No* took on different meanings. *No* came to mean many things besides a plain-old, final, everyday *no*. These salespeople began to realise that *no* could mean 'Slow down', 'Explain that part a little more', 'You haven't presented the feature I'm most interested in yet', 'You need to ask more questions about my likes and dislikes' or 'I don't want to part with that much money right now'. These salespeople realised – as one of their first steps toward professionalism – that they could overcome *all* those things instead of having to slip out the back door with their tails tucked between their legs.

To help you stay sane in this crazy world of selling, try using this approach to rejection:

> Suppose that you earn £500 for the closing of a sale. So one sale = £500. For the sake of this formula, imagine that, for every ten contacts you make, you receive one sale. So ten contacts = one sale. So every contact, whether it results in a *yes* or a *no*, is worth £50. Every rejection you get earns you £50! And you're now one step closer to that £500.

Keep working at your performance and constantly striving to improve, but avoid berating yourself when you don't succeed every time. Better instead to remind yourself that every call you make is worthwhile, whether you sell or not.

Surveying Strategies for Overcoming Failure

As a salesperson (especially if you're new to sales) you'll experience non-success (another word for failure) at least once or twice a day. How you handle that experience determines how far and how fast you start seeing sales or persuasion success.

When you demonstrate your product to an uninterested party, when you're rejected by a prospect or when you thought you had your offering sold and the transaction falls through, you can react in one of two ways: you can get angry and be unproductive, or you can investigate the reasons for the failure. We recommend the second of these two options, because when you discover what went wrong, you can prevent those pitfalls from happening again.

Look at the tremendous negatives Thomas Edison overcame when he invented the light bulb. Edison performed more than 1,000 failed experiments before he succeeded. But because of his persistence, today we have the light bulb, an invention that has changed mankind's quality of life. Can you imagine receiving a big fat *no* to what you want to achieve more than 1,000 times – and still persisting? What fortitude! The priceless part of the story of the light bulb, though, is Edison's comments in response to questions about how he felt after experiencing all that failure: 'I did not fail a thousand times. I only learned a thousand ways that it wouldn't work.' You see? It's all in the way you look at things. Failing is not failing if you learn from the experience.

When things haven't gone as well as you wished, then don't get despondent. Instead, take a breather and then, on another day, review what you did and said. Look for clues as to how you can improve for the next time. If you always practise this, then you constantly improve.

You struggle when a client gives you no negative feedback and appears to love everything presented in your offering, yet still decides not to buy. Ask for feedback, because the comments can assist greatly in increasing your future success rates.

Selling is a percentages game – a game of numbers. The person who sees more people and faces more rejection also makes more money. So, even if you haven't gambled before, you begin to do just that when you get into the game of sales. With every *no* you hear, you're one step closer to hearing a *yes*.

In life, it's not the number of times you fail that counts, but how you react when you do fail. Those who ultimately win in the game of selling and life are the ones who keep fighting back, even if they lose the last round. You only ever fail when you stop trying.

Doing the Opposite of What Average Salespeople Do

On the surface, no huge difference exists between average salespeople and top earners. They all work to find potential clients. They all qualify clients, present information and products, handle concerns and close sales. The main difference is the point where they give up when the going gets tough. Successful people keep going at the point where average people stop.

Another way successful salespeople differ from their average counterparts is in time management. Average salespeople don't plan their time effectively. Successful salespeople know what time of day is best for selling. That's when they sell, instead of doing paperwork, and they're systematised and proficient so that they can be fully ready when opportunities arise.

A final point of difference is that average salespeople just don't want to work very hard, whereas successful salespeople know the harder they work, the more they earn. Consider the wise words of a true sales leader, J. Douglas Edwards: 'Selling is the highest-paid hard work and the lowest-paid easy work there is.'

Mixing Your Personal Life with Your Professional Life

To succeed in any business, but especially a sales business, you need to focus and maintain a clear mind. So separate your working issues from your personal issues. The client you call on a Monday morning doesn't need to hear all about your woes from a family weekend gone wrong!

Having said that, selling is a 'people' process. Winning in selling is winning with people, and sharing stories and accounts of your life makes you appear real to a client.

A personal connection is more important than ever in these days of intense competition in almost every arena. Go back even 15 years and many fields of industry had one or two dominant players and little in the way of competition. Today, however, it's increasingly difficult to differentiate, when buying, between offering A and offering B. Thus, often the only real differentiator in the buying process is the individual – you.

Your prospect won't connect with you if you're only a salesperson. He'll be suspicious of much of what you say and believe that you're only talking him around to get a deal. If you connect on a personal level, however, he's more likely to like and trust you.

So, talking incessantly about your child's football games, bicycle riding, hillwalking and screaming children at teatime might be a bit much, but sharing a little when appropriate is beneficial. Indeed, it might be appropriate to share more private comments if you've already built up a good relationship with the client. We know of many times when a client relationship of several years' standing has developed into a close friendship. With these types of relationships, sharing more heartfelt life challenges might be a perfectly acceptable and even helpful approach. Your friend and client can then possibly compensate for any slippage in service that might happen whilst your eye is off the ball, so to speak.

Usually, you're able to gauge the friendliness of a business relationship. However, as a guide, you might look to share insights and comments on a par with the comments your prospect shares with you; thus, talking about your family life only on a very nominal level until he shares on a slightly deeper and more personal level with you. Then, reciprocating in a like manner shows him that he's not over-exposed or vulnerable. Sharing helps deepen your connection and is always good for sales.

Chapter 18

Setting Goals to Stay Focused

. . . .

In This Chapter

▶ Achieving balance in the goals you set

▶ Managing activities for goal achievement

▶ Writing down goals to make them real

▶ Maintaining motivation after you've achieved your identified goals

. . . .

Success should be something you feel strongly about. The journey along the path to your targeted outcome will be challenging – at times extremely so, depending upon the goals you've set – and so success has to be something that means a lot to you otherwise you simply won't achieve it. Those who achieve the most usually burn with a *have-to* not a *want-to* attitude.

If you have no concrete goals and you've been succeeding in spite of yourself, just think of how much *more* success you'd enjoy if you set your sights on a definite path and had a specific time frame in which you expected to reach your destination. If you're a newcomer to sales and you think you don't need to set goals, think again. The sooner you map a course for success, the more likely you are to achieve what you want.

Even though you don't *need* to set goals, most professionals who fail to set goals reach a certain success level and then plateau. They lack either the motivation or the direction to go beyond it. Having a set of clearly identifiable and written goals helps you to

✔ Stay motivated

✔ Stay focused

✔ Know when to celebrate

In this chapter, we give you the information you need to make goal setting a part of your daily life.

Setting Realistic and Effective Goals

When you first considered a career in sales, you probably had some vague notions of success in mind. Now it's time to turn those notions into specific, vivid pictures of your soon-to-be reality. Those pictures will keep you going on those cold, wet Monday mornings when you really don't feel like facing yet another week of hard work.

Set your personal goals when you feel relaxed and clear-headed, because you want the goals to mean a lot to you. Give yourself the time and privacy you need in order to think about what would make you happy and then write down end goals and big picture outcomes so that you stretch yourself a little into 'Wow!' territory! Your goals may change over time, but having them to focus and drive you is essential.

Goals work better when they're SMART:

✔ **Specific:** Not just 'more money', but £100,000 a year.

✔ **Measurable:** Ensure you can track progress along the way.

✔ **Achievable:** A goal that you can reach but that stretches you.

✔ **Realistic:** Within your capabilities. A goal of being company president by your next birthday, knowing that you're a newbie in your mid-20s, is a tad unrealistic!

✔ **Time-framed:** Company president by your 40th birthday may be realistic, and it has a specific timeframe too.

When you're in the beginning stages of goal setting, keep the following rules in mind to help yourself form and stay committed to what's important in your life:

✓ **The goal must be better than your best – but believable:** Don't set a goal that you don't truly believe you can reach. The trick to setting goals is to make them high enough to push you to strong levels of performance, yet reasonable enough that you can envision reaching them.

✓ **Set goals based on productivity, not just on production:** If you set goals based only on the money you want to make, you're setting yourself up for failure. Better to set productivity goals: a guideline for how many people you must contact in a week, for example, or how many calls you must make. Actively pursue your productivity goals, and increased production will result.

Breaking Down Your Goals into Smaller Steps

When you're setting goals, always begin with long-term goals and work backward to medium-range and short-term goals. The next sections help you set all three kinds of goals.

Long-term goals

Times have changed somewhat in recent years. Technological and communication advances have resulted in a pace of change faster than ever before in history. Thus you're better setting a long-term goal for 10 years' time, not for 20 or more years. The far distance in the future is too hard to imagine!

An area to include when you set your long-term goals is personal accomplishments, including health, lifestyle and net worth. When you set long-term goals, be specific. Instead of saying, 'In ten years, I want to live in a large house and be financially independent', write something like this:

In ten years, by the first of June, I will live in a £500,000 home in the suburbs of my city with an acre of gardens for my children and I to enjoy.

Get the picture? Your long-range goals, as with all your goals, don't have to be grand, but they do need to be this specific.

Medium-term goals

When you finish setting your long-term goals, cut them in half and set medium-range goals for about five years down the road. Compare your ten-year goals to your five-year goals and then determine the activity you need to keep to make those goals a reality. The question to ask is: 'What do I need to attain in five years' time to make sure that I'm on track to achieving the long-term goal?' This question might then direct you, for example, to a specific level of income that you can consider as a step in the right direction, and so it would serve as a mid-range income goal.

Your medium-range goals may well be your largest and perhaps fuzziest area, and the goals you adjust the most frequently. They do need to be specific, but possibly allow yourself a little more slack. You'll hit your end goals if you remain focused, but allowing circumstance to impact the route isn't the same as losing sight of and not hitting the goal.

Short-term goals

Your short-term goals cascade downwards from the medium-range goals. Thus you might select your short-term goal by asking clear questions such as: 'What can I attain by one year from now?' This would then lead to a direct component part of the five-year goal being chosen as the one-year goal. Your question is: 'What do I need to achieve in this year to make sure that I'm on track to achieve that goal in five years?' For example, if your five-year career progression goal is to be a proven sales manager at your company, then it might be that you aim in the short term is to become a senior account executive and actively supervise, possibly whilst the manager is on holiday.

Immediately after you set short-term goals, start taking steps to achieve them. That way they take root as real. Break your one-year goals down into six-month goals, one-month goals and, eventually, today's steps in your planner. For example, if one of your short-term goals is to improve your health, start a 'Watch what I eat and take regular exercise' plan now. So take the stairs, not the lift, and opt for salad at lunch rather than chips. Your one-year short-term goal starts with action steps today!

Looking at Particular Types of Goals

You can and should consider setting goals in all areas of your life. You're not all about work. You must consider personal health, family and community goals as well as a balance of spiritual and educational arenas too. The sections that follow offer insight into setting goals for business and your personal life.

Sales-specific goals

Selling is both an art and a science. Knowing the numbers you plan to achieve and how they break down is critical to the science side of selling. This is where you develop your own personal measurements to help you know whether you're on track to your chosen achievements.

Sales newbies may need a little extra help in setting goals for their selling lives. Your sales manager can probably assist you, but be aware that any 'goals' she helps you set may look more like company targets. You see, every manager has a certain sales revenue amount she needs to meet for the overall company goals. Most managers spread that quota out among the various members of the sales team. Usually, this is based on the manager's belief in the abilities of each salesperson to produce.

You must take control of your own personal contribution towards goals, but more importantly, take control of what you need to achieve to hit your personal target of income and progress. Here are the steps to follow to be certain of achieving the outcome goals you desire:

1. **Determine what you believe you can have as an annual income goal.**

2. **Divide the amount from Step 1 by 12 to find your monthly income goal.**

3. **Divide the amount from Step 2 by 4 (the number of weeks in a month) to find your weekly goal.**

4. **Divide the amount from Step 3 by the number of days you work each week at making sales.**

Now you know how much income you need to generate each day in order to reach your annual goal.

5. **Take the average amount you earn for yourself from
   each sale and divide it into the money amounts for
   annual, monthly, weekly and daily goals from Steps
   1 through 4.**

6. **Consider how many presentations you need to make
   to get the number of sales you came up with in Step
   5. For example, if you typically close one sale for
   every three presentations, your sales conversion
   ratio is 1:3. So, you would multiply the numbers in
   Step 5 by 3 to get the number of presentations you
   need to make.**

7. **Take your sales conversion ratio from Step 6 and
   figure out how many contacts you need to make to
   get the necessary number of presentations to make
   the sales and earn the income.**

Table 18-1 is a chart that you can use to break down your own
numbers. We've included an illustrative set of numbers so
that you can see how it works. Remember, no right or wrong
exists, merely a set of numbers that tracks your progress and
that you can focus on to always improve.

Table 18-1	Sales Goal Setting Chart			
	Annual	*Monthly*	*Weekly*	*Daily*
Income	£40,000			
Number of sales	40 (average income per sale £1,000)			
Number of presentations	400 (1:10 presen-tations becomes a sale)			
Number of contacts	2,000 (1:5 calls becomes a presentation)			

Grab a calculator and play with the numbers until you set
sales goals that feel just right. They should be a bit of a
stretch for you above and beyond where you are now, but
they must be believable!

If any of the numbers you compute along the way in this exercise cause you to doubt your belief that you can achieve the goal, stop. Think about solutions you could implement to make the goal a reality. Do you need to sharpen your skills to increase your ratio? Are you setting your expectations unrealistically high as to the number of people you need to contact *every* day based on your current level of productivity? Can you change? Are you willing to?

Personal goals

Setting personal as well as career goals is important to keep your life well balanced. If all your goals are business goals, you'll have trouble taking time out for family and friends – who are your true support system – because you'll always be pushing toward the next career goal.

Although we encourage you to pursue your business goals with fervour, we also encourage you not to pursue them at the expense of family, friends or time out for yourself. If you do, you risk becoming so single-minded that you eliminate the human qualities you need in order to succeed in sales. Nobody wants to do business with someone who's too busy to understand and care about her needs. Setting personal goals gives you life both in and after business.

Other areas of personal goal setting include making time to develop your spiritual life, exercising so you'll be in great physical condition to enjoy the fruits of your labours and setting goals for continued education outside of sales such as learning more about your favourite hobby.

Share some of your bigger picture goals with your family and friends, especially the non-work ones, so they can share in them. Their involvement can be an added lever to your achieving your goals.

Fulfilling Your Goals

Follow these five steps for goal achieving, and you'll be on the straight-and-narrow road to reaching your goals because you'll be focused both consciously and subconsciously on seeking out the means to your chosen ends:

1. **Set goals that you want more than anything**
2. **Vividly imagine your goals, and create a clear picture of them in your mind**
3. **Get your goals down on paper**
4. **Commit to your goals sincerely and completely**
5. **Review your goals daily and take the necessary action steps you've chosen**

Although all these tasks are important, two take precedence: making your goals real by writing them down and making them visual, and committing to them fully. The following sections focus on these two important actions.

Putting the goal down on paper

After you've set your goals, you need to make your final commitment to them by putting them in writing. Writing down your goals takes them from a virtual world of imagination and mental activity into a physical world of actual manifestation. Its no longer a thought, it's a physical item, even if only a piece of paper at this time. After you write them down, your mind starts seeking out whatever it takes to make those goals a reality.

Writing down your goals helps you do what we call *in-your-face goals viewing.* An even more powerful and in-your-face method is to make a vision board of the goals that you've set. Spend an hour or so searching the Internet for images that clearly relate to the goals you've chosen. So, for example, select the type of home you want to purchase one day or the type of car you want to drive. For monetary amounts select newspaper headlines or figures from lottery websites or the like. Print off the images and paste them collage-style on a board. Put your vision board in a position where you see it every morning and night so that your subconscious mind is triggered into getting what you really desire. Fire up your subconscious and dreams become reality!

Committing completely

If you want your life to change, *you* have to change it – or you'll stay pretty much the same as you are. So set some goals that excite you and get your life into gear. All you have to do is make the effort. You can change and become or do anything you want. Just want it badly enough!

Equal opportunity exists in the world of selling. Therefore, you *can* attain anything you want if you consistently take the right actions. Consider where you got the idea for your goal. Most likely you saw someone else attain it and thought 'I want that for me'. Thus if someone else can attain what you want, it's attainable. The only question is whether you want it sufficiently to work hard enough and possibly make the sacrifices along the way in order to make it happen.

The harder you work toward a goal, the sweeter the taste of success. If you doubt that, ask any Olympic medal winner. Don't think for a second that your road to success won't be painful at times. If you don't experience at least a little bit of stretching to achieve your goals and some sacrificing of the comfortable habits along the way, you probably haven't set them high enough to challenge you. And if your goals *aren't* high enough then they may be holding you back, making you content to remain at levels that are no big deal for you. You want them higher. You need to push.

So when the road gets rocky, dig in your heels and let nothing distract you from your goals. The people who persevere today produce tomorrow. Giving up immediate gratification or postponing what would satisfy you for today just for a promise of greater things down the road isn't natural in today's instant-gratification society. But don't sell yourself short by settling for what you know will bring you only temporary satisfaction. If you settle for less than your goals, that's exactly what you end up with – less.

Figuring Out What to Do When You Achieve Your Goals

The funny thing about achieving your goals is that as you get close to achieving them and you look back the struggle to achieve them doesn't seem as difficult as you'd originally thought. Time has a way of blurring the gory details of the daily grind. For example, think back now to what you were doing five years ago. Now think forward five years. Which seems longer? If you're like most people, the future always seems to loom out there longer because you don't know everything that will happen and how your life will take shape.

But when you get in the habit of setting goals, you find yourself looking toward the next set of goals before you close on those you're about to achieve – and that's a good thing to do. You don't want to wait to set new goals until you're done with the ones you have today. Keeping your eyes on the future and the opportunities it can bring your way has many advantages. Soon you get so caught up in the goal-setting process that achieving your goals becomes reward enough.

When you achieve your goals, one of the first things you want to do is celebrate your success. When you celebrate, keep these suggestions in mind:

✔ **Include in your celebration everyone you involved in the setting and accomplishing of your goals:** They were there with you in the beginning, and they'll be eager to rejoice with you in your successes.

✔ **Celebrate in proportion to your achievement:** It's good that you diligently worked on the telephone and overcame the hardest part of all for most of us, the prospecting, and so a reward is deserved – but maybe a night out, not a two-week holiday!

✔ **Keep your energy up and your focus keen:** If you do reward yourself with a holiday or a little time off, keep your energy and focus towards the end goal sharp and tuned. The longer you remain inactive, the harder it is to get revved up again. Play a while, but then head back to work.

After you celebrate, start working on the new goals you set. Keep records of all your successes. When they start piling up, you'll want to do whatever it takes to add to that pile. Remember the difficulties you overcame while you accomplished each preceding goal; mentally reward yourself for your successes. When you do set the next goal, push yourself just a tad more. Always stretch yourself; that's what keeps you growing in sales. If everything's too easy, you get bored – and selling stops being a hobby and looks more and more like a job.

The Law of Expectation

Most people have experienced the phenomenon of fulfilled expectations, but they tend to shrug off fulfilled expectations as coincidences rather than planned, envisioned events.

The Law of Expectation states otherwise:

When you think something will happen, and you feel strongly about it, you will bring about its happening.

We think this is where the phrase 'Mind over matter' came from. The Law of Expectation works with simple things, as well as with matters as complicated as achieving your ten-year goals.

For example, one evening a friend of ours left home to take a walk. All she took with her were the keys to her apartment (and, of course, the clothes on her back and the shoes on her feet). She'd been out for about an hour and was returning home right around dark when she felt a grate beneath her feet. No sooner did she feel the grate than the thought crossed her mind that if she dropped her keys into the grate she wouldn't be able to get back into her apartment because her husband was away on a three-day business trip. What do you suppose happened? You got it! The keys fell into the grate and left our friend with the dilemma of finding the best way to break into her own apartment.

Now because our friend learns from every situation, even the negative ones, after the whole ordeal she sat down to record what her experience had taught her. One of the things she learned was the power of her thoughts. But she learned something else just as important. When she finally broke into her apartment, she realised just how easy the task really was. The next day she went to the hardware store and bought various goodies that, after she installed them, made breaking in difficult if not impossible. She avoided a dangerous situation (a possible burglary) by being open to learning from what began as a negative experience.

So be your own fortune-teller. Predict your own success by making your goals happen. The more you believe in your own success, the more you'll do to turn your goals into realities. Success is no accident! You plan it, you work on it, you monitor it and you adjust it to enable yourself to enjoy a productive and prosperous life. People may look at the success you've spent years accomplishing and see you as an overnight wonder. They may even try to tell you how lucky you are to have the things you have. Well, we say you create your own luck. You control your own destiny. Lady Luck has little to do with your success, and she shouldn't get the credit for your achievements.

The harder the goal is to achieve, the more value you find in its achievement. Don't wait until you fully achieve one goal before you set your next one. Have your new goal already in place so that you're ready to start the necessary steps to make you succeed again.

Chapter 19

Selling in a Challenging Economy

. . . .

In This Chapter

▶ Maintaining sales momentum by watching economic cycles

▶ Spotting the bright lights of sales opportunity in a downturn

▶ Making technology work for you

▶ Enhancing client loyalties to sustain performance

▶ Staying positive

▶ Preparing for recovery

. . . .

*I*t doesn't matter what your product or service is, at some stage business bites. When the economy slows down, it doesn't stop. When times get tougher, sales don't totally dry up. But those with money to spend are more careful about where they spend it. So to maintain your income when things get tight, you have to be smart.

Don't panic! The sky won't fall in and the world won't end. Client accounts change, but they always bounce back, and so do economies. You don't need to fear slowdowns in the economy. By following the guidance in this chapter, you can win new business and retain existing clients, remaining secure in your job.

Understanding the Economic Cycle

Moods fluctuate, seasons shift and fashions change. Nothing in life is stable to the point of never experiencing volatility. It follows that whatever you might be involved in selling, changing fashions and tastes might affect its popularity, and local and global economic fluctuations will shift and impact what sells, and in what volumes.

Understanding that economies and buying habits change is crucial, and knowing a little about why and how they change, and even knowing enough to foresee signs of change and act accordingly, can be useful.

History demonstrates that the good times – the periods of economic boom – are linked to high consumer demand and higher production of goods, especially for export and international trade. Boom phases might last for six or seven years, before customers begin to lose their lust for acquiring ever more goods and innovators and producers stop pushing for new goods and start to consolidate what they've already created. Production slows down. A slowdown then triggers a lack of confidence and a fall in profits from businesses. This confidence issue is what ignites a recession.

Generally, in a *recession,* businesses trim back their workforces to cut their costs, if sales are down, and the rise in unemployment means that more people have less money to spend. The situation spirals into a recession because, without spending consumers, businesses cannot sell what they create. Businesses then do not purchase from suppliers, and so all business slows down.

It's not all doom and gloom, though. The good news is that these periods last approximately 12 years typically from *peak* (the boom) to *trough* (a recession), and after each recession, the new business that grows is fresh and exciting and invigorating, much like the way a forest rises again from the ashes after a fire. Often, this regrowth ushers in a new technology or advancement that everyone benefits from.

The key to your survival and success is understanding economic cycles, knowing that they happen, learning from them and expecting the best but preparing for the worst. Times may get tougher, but as the saying goes, 'When the going gets tough, the tough get going.' Your time to shine is now, and if an economic cycle takes some of the shine off, don't worry, with hard work and focus you'll soon be soaring again.

Spotting Thriving Economies

Recognising the basic indicators of economic cycles is a key skill, but so is understanding that things aren't always black and white. A recession doesn't have the same 'blanket effect' on everyone, and even when one cycle dips, that doesn't mean *all* cycles dip. For example, when fashions drive shoppers away from beef because of a health scare about cattle, they don't all avoid meat entirely, and sales of poultry or veal or pork may climb as people change what food they buy in response to the scare. Similarly, when people worry about the cost of fuel for cars, then trains and public transport thrive, as do technologies that facilitate remote rather than face-to-face communication, like video messaging. As the saying goes, 'One person's meat is another's poison.' When one area struggles, another can flourish, and the effective salesperson is one who can spot those thriving areas.

When confidence drops and spending slows down, there are two key factors you need to remember:

- ✓ **Selling activity aimed at the higher income and wealth brackets is usually less affected and more stable, so reconsider whom you are targeting.** A section of the population enjoys a level of wealth that, whilst it is affected by economics and slowdowns, isn't affected to the extent that it shows in their everyday lives. The very wealthy might see values of stocks or investments drop but still have several millions of pounds, so in real terms they aren't affected on a day-to-day basis and can continue to spend.

- ✓ **For a market to completely collapse is extremely rare, so stay calm and focus your efforts on the survivors.** In times of boom, optimism is infectious and businesses do well. Confidence becomes even more evident in the increasing numbers of start-up businesses. When times are good these new businesses can steal a little of the market share and get themselves going. However, when times slow down, the customer becomes more choosy. Consumers are unlikely to stop spending completely. A more likely scenario is that they become choosier about where they purchase from, so the market shrinks rather than collapses. The smaller, newer businesses are the ones that suffer first. Often, they aren't well enough established with a large enough client base to ride out the tough lean spending period, so they die off. This then leads to the marketplace being less thinly spread, so when one company closes others surviving in the same field often thrive as they pick up the now-defunct company's clients.

Some well-heeled and proven suppliers may not see a drop-off in their levels of trade as they already have a loyal client base that still needs what they're purchasing.

If you're to succeed as a sales professional in a challenging economy, you need to do well at spotting what's good right now. Look for job adverts where companies are still recruiting staff – usually a good indicator of their confidence and performance. Also look at where you see friends and neighbours still spending, and watch the news for stories of new contracts being awarded to companies in your area. Considering what problems people might be experiencing as a result of harder times can also be a champion strategy and can lead to new boom areas for you.

'Necessity is the mother of invention', or so the saying goes, and this is because a need or a problem somewhere usually drives a solution. Thus, if you see a need or struggle being created by a lack of spending and a recession, providing a solution opens companies up to better performances. As an example, if companies are feeling the pinch and cutting their spending, one of the first areas traditionally cut is that of advertising spend. But companies still need to attract clients, so they usually swing away from traditional advertising techniques towards technology as they perceive this to still be able to attract clients but without the huge advertising spend. As a result, many website development and Internet-marketing companies have boomed. This creates new sales opportunities.

As a final example of how to spot opportunity in a challenging economy, imagine that you're selling technology software systems that you usually sell to local governments. But during a recession, public spending dries up and you struggle to secure sales in your usual market. 'Good grief!' you think. 'That's my career in free fall.' But hang on; try approaching the issue from another angle. Go beyond the norm to think of other avenues for sales. This is a wonderful opportunity to broaden your market base and reach mainstream corporates where many office functions are extremely similar and thus your software would be appreciated.

Knowing and spotting patterns in these ways can be a lifeline. Thinking sideways or outside the box and asking questions like 'What problem is this lean time creating?' leads you to pathways where solutions are being provided and money is still flowing, even in challenging times. And another tip – keep an eye on the construction industry. House building is usually the first industry that slows when a recession is looming and the first sector to pick up again when better times are on their way.

Smoothing Out the Dip with Technology

Economic challenges put a lot more pressure on salespeople to perform. If the usual customers are spending less, or spending less frequently, then you usually feel that you must approach a greater volume of prospects in order to maintain your sales targets. For example, a closing ratio of 1:5 can slip to 1:10 and an average spend per order of £600 may now be as low as £400. So you have to see almost three times as many prospects in order to hit the same overall sales volume.

Not only do you need to reach out to more prospects, but you may find that the selling process slows as well. Times are tougher and prospects are a little warier, so they may require more time with you and more effort from you to gain the required confidence to buy.

Now's the time to embrace technology. When the economy slows, technology industries that offer the promise of cheap enquiries and easier sales' funnels all enjoy huge increases. Use:

✔ **Automated email systems:** Using an automation program enables you to massively increase the volume of mail you send and to schedule it for later if you're busy on another task. Automation allows for a huge leverage in your time, and huge increase in reach.

✔ **Customer relationship management software:** Investing time into a system such as this enables you to record details of your conversations with clients and contacts that you can then relay back to them at a later date. This shows the contact that you care, and this evidence of caring is a powerful influencer in the relationship and the customer's willingness to spend. In addition, customer relationship management software enables you to record details that directly impact added sales, such as a date by which the product needs renewing, re-licensing or servicing, and so forth. Recording information on what a customer has bought and how long the product is expected to last, and then setting a reminder for renewals, is a superbly efficient way to increase sales at any time or season.

✔ **Social media:** Developing your social media presence these days is a must. Social media creates a personal connection that directly leads to added sales purely because the time and reach of the communication have no limits. Also, you can instantly reach all of your followers and friends, meaning that marketing is seamless, costless and as far-reaching as you'd like it to be.

✔ **Video conferencing:** Video conferencing enables you to 'see' more people without losing time stuck in traffic or paying the costs of petrol and train fares just to get to them in person. When you embrace this technology, it can free up as much as 60 per cent or more of the time you'd otherwise spend sitting in traffic or travelling. Not only is this a huge cost saving, but in the time you've saved you can potentially speak to and nurture hundreds of other contacts.

✔ **Website:** Give prospects easy access to confidence-giving information so that they can easily look at committing to purchase. You can't be there all the time in person to answer questions, but you can be there all of the time virtually. Have a great 24/7 sales pitch available online.

Thus, technology is your best friend when times are tough because it facilitates the addition of numbers without stretching you into insane working hours. For the lowdown on how technology can boost your sales, head over to Chapter 6.

Keeping Your Clients Loyal

Value the clients you have now. A sure-fire way to help when times are tough is to constantly be looking to serve and to add value. Your career will rise and be secure to the extent to which you focus on helping others get what they want. Get into the attitude of helping others gain and then you'll always be in demand.

When you provide superb value for your clients, even in tougher times, they don't stop spending and they certainly never leave to spend somewhere else. You can maintain your income and your client base. Just 'love the one you're with'.

Here are some top tips for keeping your clients loyal during a downturn:

- ✔ **Look for ways to increase service levels:** Just because your client is not complaining doesn't mean that there's nothing more that you can do. Many, many times, customer relationships are enhanced and spending increased as a result of salespeople going into clients' businesses and asking how they can help over and above the expected and delivered levels of service. You might, for example, give them your private telephone number, in case they ever need it, along with your assurance that you'll be there for backup. Because a move such as this is so personal, it can often carry a huge weight, even though it might never be used.

- ✔ **Listen to your client:** Salespeople are renowned for talking, but listening is far more lucrative. Listen to your client's desires and needs and then go the extra mile to deliver them. Ask questions about all areas of their business, not just the areas where you provide a service, and then respond by introducing helpful friends and contacts so that you can become a resource should they get stuck in any area of supply. Listening to all of their issues and supply chain needs opens the door to loads of opportunity and makes you valuable as a contact, thus increasing their loyalty to you severalfold.

✔ **Be friendly:** Share family conversations and drop by unexpectedly with ideas and introductions. Selling is about relationships, and now more than ever a need exists for a supplier to be a trusted and liked friend. Sharing leisure time might be possible and feasible, but even a card at Christmas or an offer to buy a drink for them on their birthday are simple ways of showing friendship that can go a long way.

✔ **Go above and beyond the call of duty:** Deliver good old-fashioned service. Become a good networker and always be on the lookout for ways to help your client. Steer other providers their way and let them know that you'll always use your connections to help them if you can.

Adding value in the slow times is investing in your future income, and it brings with it magical benefits of an improved reputation and lasting business relationships.

Taking the time to improve your skills

'Crikey, I'm just drowning in work. I've client after client to follow up on. I'm so busy selling, I just don't have time for learning and development.'

Sound familiar? This is the kind of thing you say when business is booming and you're happily hitting your sales targets.

How about when times are tough and you have to work much harder to hit the same target? Then you may say:

'Crikey, I'm just drowning in work. I've client after client to approach. I'm so busy trying to get a sale, I just don't have time for learning and development.'

By that logic, you never make time to develop your skills as a salesperson. But when you're struggling with an economic downturn, that's when you really need to shine as a salesperson.

What can you learn today? Ask yourself that question and take steps to make those skills yours. Tough times can become a huge blessing if you direct the time wisely.

Chapter 3 contains more information on developing your skills.

Finding the Upsides to Downturns

To succeed in a selling career, particularly in times of slower economic climates and ever-changing fashions, you have to develop and work at sustaining a positive mindset. After all, sales is perhaps the only field of employment where you can get told 'no' and not sell almost 70 per cent of the time and still actually succeed! The challenge is to stay mentally strong when you face rejection from yet another customer who chooses not to buy from you today. Thus, looking at the 30 per cent who say 'yes' – that is, always looking at the good and not the bad – is a hugely positive mental habit to get into. You develop a habit of looking deliberately for an upside in a downturn.

Sometimes industries close and leave broken hearts outside the factory gates. In moments like these, shortly after a company's demise, it can seem like the world has ended, certainly for the people most affected. However, downturns and closures often drive people on to fresh pastures, new investments and new jobs, and several years later many people who once mourned their loss now look back with nostalgia and even comment how things have since improved for them.

With this in mind, a healthy idea is to always look at how you can open up new opportunities yourself after a current pathway closes. Good always comes from seemingly bad situations if you only learn to see it. Nothing lasts forever, and, as a sales professional, you come to appreciate how you can use this for positive leverage.

As a sales professional, maybe the greatest gift harder times can give you is a recognition of what you already have, and this keeps you sharp. A positive spin on a potential threat of job loss is that it can make you extremely appreciative, and encourage you to add just a little extra effort and to view it with just a little more positive determination. Remarkably, by adding a little extra when you might feel slightly threatened, you often produce more and, in doing so, attain the security you desire.

Always look on the bright side . . .

As your career develops you watch as those around you come into new roles full of hopes and dreams and positivity. But then, over a period of time, many of them fall foul of the negatives all around. They moan that they don't get the best sales support or the best sales territory or the best leads. Actually, nothing much changes – the territory, the lead flow, the basic opportunity – *their view* changes. Instead of maintaining a positive outlook they allow everyday issues and comments of others to pull them down.

How can you hope to have energy and drive and success if you're more Eeyore than Tigger? Is it going to help you to focus on what's not quite right in the world? To fixate on the media's take on corruption and scandal and workforce lay-offs? No!

Sales people for centuries have understood clearly that they need to maintain a positive outlook and that can only be managed if they limit the amount of negatives they absorb. Mix with winners, not whingers. Read and consume material that uplifts and inspires, not degrades and scandalises. Engage in conversation about the magic in the world, not the dirt. Keep a positive mindset and remember that if you want something, you can get it.

So, there can be a very real upside to a downturn when you look personally at how you can improve. You just need to be prepared to see another perspective.

If you see a slowing down in spending and sense a tough time approaching, look at potential reasons why people are no longer buying. It might be that people aren't buying as much as before because they actually need more convincing, so there is, in fact, a need for a better salesperson! Often when businesses are slowing down, a very real upside is that they actively seek sales increase and look for better salespeople and better sales practices to be implemented!

Remember this, nothing – not a service, not a product, not a jumper or a house or a car or a holiday is ever bought without a salesperson selling it. Selling is the profession that always survives and leaders in selling write their own cheque. Upsides are always there when you train yourself to only see ups.

Staying Poised for Economic Recovery

When times are good, the homeowners in your area quite likely happily buy extras for their homes. They might, for example, spend on new surround sound home entertainment systems, larger screen televisions or satellite television packages. However, when confidence is low, they most likely cut back on new electrical items and make their old ones last a little longer. They probably stop their television subscriptions too, seeing them as luxuries they can live without. These are all indicators of *consumer confidence*. When people's confidence about having a reliable income or sufficient income to cover all of their needs is lowered, their reaction is to spend less. When consumer confidence returns, you see an increase in spending on such items.

In a similar fashion, some industry sectors are viewed as indicators or catalysts for growth in spending and confidence as they generally respond to economic stimuli first. As an example, recruitment is a key indicator of the health and growth potential of businesses. An increasing number of job vacancies is generally a good sign for the future, and recruitment companies act as a barometer for business confidence and thus economies starting to grow.

You need to keep a close eye on the economy for positive signs of recovery, and particularly on your sector. Keep an eye on local and national media – read newspapers, watch the news and keep a beady eye for signs of recovery – and, especially, tune your 'radar' into such fields as the construction and recruitment industries. Then you can be the first to seize the day.

See the glass as half-full when others see it as half-empty and prospects and colleagues alike will be drawn towards your positivity. You'll trigger confidence and will be able to influence how and when people spend.

Making the very best of the situation

Ben shares a true story about his client Paul who has made the downturn work to his advantage.

Paul made over £270,000 when his business, selling fire risk assessments to other businesses, started to enjoy a fairly rapid demand after several lean years. During the last few years, Paul has noticed many businesses trying to find cheaper ways of getting these risks covered, and thus his company suffered a reduced turnover and some tough months. After talking through where else Paul could find work and learning that housing developers were a key account, he could see the benefits of getting into this market. However, housing developers were all closing sites and holding development.

In a coaching session, Ben helped Paul see the value of planning and 'digging', even though housing developers were not spending at that time and no immediate work was available. So, Paul deliberately watched for new sites being planned with local councils. In addition, he used the slower times to enhance an already-known connection into a solid friendship (with a regional manager for a national homebuilder) where they even played football together.

After a little under 20 months, the rewards of his endeavours paid off with Paul's new friendship leading to an introduction and acceptance for Paul's company to do all of the fire risk assessments at all – yes, all – of their sites nationwide as they once again started to develop. The contract was worth over £270,000.

By choosing a key sector and watching for signs and working at relationships through a downturn, the time and effort paid off handsomely for Paul. It can do the same for you!

Part VI
The Part of Tens

'. . . and the beautiful princess kissed the frog and, hey presto, the frog turned into a handsome salesman.'

In this part...

To keep you on track we've compiled two chapters of what to avoid and what to keep doing in selling. The ten great tips in each chapter are key points to keep in mind as you enhance your selling career.

Your selling career will undoubtedly have times that you enjoy and have a series of 'wins'. Equally, it will see times when sales are harder for you to come by. The simple reminders in this Part of top tips to action alongside simple traps to avoid will keep you on a smoother pathway and help to iron out some of the peaks and troughs that you're bound to encounter. Go for it and have fun always!

Chapter 20

The Ten Biggest Sales Mistakes to Avoid

In This Chapter

▶ Avoiding the worst sales pitfalls

▶ Keeping your attitude positive around your clients

*E*veryone makes mistakes in life. And you should expect to make some when you're trying something new. In this chapter, we share with you the ten most common mistakes that others who have gone before you have made, so your journey to success in sales can be shorter and much more enjoyable.

Misunderstanding Selling

In most cases, the only contact a business has with the outside world is through its customers. Yet even when the business employs a sales team, it gives very little attention to selling. Sales just happen!

This observation may seem elementary, but if you walk into most small businesses in the world today you may find it difficult to find someone who can tell you the company's current style of selling and how the company is analysing it for improvement. The company may even have trouble describing its ideal client to you. If that's the case, the company can't really be selling at all, because it doesn't understand what selling is. You can't know too much about why customers do and don't buy your product or service – and gaining that knowledge is a function of selling. It helps you not only succeed now, but also come up with new products and services to continue to grow your business for the future.

Professional selling doesn't involve becoming pushy or aggressive in any way, but it does have to be deliberate. Professional salespeople or persuaders are low-key, service-oriented relationship builders and are the lifeblood of a business – without salespeople sales don't happen, and without sales the company doesn't survive.

Thinking You're a Sales Natural

Having incompetent or untrained people serving customers is bad business. Companies may as well throw away their marketing cash if they don't sell to or convert prospects who contact the business. Selling is a task that demands constant attention to improving skills levels. If you aren't satisfied with your sales skill level or volume of sales, you *can* improve. To admit that you can improve and then not take any steps to correct the situation is simply foolish.

Sales skills are not a gift at birth. They're learned skills that anyone can master with a little study and work. Start watching others in persuasive situations wherever you go. Ask yourself why some persuaders are good and why some are bad. You'll find that identifying why salespeople are bad is much easier – when persuaders are bad, you can usually tell that they're incompetent, that they don't know what they're talking about or that they're just making mistakes in general. But when salespeople are well trained and highly skilled, things seem to move forward so smoothly that spotting the sale happening is almost impossible. That's why you tend to think of these people as naturals. Even though they may be naturally comfortable talking with others, the actual skill of persuading must be learned, just as the ins and outs of the product or service must be learned in order to succeed.

Talking Too Much and Not Listening Enough

Most people think that you've to be a good talker to persuade others. Myths surround selling in such sayings as 'He kissed the Blarney Stone' or 'He's got the gift of the gab'. These myths, however, are grossly inaccurate when it comes to the skills required for success in today's selling environment.

Typically, a good talker thinks that she can tell the customer enough about the product that she'll automatically buy, but the truth is just the opposite. When you're talking, you're only finding out what you already know. Ask questions, and you discover what your potential clients want to buy.

A good salesperson asks questions, takes notes and listens intently to the customer's spoken words, as well as to her body language.

In most cases, people who talk too much want to control the conversation and are more likely to be perceived as aggressive and pushy. Usually, they miss clues and end up in a confrontational situation when, if they had listened more, they would have heard what the other person was saying. Professional sales training involves more questioning techniques and intent listening techniques than it does speaking skills. It's knowing the proper questions to ask and knowing when to shut up that leads to closing sales. A salesperson who's been trained to ask questions *leads* the buyer down the path to the sale, she doesn't *push*.

Using Words That Kill Sales

In any presentation you make, your words paint pictures. And a few wrong word pictures can ruin the entire portrait you're trying to paint.

How many presentations do you suppose are made daily throughout the world in an effort to win approval but don't succeed just because of the sales-killing pictures that the presenter's words paint, like referring to a 'contract' someone has to 'sign' to have a product installed? Both of those terms can bring to mind negative images. *Contracts* are legally binding and most people avoid a contract unless they have the advice of a lawyer. Your parents always warned you not to *sign* anything without thoroughly reading and understanding it. By using the wrong words, salespeople create negative pictures in the minds of the people they strive to serve – giving them more reasons not to go ahead than to get involved. To master the words that are more conducive to generating sales, flip to Chapter 4.

Not Knowing When to Close the Sale

Most customers who leave a place of business without owning a product or service are shrugged off by untrained sales-people as being 'just lookers' or 'be-backs' or any number of other euphemisms that hide the basic fact that the salesper-son didn't do the job well. A professional salesperson, how-ever, prefers to see such customers as what they really are: lost sales.

Ask for your prospect's decision when you recognise his *buying signs*, such as asking more questions or using language that shows an attitude of ownership, such as, 'Will I have to clean my pool every month?' A key word to look for from the customer is the word *will* – as opposed to something more hesitant such as *might* or *would*. Buying signs also include asking for more details, wanting to see the instructions for how to operate your product and asking financing questions. Your prospect may ask questions that refer to delivery, such as, 'Is it in stock?' or, 'Is there a delivery charge?' When you see such signs, *yes* is usually right around the corner.

If you don't close a sale when you recognise the buying signs, the prospect could very well cool off and give the purchase second thoughts that include not making a decision today, or worse still, buying from a competitor.

Not Knowing How to Close the Sale

In many cases, all you have to do to close the sale is ask. If a customer asks, 'Do you have it in red?' and you say, 'I believe I do have a red one,' what do you gain? Nothing.

A better approach is to reply with an 'If I could . . . would you?' question. For example, you say, 'I'm not sure right now whether we have this in red. I'll have to quickly check. But can I ask, if I can get you a red one, would you like to buy it today?'

In other words, ask a question that moves the prospect into a position of having to make an either/or decision about owner-ship. You can find even more simple yet powerful closes in Chapter 12.

Being Insincere

If you're trying to persuade someone else to adopt your point of view, to own your product or to start an account with your service, you must first help her to see that you're talking with her for her benefit, not yours.

Never let greed get in the way of doing what's right. If you don't sincerely believe that what you have to offer is good for the other party, yet you still try to convince her to own it, one of two things happens:

- ✔ She recognises your insincerity, doesn't get involved with you and tells at least 11 other people how terrible her experience with you was, thus ruining your reputation.

- ✔ She's persuaded, even though what you're selling isn't good for her, suffers the mismatch consequences, per-ceives you as nothing more than a con artist and takes every measure possible to see that you're punished as one.

When you're professionally selling or persuading others, it must be your sincere desire to serve others and help them get involved in something that's truly beneficial for them. Honesty and integrity are the key elements to every success-ful selling career.

Failing to Pay Attention to Details

When you wing it on your presentations, skim over details and ignore important cues from others, you also skim over big potential wins for yourself. Lost or misplaced information and orders, correspondence with typographical errors and missed appointments or delivery dates all ruin your credibility with your clients. They also take away from the high level of competence that professionals strive so hard to display. If your clients don't have the impression that you're doing your best for them, they'll find someone who will – maybe even someone else in your own office. Ooh, that would hurt, wouldn't it?

Letting Yourself Slump

Getting out of a slump takes a lot out of you, both mentally and physically. Why put yourself through hard times when, with a little bit of diligence, you can keep things on an even keel instead?

Most people have patterns to their selling cycles and efforts. Try charting your daily activities, productivity and winning presentations on a graph for not less than 30 days, preferably for 90. If you watch your cycles carefully, you'll see a slump coming long before it hits and you'll be able to correct the errors of your ways to even out your successes.

Neglecting to Keep in Touch

Most people who switch from your product, service or idea to another do so because you're being apathetic and someone else is paying them more attention. Someone else is keeping in contact on a regular basis and making them feel important. When all it takes is a bit of regular contact to keep people doing business with you, why would you ever get so lazy as to let them go?

When you invest in a Customer Relationship Management system (CRM) or contact management system, it will remind you of the need to communicate on a regular basis according to the information that you enter into it, and by doing so you remain present in the mind of your customer. This discipline and use of a system could save you a fortune in lost customers. (See Chapter 6 for more info.)

Chapter 21

Ten Strategies for Improving Your Selling

*W*hen you attain a certain level of professionalism, you find that you sell more. This increase in sales is a culmination of a lot of things: you're finding the best people to sell to, you're building a great rapport and relationship with them, you're recognising buying signs so that you're closing more sales and, most importantly, you're enjoying it all. This chapter reveals how to get started on your rise to that fun level of professionalism.

Prepare Yourself

Prepare yourself both mentally and physically for the challenge of persuading others. Dress appropriately. Give yourself an attitude check. Clear your mind of everything except what you need to think about for the presentation. Review any notes or information that may be vital within a few hours of meeting with your potential client. Professional salespeople know what they need to know, have to hand what they need and are prepared for twists with a Plan B for backup.

Be Disciplined

If you crave the financial and personal freedom that a successful sales career can provide, you have to be willing to go the extra mile. If that means working on a Friday night when all your friends are at happy hour, then so be it. If that means getting up hours earlier each morning until you master your new skills, then that's what you must do. The sacrifice you make today will pale in comparison to the reward you'll enjoy later.

Be a self-disciplined self-starter, and eventually you'll reap rewards. Stay on your feet and run the race to the finish. Remaining sharp and focused can sometimes be challenging, but doing so always pays off. You might be inspired to work harder when you're enjoying a successful period, to capitalise on the momentum, whereas other people might feel that a successful period entitles them to back off a bit and conserve their energy for when things get tougher again. There's no rule here; you must work in the way that suits you best. The real trick is to remain balanced during your successes. Although it can be almost impossible at times, always strive to keep your activities and attitudes balanced.

Rehearse, Perform and Critique Your New Skills

After you internalise some of your new selling techniques, you need to practise them. At first, go over them by yourself until you feel confident enough to practise them in front of peers who can give you valuable feedback.

When you get advice from people you respect, listen! On the other hand, if you get unsolicited advice from people you don't respect, don't let them share in your learning experience: their responses may damage your delicate psyche.

Give yourself permission to be a novice, but be sure to follow novice rules:

✔ Give yourself many, many opportunities to perfect your new selling techniques

✔ When you look back, feed the positive – celebrate all the things you did right

✔ Hold on to your novice enthusiasm even when you become a polished sales professional

Honestly critique your selling performances and persuasion skills with a critical but fair eye, and have a tool by which to measure your success. For example, if you've been in sales for a while but haven't been able to reach the level of success you'd hoped for, you may want to jot down your sales ratios and compare the old with the new as you move forward. Seeing positive results gives you something tangible to encourage a continued pattern of improvement.

If a specific stumbling block keeps inhibiting your sales growth, ask another sales professional whom you respect for some advice. Sometimes taking such a person along on a presentation or recording a meeting and critiquing it together can be a big help. In fact, you may be surprised to review a recorded presentation and discover all the things you could have done differently. Critiquing a recorded presentation gives you some distance from the excitement and anxiety of the actual meeting and allows you to look at your performance more objectively. Some of your recordings will hold great entertainment value. You'll be amazed at how many things you don't remember and how many things you'd swear you never did or said – it's a real eye-opener and a great learning opportunity.

Make a Good First Impression

You won't hear too many winning stories about people who overcame bad first impressions to go on to land a major account or persuade an important person to their way of thinking. The first impression is a critical part of the selling profession and one that you must focus on and always improve. Going in confidently and handling the initial rapport-setting stage properly goes a long way toward closing a sale or landing a new client.

Make a good first impression with everyone you encounter in a client's company, not just the decision-maker. A time may come when you need the assistance of someone else in that company.

Quickly Determine Whether You Can Help Your Client

By asking a few simple questions and improving your prospecting skills, you can determine quickly whether your product or service is right for a prospect and whether meeting and presenting is a worthy time investment. By doing this, you maximise your efforts and constantly develop your sales performance figures by giving presentations only to people who are best positioned to become clients.

Give Every Presentation 110 Per Cent

Never sell a prospect short. In doing so, you show a lack of respect toward him, and you'll probably lose whatever credibility you had with him. Don't take shortcuts either – drop a step and you may lose a sale.

By making every presentation as though it's the most important thing in your life at that moment, you show the decision-makers that you're sincere about their needs and that they're important to you. Generally, people will be whatever you expect them to be. So expect your prospects to be vital to your overall success – not just in business but in life too – and treat them with the proper amount of respect. This approach will take you far.

Address Concerns Completely

If and when your prospect voices a concern about something, don't ever glide over or minimise it. Let it stop you momentarily. Think about what the prospect said and what you may have said or done to trigger the comment. Then carefully and thoughtfully address the concern. For example, say your prospect is concerned over the expense. You say, 'What I understand from your comment, Mr Friedman, is that you're concerned about the payment process for the new photo-copying machine. Is that correct?' Mr Friedman will most likely respond 'Yes' and you can then examine how you can meet and agree terms, instead of arguing about whether or not the copier is too expensive.

Confirm Everything

Miscommunication costs people loads of money, time and effort. Missed appointments or phone calls can destroy in minutes what may have taken months to build. Taking just a few seconds to confirm (and reconfirm) everything brings you more success.

Never fear re-stating the details to your clients. They won't think you're brain damaged. Rather, they'll appreciate the clarity it brings to what they've agreed to.

Ask for the Decision

You have nothing to lose by asking a prospect for a decision. If he's not ready to make a decision and that's what you find out by asking, great. But if he is ready and you don't ask, you lose everything. If you truly believe in the good of what you're doing, you should have no reluctance in asking the other party to commit his time, effort or money to your cause or for your product or service.

Hesitation is an indication of doubt – and you should never be the one having doubts when you're in the persuader's seat.

Tell Your Clients about Others

Few people want to be guinea pigs. They don't want to be the first to try something – they want to know that others have preceded them. Social proof is a vital element in the selling process. By sharing experiences you've had with others just like them, you give your prospects permission to be like those others and invest in what you're selling. They'll recognise the landscape and understand that they're not going into uncharted waters. Overcoming their fears takes you far in convincing or persuading people, especially if you can use examples of people they know.

Make a Commitment to Lifelong Learning

Think of every technique you read in this book as one link in the chain of your success in sales. If you have weak links in your chain, then you may need to review a chapter or two to build, say, your prospecting or presentation skills (see Chapters 7 and 10, respectively). If you don't go back and make the weak link stronger, your career chain will never carry the weight it needs to carry in order to haul you up to top-producer status.

When you find yourself in the fortunate position of a competition-winning star performer, you'll probably get asked to share some of what you know with others. In fact, you may be asked to train at a sales meeting.

When you teach, you learn. By teaching your techniques to others, you clarify your own skills and reinforce your knowledge of what makes an effective salesperson. Teachers are students too. If you can remain flexible – sometimes the teacher, sometimes the student – the opportunity to learn in diverse situations constantly presents itself, and you're prepared to learn from the experience.

Even though you want to make more profit and more sales, you're most likely to accomplish these goals only when you put your customers first. When your clients know that you're putting their needs before your own and when they recognise your integrity and honesty, most clients are happy to go the extra mile with you to make meetings mutually beneficial. People are the key to your sales success.

Index

About the Authors

Tom Hopkins is the epitome of sales success. A millionaire by the time he reached the age of 27, Hopkins now is Chairman of Tom Hopkins International, one of the largest sales-training organisations in the world.

Thirty years ago, Tom Hopkins considered himself a failure. He had dropped out of college after 90 days, and for the next 18 months he carried steel on construction sites to make a living. Believing that there had to be a better way to earn a living, he went into sales – and ran into the worst period of his life. For six months, Tom earned an average of $42 a month and slid deeper into debt and despair. Pulling together his last few dollars, he invested in a five-day sales training seminar that turned his life around. In the next six months, Tom sold more than $1 million worth of $25,000 homes. At age 21, he won the Los Angeles Sales and Marketing Institute's coveted SAMMY Award and began setting records in sales performance that still stand today.

Because of his unique ability to share his enthusiasm for the profession of selling and the successful selling techniques he developed, Tom began giving seminars in 1974. Training as many as 10,000 salespeople a month, he quickly became known as the world's leading sales trainer. Today, he presents approximately 75 seminars a year to over 100,000 people throughout the world.

Tom was a pioneer in producing high-quality audio and video programmes for those who could not attend the seminars or who wanted further reinforcement after the seminars. Recognised as the most effective sales-training programmes ever produced, they're continually updated and are now being utilised by more than 1 million people.

Tom Hopkins has also written nine other books, including *Sales Prospecting For Dummies* and *Sales Closing For Dummies*, as well as the best-selling *How to Master the Art of Selling*, which has sold over 1.3 million copies in 8 languages and 27 countries.

Tom Hopkins is a member of the National Speakers Association and one of a select few to receive its Council of Peers Award for Excellence. He is often the keynote speaker for annual conventions and is a frequent guest on television and radio talk shows.

Ben Kench is Britain's leading small business growth specialist, enjoying a reputation for delivering quite incredible results.

Ben's pedigree and character have been formed over a lifetime of adventure and achievements that culminate in a rich spectrum of knowledge that's life-based with family values and an underpinning of integrity and honesty.

His selling career began with an early foray into double glazing sales as an impressionable 19-year-old, and while his initial success was nationally recognised he also learned hard lessons about life, success, and attitude, eventually falling out with family and loved ones as arrogance overcame the youth. A few months taught lifelong lessons. Moving on and learning, Ben's first major role in selling was to industry selling air compressors and related tools. Aged 20, he learned to face the 'we've been doing it this way for longer than you've been alive, lad' rejection.

Over the years, Ben has enjoyed success in roles selling higher-value equipment to corporate clients, selling to the small business market, and selling to the home owner. He's experienced in selling in the consumer marketplace in industries as diverse as unregulated timesharing to heavily regulated financial services. Each have presented their particular challenges and each has added their own unique refinement to the art of selling.

Ben also raised his daughter from the age of 20 months as a single parent and knows well the struggle to balance work and family whilst also appreciating the real value and meaning of family life. Ben is first and foremost a family man, with old-fashioned values, where truth and integrity are non-negotiable and where business relationships become friendships that last. Those sentiments echo throughout the advice in this book to help you succeed in your selling career.

Ben's programme, 'The Business Booster', is gaining national recognition and his company is often approached by major institutions to assist with their performance objectives. He's approved as a member of The National Consultants Register and is often asked to speak at conventions for The Institute of

Sales and Marketing Management (ISMM), and The Federation of Small Businesses (FSB), as well as major business-to-business exhibitions nationally.

Ben has also written a book on small business growth entitled *How to Grow Your Business and Enjoy More Money, Less Stress!*

Today, Ben's time is spent dedicated to helping individuals improve their performance through a variety of sales and business education programmes.

Dedications

From Tom: This book is dedicated to all my teachers and my students. Some of you have been both to me. Thank you for your loyalty and for sharing your successes with me. You are the reason why my life has been so filled with love, laughter and abundance.

From Ben: This book is dedicated to the thousands of people who have helped me along my path. Literally every step is remembered with fondness. Lessons learned from teachers mingle with lessons learned from life and the many situations I've been presented with. This book is dedicated to each and every person or situation along the way.

Above all, this book is dedicated to my great friend and sales leader, Dave Brazier. Dave you showed me (when I wasn't best disposed to learn!) much of the foundation basics relayed in this book. You showed me the huge value in discipline, order and record-keeping to become a professional. You showed me the adaptation from direct to consumer sales into selling business to business and all of the variations that entailed. You showed me how to handle prejudice and overcome stacked odds as a young man in an old industry. In short you were a cornerstone and as vital on my journey as snow is to skiing. This then, Dave, is my way to say thank you. You probably don't know or dare think about how much you have influenced me but, for the record, I still bear the scars from those first lessons you taught me!

Authors' Acknowledgements

From Tom: I must acknowledge my wonderful wife, Debbie, who has brought so much joy into my life. I'm grateful for your patience and understanding when my life's work takes me away. I'm also grateful for your valuable input into my teaching, and particularly in this book.

I thank Judy Slack of Tom Hopkins International for writing and managing all my material for so long. I also thank Laura Oien, my company President, and Spence Price, CFO. You all work hard to make my life easy, allowing me to do what I do best – teach.

From Ben: As is almost always the case, any achievement involves support staff and friends who, whilst out of the spotlight, are nonetheless much needed component parts.

For my part, I have to primarily thank both the fabulously helpful author support team at Wiley – Steve Edwards and Claire Ruston, who steered me, advised me and managed to hide their frustrations! And thanks, of course, to my wonderful back office admin girls who keep me organised and on-track, even when my entrepreneur mind wants to go off on exciting new ventures! Kimberley, Paula and Sally – thank you.

I must recognise publicly the clients who constantly challenge me as I work with them and coach them in their business situations. In doing so, I am rewarded with an ever-present 'saw-sharpening' opportunity and am never, ever allowed to sit back on past performance and reiterate old 'stuff'! To my clients, thank you for keeping me pushed and in 'real time'.

And thank you to for the thousands of people in business who inspire me and keep me motivated as I am blessed to speak to them in audiences all over Europe. I am eternally grateful as you share your thoughts, struggles, ideas and successes with me, as this task is why God made me.

For allowing me to do my life's work, I thank you all.

Publisher's Acknowledgements

We're proud of this book; please send us your comments at http://dummies.custhelp.com. For other comments, please contact our Customer Care Department within the U.S. at 877-762-2974, outside the U.S. at (001) 317-572-3993, or fax 317-572-4002.

Some of the people who helped bring this book to market include the following:

Acquisitions, Editorial, and Vertical Websites

Project Editor: Steve Edwards

Commissioning Editor: Claire Ruston

Assistant Editor: Ben Kemble

Development Editor: Charlie Wilson

Proofreader: Cate Miller

Production Manager: Daniel Mersey

Publisher: Miles Kendall

Cover Photos: © Yunus Arakon/iStock

Cartoons: Ed McLachlan

Composition Services

Project Coordinator: Kristie Rees

Layout and Graphics: Jennifer Creasey, Andrea Hornberger

Proofreaders: Lindsay Amones, Jessica Kramer, Susan Moritz

Indexer: Ty Koontz

FOR DUMMIES®

Making Everything Easier!™

UK editions

BUSINESS

Bookkeeping FOR DUMMIES
978-1-118-34689-1

Pop Up Business FOR DUMMIES
Dan Thompson
978-1-118-44349-1

Starting & Running a Business ALL-IN-ONE FOR DUMMIES
6 BOOKS IN 1
Colin Barrow
978-1-119-97527-4

MUSIC

Mandolin FOR DUMMIES
978-1-119-94276-4

Ukulele FOR DUMMIES
Alistair Wood
978-0-470-97799-6

DJing FOR DUMMIES
John Steventon
978-0-470-66372-1

HOBBIES

Stargazing FOR DUMMIES
Steve Owens
978-1-118-41156-8

Keeping Chickens FOR DUMMIES
Pammy Riggs
Kimberly Willis
Rob Ludlow
978-1-119-99417-6

Beekeeping FOR DUMMIES
David Wiscombe
Howland Blackiston
978-1-119-97250-1

Asperger's Syndrome For Dummies
978-0-470-66087-4

Basic Maths For Dummies
978-1-119-97452-9

Body Language For Dummies,
2nd Edition
978-1-119-95351-7

Boosting Self-Esteem For Dummies
978-0-470-74193-1

Business Continuity For Dummies
978-1-118-32683-1

Cricket For Dummies
978-0-470-03454-5

Diabetes For Dummies, 3rd Edition
978-0-470-97711-8

eBay For Dummies, 3rd Edition
978-1-119-94122-4

English Grammar For Dummies
978-0-470-05752-0

Flirting For Dummies
978-0-470-74259-4

IBS For Dummies
978-0-470-51737-6

ITIL For Dummies
978-1-119-95013-4

Management For Dummies,
2nd Edition
978-0-470-97769-9

Managing Anxiety with CBT
For Dummies
978-1-118-36606-6

Neuro-linguistic Programming
For Dummies, 2nd Edition
978-0-470-66543-5

Nutrition For Dummies, 2nd Edition
978-0-470-97276-2

Organic Gardening For Dummies
978-1-119-97706-3

FOR
DUMMIES®

Making Everything Easier!™

UK editions

SELF-HELP

Cognitive Behavioural Therapy
FOR DUMMIES

978-0-470-66541-1

Creative Visualization
FOR DUMMIES

978-1-119-99264-6

Mindfulness
FOR DUMMIES

978-0-470-66086-7

LANGUAGES

Spanish
FOR DUMMIES

978-0-470-68815-1

Polish
FOR DUMMIES

978-1-119-97959-3

British Sign Language
FOR DUMMIES

978-0-470-69477-0

HISTORY

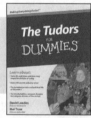

The Tudors
FOR DUMMIES

978-0-470-68792-5

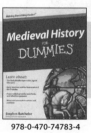

Medieval History
FOR DUMMIES

978-0-470-74783-4

British History
FOR DUMMIES

978-0-470-97819-1

FOR DUMMIES

Making Everything Easier! ™

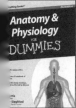
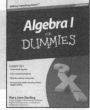

Think you can't learn it in a day? Think again!

The *In a Day* e-book series from *For Dummies* gives you quick and easy access to learn a new skill, brush up on a hobby, or enhance your personal or professional life — all in a day. E

Football Rules & Positions FOR DUMMIES *in a day*

Improving Your **Golf** Swing FOR DUMMIES *in a day*

Buying & Serving **Wine** FOR DUMMIES *in a day*

Getting Started with **Crowdfund** Investing FOR DUMMIES *in a day*

Boost Your Confidence FOR DUMMIES *in a day*

Giving a Presentation FOR DUMMIES *in a day*

Knitting a Scarf FOR DUMMIES *in a day*

Launch a WordPress.com **Blog** FOR DUMMIES *in a day*

Rugby Union Basics FOR DUMMIES *in a day*

Cricket Rules FOR DUMMIES *in a day*

Become More Mindful FOR DUMMIES *in a day*

Running **Great** Meetings FOR DUMMIES *in a day*

Planning a **PRINCE2** Project FOR DUMMIES *in a day*

Building Rapport with NLP FOR DUMMIES *in a day*

Ukulele FOR DUMMIES *in a day*

Become More Relaxed FOR DUMMIES *in a day*

Available as PDF, eMobi and Kindle